Kids Cook Real Food
Cooking Class Curriculum

by Katie Kimball

www.KidsCookRealFood.com

Working in the kitchen, as with most real activities in life, comes with inherent risks. We emphasize safety throughout the curriculum but strongly encourage you to stay close to your kids and above all, use common sense. Neither the author nor the publisher assumes responsibility for any accidents resulting from the use of this book.

Published in the United States by Kitchen Stewardship, LLC
www.KitchenStewardship.com

To order more copies of this book or to order the companion recipe books visit:
www.KidsCookRealFood.com/PrintBook

Contact the publisher at *mailadmin@KitchenStewardship.com*

Cover design by Mary Voogt.
Cover photos by Alli Jagoda Photography.
Photo of Katie Kimball by Allison Martin Photography.

Publisher's Cataloging-in-Publication data
Kimball, Katie
Kids Cook Real Food : Cooking Class Curriculum / Katie Kimball
388 p. ; 21 cm.
ISBN: 978-1-947031-77-7
1. CKB120000 COOKING / Cooking with Kids I. Kimball, Katie II. Kids Cook Real Food
LCCN: 2017904881

First Edition

Table of Contents

Congratulations!

You're one of the elite few who are stepping out of their comfort zone, going against the norm of the culture and getting kids in the kitchen. I'm thrilled that you've committed to sharing real food with the next generation by teaching children to cook.

Sharp knives. Fire. And...vegetables!

You're brave. And very smart. I'm so honored to join you on this journey, to help teach children lifelong independent skills and build healthy bodies for their future and ours.

This course is designed for families to teach in their homes, but it has also worked well in group settings like homeschool co-ops, after-school programs, and more. All ages can work on their own skills at the same time, and what they create comes together to create one meal or snack. (If you work with just one age group/skill level at a time, it still works out.)

For helpful tips on how to juggle the age groups, find a play-by-play plan at the end of each Adult Guide Section.

As you'll see in the Curriculum Map on the next few pages, the course is divided into Beginner, Intermediate and Advanced Levels. Use the Map to guide your planning, check off skills that the kids master, and get excited about what's to come. Many families bookmark or tear out those pages so they can check off sections as they go.

You'll find details about the lessons for each level on their own page, but if you are working with multiple ages, be sure check page 13 for the overview where you can see how the lessons mesh together on any given day.

I recommend that you, the "Adult Guide," start by reading through the introductory section on pages 15-29. This will give you details about how everything is structured, what to expect, and our philosophy of teaching.

If you want to jump right in, you can teach the Foundations 101 classes (page 31) without much prep or special grocery shopping. They teach basic skills that will be used many times in the other classes. Feel free to start with them first, or you can use them just before especially appropriate lessons.

Keep in mind that this course was originally written to be used with video lessons, so you'll get to demonstrate a lot for the kids yourself instead. You'll understand why demonstrating is important in a few more pages.

If you'd like to obtain access to the video lessons, we'd love to have you join us as a full member in the Kids Cook Real Food eCourse. Go to *www.KidsCookRealFood.com/printbook* for a special entry!

Navigating the Book

Adult Guide Notes: Each class has 3 lessons at skills levels (Beginner, Intermediate and Advanced) plus an "All-Kid" lesson that teaches all ages a basic skill together. The Adult Guide information will walk you through the All-Kid lesson as well as tips for teaching the module levels.

Lesson Plans: Every lesson plan lists food and supplies right on the first page, which is a great at-a-glance overview of everything you'll need to prepare. Plus we have one-page grocery lists for each module and an overall supply list (not food) in the resources section starting on page 319.

Resources Section: You'll also find flash cards and daily nugget cards in the resources section, intended to be torn out and cut apart to help everyone remember the fun memory phrases you'll encounter in the lessons. All the recipes referenced in the lessons are in the separate *Recipes for Kids Cook Real Food* book. If you don't have it already, find it at *www.KidsCookRealFood.com/printbook*

With the purchase of this book, you have permission to photocopy anything in the resources section and may share flash cards and daily nugget cards, as well as the Curriculum Map, with any number of children to whom you teach these lessons. Lesson plans do not have copy permissions.

Tools Needed: The course requires very simple equipment, but if you'd like some ideas of what we've found to work best in our kid-friendly kitchens, the online resources page will help you: *www.KitchenStewardship.com/kcrfresources*

Updates: If there are ever any changes to the lessons, additions, or new tips and suggestions, you can find those at *www.KidsCookRealFood.com/ printbook* along with special instructions for how to become a full member of the course and get access to the videos. That page also includes links to online recipes and resources that may be helpful.

Meet the Teacher

I'm Katie Kimball, and as a mom of 4 I hit this point where I was too busy and too stressed out to even think about inviting my kids to help me in the kitchen.

But...I needed help so I could stop being so busy and spend time enjoying my children.

For the good of my whole family, it was time to teach my kids to cook.

My educational background is in elementary education and English, but as I began cooking for my children and reading about nutrition, I quickly became a home chef and researcher.

Even though I love cooking myself, sometimes having my kids in the kitchen was as painful as doing crafts and finding glitter on everything two months later.

But I didn't want my kids leaving for college not knowing how to cut a vegetable and ending up relying on frozen dinners the whole time!

I gave myself many pep talks so I'd remember how important it was, and once I began to see the fruits of my labor, I realized I needed to share our methods with more people.

That's why I created the Kids Cook Real Food Course, and why I can't wait to share it with your family.

-XOXO-
Mrs. Kimball

The **Kids Cook Real Food Course** was originally created to be an internet-based eCourse.

If you would like access to the videos that compliment each lesson go to
KidsCookRealFood.com/printbook
to learn more.

Kids Cook Real Food Curriculum Map: All-Kid Lessons

Class 1	Getting Started: The Ultimate Guide to Working in the Kitchen for Kids
Class 2	Cut! It's Knife Safety Time
Class 3	What's That Smell? Spice Exploration
Class 4	Keep It Flat! Measuring Ingredients
Class 5	The Bean-y Science Experiment
Class 6	Flip It! Using a Spatula
Class 7	Clean It! Washing Produce
Class 8	Make It Up! Being Creative in the Kitchen

Kids Cook Real Food Curriculum Map: Beginner

	Title	Skill	Applications	Skills Revisited	Recipes
Class 1	Spreading and Peeling	spreading with a dull knife; peeling vegetables	spreading butter on bread, PB on celery; peeling carrots and cucumbers	Class 3, 7, 8	• Ants on a Log • Buttered Toast • Crudités Platter
Class 2	Dull Knife Skills, Level 1	slicing soft foods with a dull knife	slicing bananas, melons, cheese	Class 3, 7	• Fun Fruit Salad
Class 3	Dull Knife Skills, Level 2	slicing solid foods with a dull knife, cross-hatch dicing	slicing cucumbers, zucchini; dicing cooked potatoes, mushrooms	Class 7	• Stir Fry • Potato Hash
Class 4	Measuring Ingredients	measuring dry ingredients, teaspoons and measuring cups	making homemade seasoning mixes	Class 5, 6, 8	• Taco Seasoning • Ranch Salad Dressing Mix
Class 5	Soaking Dry Beans	preparing dried beans	rinsing, picking, and soaking dry beans	Class 7	• Homemade Refried Beans
Class 6	Pouring Skills	pouring: wet and dry	special practice activities, making gelatin cups	Class 7, 8	• Gelatin Gellies • Gelatin Cups
Class 7	Salad Masters	washing and tearing lettuce	making a colorful salad	none	• Basic Salad Ideas
Class 8	Working With Dough	rolling balls of bread dough	making rolls	none	• Happy Rolls • GF Corn Bread

Kids Cook Real Food Curriculum Map: Intermediate

	Title	Skill	Applications	Skills Revisited	Recipes
Class 1	Following a Recipe	following a recipe well; wet and dry measurement review	making homemade salad dressing	Class 4, 5, 6, 7	• Ranch Salad Dressing or Dip
Class 2	Intro to Sharp Knife Skills	slicing soft produce	slicing pineapples, strawberries, mushrooms	none	• Fruit Salad
Class 3	Cracking Eggs	cracking eggs with minimal mess	cracking eggs for various dishes	Class 4, 6	• Omelet • Scrambled Eggs • Fried Rice
Class 4	Making A Whole Recipe Without Help	mixing simple recipes start to finish with independence	making pumpkin muffins or your favorite kid-friendly recipe	Class 5, 6, 7	• GF Pumpkin Muffins • Whole Wheat Pumpkin Muffins
Class 5	Stovetop Safety and Cooking Rice	proper stovetop safety, preparing and cooking rice	preparing basic rice	Class 6, 7, 8	• Plain Rice • Mexican Rice
Class 6	Flipping Pancakes	flipping something on the stovetop	making pancakes	Class 7	• Wheat Pancakes • GF Pancakes • Grain-Free Pancakes
Class 7	Rolling Dough	rolling out dough	making homemade tortillas	none	• Homemade Whole Wheat Tortillas • Homemade GF Crackers
Class 8	Browning Ground Meat	browning ground meat	browning ground meat	none	• Taco Beef

Kids Cook Real Food Curriculum Map: Advanced

	Title	Skill	Applications	Skills Revisited	Recipes
Class 1	Sharp Knife Skills Level 1	cutting straight	cutting carrots and cucumbers into sticks and wheels; dicing celery	Class 2, 3, 4, 5, 7, 8	• Crudités Platter • Simple Chicken Rice Soup
Class 2	Sharp Knife Skills Level 2	slicing and dicing round vegetables	slicing and dicing onions and peppers	Class 3, 4, 5, 7, 8	• Pepper and Onion Freezer Prep
Class 3	Sharp Knife Skills Level 3	crushing garlic, stovetop safety review, sautéing vegetables	making a basic stir fry	Class 4, 5, 7, 8	• Basic Veggie Stir Fry
Class 4	Sharp Knife Skills Level 4	cutting whole fruits, oven safety	apples and melons, baking something	none	• Pumpkin Muffins • Oven Baked Apple Crisp
Class 5	Cooking Dry Beans	cooking dry beans	making homemade refried beans	Class 7	• Homemade Refried Beans
Class 6	Cooking Eggs	scrambling and frying eggs	making eggs for breakfast	none	• Best Scrambled Eggs • Best Fried Eggs
Class 7	Using A Small Appliance	using a food processor	shredding cheese, slicing veggies, and mixing a dinnertime recipe	none	• Chickpea Wraps • Chicken Rice-A-Roni
Class 8	Making a White Sauce & Steaming Veggies	making a roux and béchamel sauce, steaming veggies	homemade cheese sauce and steamed broccoli	none	• Simple Cheese Sauce • Simple GF Cheese Sauce

Kids Cook Real Food Curriculum Map: Module Integrations

When you have kids in multiple age groups, they often work together to create a meal or a snack!

	Beginner Lesson	Intermediate Lesson	Advanced Lesson	Family Snack & Meals
Class 1	spreading butter on bread, PB on celery; peeling carrots and cucumbers	making ranch dip	cutting carrots and cucumbers into sticks and wheels; dicing celery	• Crudités Platter • Ants on a Log
Class 2	slicing bananas, melons, cheese	slicing pineapples, strawberries, mushrooms	slicing and dicing onions and peppers	• Fruit Plate • Cheese & Peppers Snack Platter
Class 3	slicing cucumbers, zucchini; dicing cooked potatoes, mushrooms	cracking eggs for various dishes	making a basic stir fry	• Veggie Stir Fry • Egg-Fried Rice • Potato Hash
Class 4	making homemade seasoning mixes	making pumpkin muffins or your favorite kid-friendly recipe	apples and melons, baking something	• Homemade Muffins with Fruit • Apple Crisp
Class 5	rinsing, picking, and soaking dry beans	preparing basic rice	making homemade refried beans	• Refried Beans and Mexican Rice
Class 6	special practice activities, making gelatin cups	making pancakes	making eggs for breakfast	• Pancakes and Eggs (syrup poured by beginners) • Gelatin Snacks
Class 7	making a colorful salad	making homemade tortillas	shredding cheese, slicing veggies, and mixing a recipe	• Chickpea Wraps with Homemade Tortillas • Side Salad
Class 8	making rolls	browning ground meat	homemade cheese sauce and steamed broccoli	• Leftover Bowl (Meat, Veggies, Rice +Cheese Sauce) with Rolls

Getting Started and Being Prepared for the eCourse

As we get started working with kids in the kitchen, I want to thank you again for making this commitment. It's not easy to slow down and bring children along while preparing food, but I am convinced **that it will make a difference in their long-term health**. And quite frankly – they'll be better adults if they know how to cook, hands down.

I want to encourage you to keep at it!

Many things are minorly annoying – like opening a bag of flour or sugar. There's stuff in the seal every single time and it gets all over the counter no matter how careful you are...but no one stops buying flour or sugar JUST because of the mess it makes (although you might stop for other reasons!).

Just so with kids – we need to simply **accept that they'll make messes** and teach them to clean them up, not boot them from the kitchen every time we're working.

Why Train Kids in the Kitchen

In case you're still wavering in your resolve, remember how many, many great reasons there are to teach kids to cook:

1. They gain **life skills** they need.
2. Kids learn the value of a **hard work ethic** and shared responsibility.
3. Learning real life skills gives them **confidence** that extends into all areas of life.
4. Being involved with food makes them **more likely to eat it.**
5. Parents get a chance to **connect one on one with their kids**, practice good discipleship and great parenting. Other caring adults have a super opportunity to be a mentor to a child as well, and cooking is a perfect background for conversation.

I'm hoping we all want our kids to **eat better than frozen dinners** and take-out pizza when they're on their own as adults, so teaching them life skills in the kitchen at an early age is one way to prepare them for real life.

Whether kids grow the food in a garden, choose something at the grocery store, help prepare it or choose the recipe, **any involvement in the cooking process** may increase the chances of them trying and enjoying a food (but not always, sadly).

In our house, **family responsibility is important** and this is an area that everyone participates in – everybody has to eat! – so it's part of good parenting to invite and train them in the kitchen, for all ages and genders. It's good for kids to understand that nothing happens without work from someone.

In addition, my kids love to get the chance to show off to visitors and guests by sharing the food they've made. It's a great way to **build in opportunities to praise a child** for a (real) job well done and help them gain confidence in general.

Your Role, My Role

We're a team here, you and me. I call you "Adult Guides" for two reasons:

1. The course isn't only for parents and children, but can be taught by any adult who wants to help a child in their life learn to cook.
2. The adult's job is to guide the child from a place of zero or beginning experience to complete independence in the kitchen. You are their Yoda.

And I am *your* guide, in a sense. I've thought through the order of the skills and the activities/recipes so you don't have to, I'll help you demonstrate skills for the kids, and I can be the scapegoat when your kids don't want to do what you say. Just pull the "Mrs. Kimball says..." card and push the blame on me. (You're welcome.)

I've been a third grade teacher and am a mom of four kids, and I've been cooking from scratch for ten years. I apply all that experience to this course, and I'm excited to work with you and your kids!

The course is definitely designed to be multigenerational, taken by an adult and a child (or children) together. The lessons help teach YOU, the adult guide, how to teach your children.

With over 30 skills in the eCourse, your kids will learn a lot by the time they're finished – but I couldn't include everything.

There are elements of many skills that are **unique to each household** based on personality, tools available, and kitchen setup. You'll want to demonstrate and explain to your kids these nuances so they feel completely at home in your kitchen.

We deal with some of this in the lessons already. Even something as simple as cooking eggs is radically different based on what kind of pan surface and spatulas you have, so I'll remind you in that lesson to **introduce your own cooking tools** to your kids. Similarly, sometimes I just can't teach a certain skill because there's too much variance among households, like making toast. My toaster oven probably doesn't behave at all like my neighbor's upright toaster.

I didn't choose to teach much about cleaning up just yet, partly because **cleanliness reflects much personal preference**.

Cleaning up *is* important so you don't burn out and so they learn real responsibility! But teach your own style, and be sure to include washing dishes once kids are responsible enough to do a good job.

What Level is Right for Your Child?

If you're not sure what module level to start with, here's a quick overview:

- **Beginner:** for young children, or anyone who needs to brush up on these skills)
- **Intermediate:** for those who have mastered the beginner level skills
- **Advanced:** for those who have mastered the beginner and intermediate level skills (especially stovetop safety and some sharp knife experience)

I recommend checking out the Curriculum Map on page 9 to get a complete overview of the course, but here's a quick synopsis of skills:

BEGINNER

1. Spreading and peeling vegetables
2. Dull knife skills, level 1
3. Dull knife skills, level 2
4. Measuring ingredients
5. Soaking dry beans
6. Pouring skills
7. Making a salad
8. Working with dough

INTERMEDIATE

1. Following a recipe
2. Introduction to sharp knife skills
3. Cracking eggs
4. Making a whole recipe without help
5. Stovetop safety and cooking rice
6. Flipping pancakes
7. Rolling dough
8. Browning ground meat

ADVANCED

1. Sharp knife skills, level 1
2. Sharp knife skills, level 2
3. Sharp knife skills, level 3
4. Sharp knife skills, level 4
5. Cooking dry beans
6. Cooking eggs
7. Using a small appliance
8. Making a white sauce & steaming vegetables

I encourage you to **choose the level based on your child's prior experience, abilities, personality, and motivation,** not solely on their age. There's no shame in an older child taking some of the beginner course, and some young children might be able to learn quite a bit of the intermediate and even advanced skills.

The Structure of the Course (What to Expect)

- The **"Adult Info" materials**, like what you're reading now, are just for you. You should read the adult info section of each lesson before working with your children.

- **Each module level has its own section**: Beginner, Intermediate and Advanced. Each level will give the adult an overview of the class, including supplies and food necessary and what you might need to prepare before working with the kids. It also includes step-by-step instructions for how to teach the skill.

This book also includes a number of documents for the entire course that you may want to go over before day one:

- Curriculum Map, pages 9-13
- Daily Nugget Cards (one set for each module), page 349
- Flash Cards with Key Terms (one set for each module), 363

Curriculum Map
For those who love planning and having a visual of your destination, the Curriculum Map will be your best friend. It includes all the skills taught at each level, how those skills will loop back into future lessons, and even how the skills taught on the same day/week can connect across the age level modules, for those teaching multiple age groups at once.

Daily Nugget Cards
Each lesson includes a "Daily Nugget," which is a little bite of information so that kids are learning *about* food while they learn how to make it. The nuggets are more academically minded than the rest of the course. If you'd like to discuss and review the factoids with your kids throughout the week, the Daily Nugget cards will help you remember.

Note: You may want to preview the Daily Nuggets, because science is a bit of a moving target when it comes to food. Depending on how you eat, you might need to be prepared to discuss with your children any you disagree with, or you can just skip them.

Flash Cards with Key Terms
One gem of the *Kids Cook Real Food* Course is the kid-friendly vocabulary we use and the catch phrases that help all of you remember

proper skills in the kitchen. The flash cards include these phrases and are designed to be cut out to the size of an index card.

You can bring them easily into the kitchen while you teach the lesson initially to help you remember what phrases to practice, since repetition is vital for memory. Then tack them to a board, put them on the fridge, or make them into a book so that kids can return to them again and again, especially during the first week after the lesson. Repetition is vital for memory. (Got it?)

Teaching the Lessons

Once your "cooking class" is ready to start, invite your children into the kitchen and demonstrate the new skill(s).

If you do allow your **older kids to read through a section without you**, be sure you keep up with their new vocabulary and ensure that you can help them be accurate with their skill. Expect to do a lot of "co-working" at all levels, because we don't expect a child to be able to make a recipe completely on their own the first time they see it unless they've done something like it before.

Your goal should always be to **"co-cook" the first time around on a recipe**, or at least be close for Q&A. Once the child has seen the entire recipe in action, they will be able to take more independence (at the intermediate and advanced levels of course).

Most of the lessons have **extension recipes** – more that you can do with that lesson's skill. In order to really gain proficiency in the kitchen, your kids do need to practice again and again, so always look for opportunities in the kitchen for the kids to practice.

When you invite them to work with you, **I recommend saying, "Time for cooking class!"** or "I have a way for you to use your _____ skill for dinner today," instead of, "Somebody come help me out with dinner please!"

You can plan the classes about once a week OR move faster or slower if you choose. Once a week would give you two months of official "cooking class."

Creating a Kid-Friendly Kitchen

Don't worry, I'm not suggesting a kitchen remodel! A kid-friendly kitchen simply means **providing accessible materials for kids**. Think, "What do the kids need day to day that they can get themselves if I put it down low?" We have all our kid-sized plates, bowls, and glasses in a low cupboard, and I'm learning to move key ingredients lower as well as my kids add to their recipe repertoire.

Similarly, you'll want to think ahead about the **best place to work for each child's height:**

- A chair at the kitchen counter?
- A small stool at the counter?
- At the table standing on the floor?
- At the table kneeling on a chair?

Some really neat tools are available to help kids get high enough at the counter while staying safe, and I've included some ideas on the KCRF resources page: *www.KitchenStewardship.com/kcrfresources*

If you have more than one child working through the course with you, it will take a bit more planning to make sure everyone has something to do and you aren't pulled in a million directions.

Often you can get kids started on their different tasks and allow them to **work at the same time**. I like to take that approach personally, and I've included suggestions in each class for juggling multiple ages. Make sure you have enough space to make that happen (using the table can really help!).

Some families prefer to have each child work one at a time, youngest to oldest. With knife skills, for example, everyone watches and learns from and helps each other.

For more, check out the "Tips for Working with Multiple Age Groups" section on page 27.

Allergy and Substitution Notes

I've made every effort to make the *Kids Cook Real Food Course* allergy-friendly. For each class, if a dietary restriction makes the demonstrated recipe a poor fit, I've included suggestions for **other ways to apply the skill**. If the skill itself isn't needed in your household (cooking rice for a Paleo family or making eggs for an egg-free child, for example), I've even included ideas for **alternate skills** you could teach that would be age appropriate.

Allergies aside, please remember that **you don't have to use every item on our list**, every time – and the recipes are just one way to use the skill. Feel free to use your own favorites, omit foods that aren't in season, and make substitutions that your family will enjoy.

Quick Start Guide:

I'm long-winded. If I've overwhelmed you with all this information, focus here. Just **follow these simple steps** and you're off the races! (er, kitchen!)

- Look at the supplies/food needed, time required and the skills taught for the module levels you'll be teaching.
- Schedule class 1 in your calendar. Treat it like any other extracurricular and make it happen.
- Collect all the supplies/put food on your grocery list if necessary.
- Read the Adult Info section and any module sections you'll be teaching ahead of time.
- Tell the kids you're having "cooking class" soon.
- Thank you for making real food a priority for kids in your life!

Adult Info: Background Basics

You don't have to be a certified teacher to do a great job teaching your kids.

The basic step that most adults forget precisely *because* we're all grown up is how much we need to break down a technique into tiny, simple steps for children.

The section you're reading now will teach you how to do that and give you a great foundation for all your work with kids in the kitchen...

Basic Philosophy to Keep in Mind
While Inviting Kids to Join you in the Kitchen

1. Kids should feel good about being in the kitchen, before, during and after.
2. Everyone gets to (and needs to) participate in family life.
3. Children will acquire real life skills with competence and confidence.
4. Take incremental steps as the child is ready, based on *them*, not a chart.
5. Keep a positive atmosphere at all times.

If keeping a positive atmosphere while kids are infiltrating your kitchen is difficult for you, you're not alone. (Note the connotation of the word "infiltrating," ahem.) It is often faster to just do a task yourself than it is to teach kids what to do, step by step.

I'm here to promise you that it will be worth it. Yes, kids are going to make a bigger mess than you would on your own. They're not even going to notice, or clean it up (that's on you to teach them how!).

The time you spend with your kids in the kitchen is an investment. When your children are grown and on their own you'll have confidence that they know how to cook real food for themselves, and they won't have to rely on fast food or freezer meals.

Not to mention, I bet you could use a break from the kitchen, right? The time you spend teaching your kids how to cook is time well spent, and your investment will yield great rewards when your kids know their way around the kitchen and can offer you *real* help, or even cook dinner on their own someday.

So, let's acknowledge the fact that they're just going to make some messes, and be ready for it. In the end, it'll be worth it. I promise.

The 3-Step Process for Training Kids in the Kitchen

When you work with kids on kitchen skills, I want to encourage you to **think small.**

In other words, think about the smallest piece you can do of a skill, and explain that to your child. Examples might include the angle at which to hold a knife or peeler, how much pressure to put on a tool, where to put your thumbs, and more.

In the *Kids Cook Real Food Course*, every lesson includes three steps for adults:

1. **Demonstrate**
2. **Guide**
3. **Coach to Independence**

We even created a "flash card" just for you, to help you remember. (page 369)

Because it doesn't always come naturally!

It's downright *weird* to go as slowly as the "demonstrate" step requires, but it's worth it.

Step One: Demonstrate

When you introduce a skill to your kids, you won't let them pick up the tools or food right at first. They won't like it, but do it anyway. Show them how to do it with a running commentary.

As you demonstrate the skill, explain those minute, incremental steps. I'll help you along.

Be sure to demonstrate the entire skill, and you might even make some mistakes on purpose to help kids understand how to avoid or fix those mistakes if they happen. Be really clear about when you're doing it wrong, by the way, since the visual will stick in their head longer than your words.

You'll need double the number of pieces of food to demonstrate for skills like cutting and spreading. Don't forget to count yourself when you make a supply list!

Step Two: Guide

Guiding is a tandem work – for some skills and some ages, you can allow the child to have the tools in hand and give it a go with only your words to guide them. For others, like very young children or dangerous skills like sharp knives, you may want to begin with some hand-on-hand guided practice.

Invite your child to put his/her hand on top of yours as you complete the skill. This will allow them to get a sense of how much pressure you apply, the direction you move, your speed, etc. Then switch and ask the child to hold the tool while your hand is on top, guiding them in their motions.

I do this a lot with cracking eggs, stirring hot things, and cutting skills. The guide process is how you will feel comfortable allowing children to use sharp knives on their own.

If you've been baking together with your young children, that traditional side-by-side work is a perfect opportunity for some guided practice. Use the hand-on-hand technique with your stirring, measuring, and egg cracking, and you'll be training your littlest ones to be ready as soon as their small motor development allows them the ability to execute some of those techniques on their own. (My daughter was cracking eggs like a pro by age 4 or 5, completely independently.)

Step Three: Coach to Independence

Once you're confident that the child understands the technique, it's time to let them try it themselves – but that doesn't mean you just walk away!

The Adult Guide is like a coach of a sports team – you stay close, watch, use words and phrases to redirect actions if necessary. You remind them of the Flash Card catch phrases and safety tips.

We need you close so that your kids set a solid foundation of good habits, especially when it comes to knives and stoves. A good coach helps the team execute their best performance, and that means focusing on the little things as well as the big picture. It also means knowing when to step to the side and allow the child to experiment a little and learn on their own, as long as they are safe with the skill.

And a good coach, of course, has practices for his team often. That's your job too! Both on the initial teaching day and in the days and weeks to follow, provide opportunities for each child to practice their skills over and over.

It may take time – even years – to move through all the steps for a given skill. You might also repeat the 3-step teaching process with some skills, either if the child has forgotten something or if they're leveling up on the same skill, such as cutting with butter knives vs. Chef's knives.

Repetition is key! The more a child sees you doing something, the more times you say the same teaching phrases, the more the child gets to practice while you observe and coach, and finally the more regularly the child gets to perform the skill once learned, the better.

Have "cooking class practice" just like a sports team would have football practice, and invite your kids into the kitchen regularly to help out with food prep.

Finally, see if you can find opportunities for your kids to teach others their skills – whether that's a younger child in your family, your spouse, a friend, or even yourself. Teaching cements learning and is a powerful tool to take advantage of.

As you work with your kids, remember:

Demonstrate, Guide, and Coach to Independence.

Adult Info: Tips for Teaching Multiple Age Groups

As a mom of four kids, I understand the tension you feel when you're trying to juggle more than one child in the kitchen, especially more than one age group, *especially* if you have a toddler or baby vying for your attention too!

In fact, that's exactly the reason I felt it was easier just to cook by myself for a couple years and mostly kept my children out of the kitchen. When I stepped back and realized what I was doing, I decided to create this course to force me to teach my own kids to cook (and it's working!).

That's good for you, because it means this course is totally set up for families!

I've taken great pains to tie together the skills in a given module with threads going throughout various lessons, looping skills back for practice. I've *also* created vertical threads that tie together the different modules, which is really cool for families with multiple age groups.

On most cooking class days, you'll notice a connection between the skills on the curriculum. So even though everyone is doing something different, something appropriate for their age and skill level, they end up working together to create a meal or snack that everyone can enjoy.

Just because it's beautifully designed, however, doesn't mean it's automatically easy to implement. Family life can still get crazy.

Some Ideas to Lighten the Load

To make cooking class a more positive experience for everyone (including you, the Adult Guide) see if any of the following suggestions will work for you:

1. **Set up different workspaces.** Some kids might work at the table while others are at the counter, which will open up your kitchen and reduce your stress level.

2. **Invite the children to help each other out.** Older children might be willing (and may enjoy) helping younger ones with their pouring skills or reminding them to measure flat.

3. **Set up activities** for your kids so you can cycle through one age group at a time (or get each group started for ten minutes while the others are waiting). Kitchen-related ideas include: dough to work/play with, sugar and flour to practice measuring with (from class 4, Beginner), pouring works (from class 6, Beginner), something to prepare for dinner or snack using a previous skill, or just eating a snack to keep them busy.

4. **Many lessons are set up for multiple ages** to be busy almost all at once, and I'll walk you through the order in which to do things in the Adult Guide notes for each class. I'll also alert you about the classes that really aren't good to balance all at once.

5. **Add more kids!** It sounds counter-intuitive, but it really worked for us to increase the number of children I was teaching. Inviting friends to join meant that my kids had someone fun to play with for downtime and someone to work together with, which I'm sure helped us avoid bad attitudes before they could even start. It also meant that I scheduled my classes and stuck to them, because other families were depending on me too. "Cooking class" felt more official for everyone. Plus, our closing meal, where the kids all cooked for all three sets of parents, was an event that will always be a treasured memory!

   Having more than two kids at each level might get tricky, and you definitely don't want more than three at the Intermediate and Advanced levels, because it would simply be impossible to share the space at the stove at the same time.

6. **Try a babysitting swap.** If you have a toddler or baby, see if another family will trade with you – you teach their older kid(s) to cook while they watch your tiny one(s). Or just get a good sling or carrier and strap that baby to your back and bounce. It's reality sometimes, isn't it?

Foundations 101

Note: These lessons are designed to be taught at any time, to "lay the foundation" with basic skills. There is a space left in Class 4 during the All-Kid lesson if you haven't gotten to them yet, although the Intermediate and Advanced groups need them before Class 1 and 3 respectively. See pages 145-149 for Adult Guide tips for this section.

Stirring Specialties
2 Elements of Great Mixing and 5 Ways to Stir
(for all ages and experience)

2 Elements of Great Mixing

Yes, mixing well really is a skill.

Teach the kids two really important elements about stirring well:

1. Hold the Bowl
2. Look for a Uniform Mixture

I hope holding the bowl is obvious to the adults. You can talk to your kids about different groups of people who wear *uniforms*. What does the uniform make them all look like? (*The same.*) So when we look for a uniform mixture, we want everything to look the same. No pockets of flour. No bit of spices or salt that we can see. Nothing that isn't completely mixed in.

5 Ways to Stir

To get our uniform mixture, we'll use one of these 5 ways to stir:

1. Merry Go Round (basic stirring around and around)
2. Pogo Stick (stirring up and down, like in a tall, narrow container)
3. Roller Coaster (flipping the food up and rolling it over toward the center of the bowl)
4. Lawn Mower (scraping the bottom back and forth, back and forth, trying to cover all the ground)
5. Hula Hoop (mostly for whisk, that small circular motion you make with your wrist)

One element of stirring that is worth teaching which helps achieve that uniform mixture is the skill of scraping down the sides of the bowl. Even our littlest helpers can usually learn how to use a spatula to rudimentarily scrape straying ingredients from the sides of the bowl back into the batter (and then adult guides can do what we call "finishing touches" and catch what they miss).

Language for Measuring with Young Children
Gaining Independence with Measuring Spoons and Cups
(for Beginner and some Intermediate Level kids)

When my oldest was little, I realized how frustrating it can be for an adult to ask a child, "Can you get the teaspoon ready?" and receive a blank stare. It's equally frustrating for the child to want to help bake but their parent ends up doing almost everything. I had to find a way to communicate which spoon to pick up so that my kid could really be a helper while we baked beyond just dumping stuff in the bowl.

Kid-friendly Vocabulary for Measuring Spoons and Cups

We came up with a family of measuring spoons and cups, creating the beginning of a new kitchen vocabulary that we're excited to share with you now.

There are pretty much 4 standard spoons or cups in a set, and we call them:

- Dad – tablespoon / cup
- Mom – teaspoon / half cup
- Kid – half teaspoon / third cup
- Baby – quarter teaspoon / fourth cup

You can call the "kid" a "big brother" or "big sister" if you like.

For the Beginners, this language really is necessary. For our Intermediate crew, we want to start to bridge to the proper terminology, but it's nice to have these terms to fall back on to remind them what they need if you're across the room. Hopefully our Advanced kids don't need this crutch, but the other measuring lessons should be a good reminder.

I highly recommend creating time to bake with your 5-and-under crowd while you are working through the course – the plain old "work together on a recipe" kitchen work that most parents do already. It's important to be able to use this language and practice measuring flat WITH an adult often so that it becomes second nature. Teaching one lesson won't make it stick.

Measuring Mastery, Part 1 & 2
Dry Measuring, Fats, & Liquids
(for all ages and stages of experience)

Measuring is a very basic skill at which everyone needs to be not only proficient, but become masters. We use some very specific and fun language for measuring skills in the *Kids Cook Real Food* Course, so I recommend that kids of all ages participate in this lesson.

- Part 1: dry measuring, including flour
- Part 2: liquid measuring and how to measure fats

Part 1 is definitely necessary for Beginners for Class 4, and they should go over part 2 (although they only need the liquid measuring skills) by Class 6. Intermediate kids should lay this foundation before they even begin Class number 1, and Advanced kids may think they have measuring down, but many older kids (and even some of the moms!) may pick up some important tips. That level first makes a recipe in Class 3.

5 Basic Measuring Strategies

1. **Keep it Flat.** Starting with a set of measuring spoons and a bowl of sugar or salt (the Beginner kids will use this again and again), demonstrate the importance of level measuring. We say, "No Holes, No Hills" to help kids watch for problems.

    - Scoop the food.
    - Level it with a butter knife or sometimes "cheat" with a straight finger (no fingers for Beginners).
    - Sometimes you can just jiggle it back and forth, especially if you're inside a spice jar.

I recommend an extra "spill bowl" for Beginner, Intermediate, and messy Advanced kids. They can measure over the little bowl and then pour any spills back into the container so you don't waste.

2.   Flour Falls like Snow. Measuring flour is a lot like spices or sugar, but it's more important not to pack it down. We say, "No Sand Castling It." And no jiggling. Use that butter knife or scoop to *Snowplow It Flat*.

If you like, you can demonstrate what happens when you do pack it by doing a side by side comparison. I recommend that adults do it the wrong way so that children aren't practicing it "wrong!"

- Measure with the same size measuring cup correctly ("Let It Fall Like Snow") and then incorrectly by packing it down ("Play Sand Castle").
- Pour into two bowls of exactly the same size – are they different? Why? If you have a kitchen scale, you could also demonstrate the difference by weight.

Let the children touch the flour to see how soft it is. This can remind them to treat it softly and Snowplow It Flat.

Note: For those in warmer climates where snow is not familiar, try terms such as "let it fall like a digger into a dump truck" if your child has used a digger toy in the sandbox or "like pouring water in the bathtub." Think of anything your child is familiar with that would be poured from up high into another container. For the snowplow image, try "sweep it flat" or "use the bulldozer."

3.   Pack the Fat. Show how to put fat evenly into a measuring cup, filling in holes, and scraping flat. A butter knife is essential to the process. It takes a reeeeeaaaalllllly long time to let kids do it, but the Intermediate Level *can* be independent in it if you have enough patience to let them! You just might have to walk away and not watch.

4.   Sometimes We Do Pack Dry Ingredients. If you use brown sugar, coconut flour, or anything else that should be packed, demonstrate packing it into a measuring cup.

5.   Cut the Butter Sticks. Because butter has the little marks on the package to help us measure it easily, you can demonstrate and discuss how those work.

Basic Liquid Measuring Skills

Show the kids a liquid measuring cup. Using water, show how different the measurement looks when you're standing up and when you look straight on. Our phrase is "**Get Level with Liquids**."

I like to celebrate the importance of the Beginner age group by pointing out that they're usually the perfect level to do this skill and allow them to "be the boss" and tell me when to stop.

Season Like a TV Chef

(for more experienced kids)

I always wanted to look so cool like the chefs on TV who just throw in a little of this, a little of that. They look so carefree, and yet their recipes always turn out wonderfully! I finally decided to teach myself what "about a teaspoon" of spices looks like. For your Intermediate and Advanced kids, this is a really fun extension and something that will be helpful in efficiency and creativity throughout their lives.

Practice measuring a teaspoon or half teaspoon of sugar or salt into your hand (depending on the size of the hand) to see how much space it fills, what it really looks like. Do this a few times. Then let the child guesstimate "about a teaspoon" in their hand, and measure it out of their hand to see how close they are.

Be sure to discuss WHEN it matters to be perfect and when you can fudge it. In baking recipes, the leaving (salt, baking powder, baking soda) really needs to be measured precisely, but the spices (cinnamon, ginger, pepper, etc.) can be more varied. In cooking, nearly everything can be guesstimated, as long as you're okay with variability in your recipes.

They can choose to do independent practice now, back and forth between measuring and guessing. Definitely take advantage of natural opportunities as you cook and bake. In other words, anytime you are measuring anything, remind your child to pour it into their hand first to get practice eyeing it up. Then sometimes see if they can guesstimate measuring something, checking it before adding it to the recipe (especially if it's a "non-fudge" ingredient).

Class 1

Welcome to Kids Cook Real Food!

The lesson this week will help you, the adult guides, teach children in your life basic cooking skills. Remember that great teaching and learning includes demonstrating, guiding, and finally coaching to independence. You are a vital part of that process!

You should demonstrate each step of today's skills for your child learner(s). Nothing can replace the guidance you will provide as your child first attempts today's new skills. Be sure to help them on each step - and then step back.

As the child begins to be comfortable with the skills, use your voice to redirect them or refocus them if necessary, but the ultimate goal is for you to fade into the background. Let's dive into today's skill so you feel prepared to work with the children.

What Adult Guides Need to Know

The "adult info" section of each class will give you a quick overview of each day's lesson for ALL the module levels, some challenges to be ready for, an explanation of why the skills are developmentally appropriate for these age groups and some tips for juggling multiple age groups at once.

Today everyone is making something appropriate for snacking or appetizers, but no one is actually cooking with heat yet.

You'll get practice with the "demonstrate, guide, coach to independence" strategy that I want you to use. You should demonstrate for your kids so they can see the skill in real life.

Being very precise with your motions and expecting them to do the same lays the foundation for care in the kitchen at all module levels. Focus on developing good habits and basic skills that will serve your kids well their entire lives.

Remember that demonstrating means you'll need at least one extra for each item so you have one to show. It's best to have multiple extras on hand.

Although I suggest specific fruits and vegetables, that doesn't mean you must use exactly those foods or all of the options. Consider what is in season, available, and fits your family's needs. Your goal isn't to cut a specific food necessarily but to practice a skill. Each module has suggestions for alternate foods.

Challenges You Might Encounter

Bad Attitudes. Yours or theirs? Although it may not have been a great experience in the past working in the kitchen with your kids, don't let that get you down. Pretend you're an optimist. ;) I was thrilled to get this feedback from one mom after her first *Kids Cook Real Food* class: "I loved that I was able to work with my kids in the kitchen and not get frustrated!" One way to set this course apart is to call it "cooking class" and wear aprons to set aside the activity from other day-to-day tasks. Starting off well can help everyone stay positive.

Too challenging or not challenging enough. If your kids feel like the class was too easy or too hard, ask them for details. You might be able to simply add a bit more to the lesson (like having Advanced kids make a ranch dip if you don't have the Intermediate level). If kids are really struggling with the skill, there's no shame in going backward to a previous level (or if they're Beginners, I'd recommend only spreading and not peeling today).

Developmental Readiness and Kid-friendly Reminders

Today's skills get the kids jumping right in to learn something they can do on their own to help the family out and provide a snack for everyone right away – this is way better than craft time!

Beginner

The Beginner group is learning two skills: spreading and peeling. Very small children will have trouble with the peeler, so they might stick with just the one skill of spreading. But with this low-risk skill, they will be able to help prepare an Ants on a Log snack and butter toast for the whole family, so they're helping out immediately!

The dexterity they'll practice with all of the dull knife skills we teach in the eCourse will actually help them be successful in school as well, because the same muscles are used to hold a pencil and cut with scissors. The other fine motor skill kids work on is using both hands together, which is something we generally wouldn't think of as important, but it totally is!

Intermediate

Intermediate kids are using their expanding reading skills to follow a recipe properly and to practice careful measuring and pouring (from the Beginner Level). They now have the organizational capacity to keep track of ingredients – and if they don't, this will be good practice! (Non-readers can still take the Intermediate Level; they'll just need the parent to read the recipe for them.)

I quickly learned while working with my 7-year-olds that abbreviations and fractions in recipes were too much to handle all at once for these somewhat new readers. That's why you'll see the recipes in the *Kids Cook Real Food Recipe Book* written out ("one-fourth teaspoon" and "one cup"). I do include the fractions as well to help bridge the children as they continue to grow in their skills.

The terminology we use to describe measuring spoons is covered in the Foundations 101 section on page 35. You should go over the Foundations 101 material with your Intermediate kids, too.

Advanced

Our Advanced level is moving right into sharp knife skills with a big chef's knife. They ought to have the self-control and manual dexterity to handle a sharp knife, but if they're on the young side (8 and 9) you may want to put them through the Intermediate Level first and/or wait until their small motor control gets better with smaller sharp knives. You can always bridge them by doing some of the larger cutting with your own knife and allowing them to finish the job on smaller pieces with a medium-sized sharp knife.

All-Kid Lesson

Remind your children about the absolute basics of working in the kitchen. These are basic food preparation habits that people of all ages should practice:

- Wash your hands before working with food.
- Put your hair up if it's long.
- Wear an apron – this helps to set apart the activity from other work and also keeps clothing cleaner.
- Keep hands out of noses, mouths, and off feet while working.
- Listen to your adult and have a great attitude – working in the kitchen can be so much fun!

Tips for Teaching Multiple Age Groups

The activities in this class are perfectly suited to dovetail into each other. Try working in this order to juggle all 3 levels at once:

1. Get the Beginner group going (at the table) with buttering bread, and they can eat that snack if they have any wait time. I recommend asking them to butter extra bread for everyone in your family before they eat.
2. Also at the table, start the Intermediate group on their dressings. You should be able to be nearby but not 100% involved in their entire process.
3. Move the Beginner group on to peeling – this skill generally takes some time for little hands to accomplish. The cucumber they peel can be used in the Advanced module.

4. Then teach the Advanced group so they can cut celery for the Beginners. The counter or table is appropriate for these skills. Remember to grab a stool or chair for the counter so your child is above the food. You should be quite involved until you feel comfortable walking away while they cut!

5. *(While they have been waiting for you to get the others started, your Advanced kids could either be doing an outside activity like homework or playing or might be well-suited to help the younger kids with their tasks.)*

6. Everyone's skills will sort of move forward bit by bit, and after all your kids taste the ranch and veggies, pack the rest up for dinner (at which time you can applaud everyone for helping the family).

7. If you leave Ants on a Log for last with the Beginners, they can make a snack for tomorrow – just store the celery sticks in an airtight container in the refrigerator.

Don't forget to read the information on "Tips for Teaching Multiple Age Groups" on page 27 – there are some overall strategies for success that may be game changers for your family.

Spreading & Peeling: Beginner

How We Apply the Skill Today:
- Spreading peanut butter on celery to make Ants on a Log, spreading butter on bread, peeling cucumbers and carrots.

Skills That Loop into this Lesson:
- Child should be able to hold a crayon and color.

Time Needed:
- Hands on Time: 20 minutes

Tools Needed:
- Small plate
- Dinner knife (butter knife) or spreader or both
- Sometimes holiday dip or cheese sets have the perfect sized little spreader.
- Vegetable peeler (kid-sized are available)
- Cutting board

Food Needed:
- Celery
- Peanut butter
- Raisins
- Butter (softened at room temp)
- Bread (or toast)
- (or alternative to spread: cream cheese or hummus and crackers or cucumbers, jam on toast, guacamole)
- Firm cucumbers
- Whole carrots

Today's Recipes:
- Ants on a Log
- Buttered Toast
- Helping on a Crudités Platter

Adults Should Prepare:
- Wash cucumbers and carrots
- Wash and cut celery (unless you have an Advanced Module student; then they will cut celery)
- Set butter and peanut butter (if refrigerated) out to soften the day before
- Optional: toast bread so it's more solid

Allergy Notes and Substitutions:

- If kids don't like celery, try peanut butter on apple slices.
- To avoid nuts, cream cheese or hummus on crackers works. Guacamole is also yummy on veggies if you don't want to use peanut butter.
- For grain-free, try veggie slices with a thick ranch dip, hummus, or nut butter. Cucumber slices, chunks of red pepper, or apple slices are fun. Pull in the veggie the child has just peeled, and spread hummus on a cucumber slice.

Daily Nugget:

"Bread with Butter is Better"

Different foods help your body be healthy in different ways. We should eat things from more than one food group together – butter with your bread, veggies and nuts, fruits and cheese or yogurt. Balance!

Adults may want to understand: Fat slows down the digestion of starch and helps the body use vitamins in vegetables better.

Notes:

_____

_____

_____

_____

_____

_____

_____

Lesson Overview: Spreading

Spreading is a great low-risk activity for little hands. A mistake won't cause an injury or mess up a recipe result. The worst thing that can happen is a delicious mess of peanut butter or butter!

For this age, adult guides will want to prepare the materials thoroughly so there's no downtime for little attention spans.

All ingredients should be accessible:

Catch Phrases to Remember:

Catch phrases help kids to remember the principles and the skills that they are learning. Try to incorporate these phrases into your lesson to help these ideas stick in your kids' minds. Additionally, be sure to cut out or photocopy the flash cards (page 363) and keep them handy throughout the week.

Spreading

- Hand over Teeth
- Tip of the Knife in the Spread
- Corner to Corner, Edge to Edge

- If your peanut butter is almost empty, open a new one.
- Make sure anything you're going to spread is softened if usually refrigerated.
- Consider toasting the bread so it's easier for the child. (Frozen bread sounds like a good idea but it makes the butter too hard to spread.)

How to Demonstrate

It can seem like a no-brainer to adults to spread butter on toast – but if you just give your child a butter knife and let them go at it, you'll be surprised at how many different ways mistakes can be made! It's worth the time to break it down into little steps and demonstrate:

1. Show your kids the teeth on the butter knife. Let them feel how the teeth are not very sharp – but can be a little bit if you press hard or saw back and forth.

2. Hold the knife firmly with the palm on top. We call it "hand over teeth" so the hand is on top and the teeth on bottom.

3. Explain that it's not like holding a crayon or a pencil, nor like holding a fork – more like holding a hammer.

4. Use the very tip of the knife to dip into the peanut butter or butter. Demonstrate how much they should scoop.

5. Spread the pile around on the bread. Remind kids to spread their piles in different places so that they have butter from corner to corner, edge to edge.

6. Tell your child how you want them to hold the food – should they set it on the plate and steady the plate with their non-dominant hand or hold the food? It depends on how big they are. (If the item you're spreading on is large like bread, leave it on a flat plate. If it's small like celery, it's ok to pick it up, but if you're having trouble, set it back down.)

"Hold the knife firmly with the palm on top. We call it 'Hand Over Teeth' so the hand is on top and the teeth on bottom."

7. Set the knife down before you pick up food to eat or move it. This doesn't seem important with dull knives but is a key safety habit!

8. Demonstrate some common mistakes:
    • No fingers on the butter.
    • We never lick knives (unless we have permission).
    • If you lick the knife on accident, don't put it back into the serving dish.
    • What to do if you get too much? Don't put it back.
    • Pull the piles out (when there is too much in one area of the bread).

How To Guide

For just a swipe or two (more for very young children) allow your child's hand and your hand to be on the knife at the same time. This will help them learn the stroke pattern and how to hold the knife.

Many young children will need to choke up on the knife and hold it at the top of the handle, unlike how an adult might do it. This will give them greater control.

How to Coach to Independence

As quickly as possible, allow your child to move on to experimenting for themselves – a low risk activity means it's easier to just let the child go at it!

Lesson Overview: Peeling

Note for adult guides with 2-3-year-olds: If you're not comfortable with your child having anything with a blade (which includes veggie peelers since they could actually nick skin and hurt),then just focus on the spreading for today, or add something blade-less like separating orange sections, snapping beans, or peeling leaves off kale stems.

Both shapes of peelers (Y-shaped and straight) should work fine for peeling, although I personally prefer a Y-shaped peeler. We even have one that fits little hands. *(Find the KCRF Resources page at www.KitchenStewardship.com/kcrfresources)*

Feel free to include your little ones in the produce washing process or do it before you start – your preference.

How to Demonstrate

We start with the carrot because it's far easier to peel. The solid carrot allows the peeler edge to "catch" better than the cucumber.

Note: I don't usually peel organic carrots, only conventional ones – both for nutrition and as a time saver. However, bitter cucumber peels need to go!

The peeler goes in the "Crayon Hand" (that's the hand the child uses with a crayon, or the dominant hand). Show your child how you hold the peeler with your fist on top, firmly. The other hand holds the carrot on the far end. Holding the vegetable with your thumb down and out of the way is good practice for knife skills.

We show kids that there's an imaginary wall in the middle of the carrot to keep our hands safe. The peeler and the hand both never cross the imaginary wall – "Bonk!" We tell kids to keep the peeler far from their hands "so you don't peel yourself!"

Demonstrate how to get the peeler to "catch" the vegetable and the angle you have to hold it at (not straight up and down). Talk about nice long strokes and touching the lines together. Only peel *away* from your other hand. Show how you turn the vegetable bit by bit as you peel. You can have some fun demonstrating what happens if you don't turn it – you'll end up with carrot "tongues."

> "We show kids that there's an imaginary wall in the middle of the carrot to keep our hands safe."

When one half is done, turn it around "like a board game spinner." Get the same invisible wall in place and peel the other side. Your hand still never crosses the center!

Show the kids how to "Clear the Peels" from the cutting board, always with the peeler out of your hand. Kids like to help with this and that's perfectly acceptable even at the demonstration level.

How To Guide

Because angles and pressure are key to making the peeler work properly, the guiding step is important for this skill. Start with your hand on the peeler and the child's hand over yours, then switch.

As the child is working, they'll likely miss some spots. Ask them, "Do you see anything else you'd like to peel?" or somehow use a question rather than a correction. This helps the child learn how to evaluate their own work and set expectations for themselves.

> "Have fun reminding them not to cross the wall – 'Bonk!'"

Have fun reminding them not to cross the wall – "Bonk!"

How to Coach to Independence

In our house, we have cucumbers and carrots at almost every dinner, so our little ones get plenty of chances to practice peeling. A cucumber shows what you miss better, but a carrot is easier to peel by a long shot. Try to find firm cukes OR just stick with carrots for practice until they're more proficient.

"DO NOT clean up for them! It's an investment in your future."

Always insist that the children clear the peels to trash before moving on. DO NOT clean up for them! It's an investment in your future.

Let them do and redo if they need to / want to. Practice makes perfect! (or at least close enough!)

Challenges You Might Encounter

The Licker. It might take too much self-control for your child to NOT lick the knife while they're working. If you want to avoid contaminating the serving container, scoop out a small amount of peanut butter or hummus into a bowl for them.

Big Ol' Pile of Butter. Kids can get stuck in a rut, literally, and keep putting butter on the same part of the bread (or whatever you're using). We just say "pull the pile out" and remind "corner to corner" and they'll get it eventually!

The Painter. Look out for those who wish to paint the table with their spreads! :)

Stamina. With two skills today, you might need to split the lesson into two parts. Gauge the child's stamina after spreading and see if they seem ready for more.

Tough cucumber peels. We peel carrots first because they're easier for the peeler to "catch" the peels. If the child has trouble getting the peeler to "catch," help them angle it more upward a bit or ask them to get on their knees to get a better angle for themselves. You might even need to peel a stripe around the middle of the vegetable so there's a piece of peel for their peeler to grab hold of. Use firm cucumbers to try to avoid this problem.

Don't forget to create opportunities to practice this skill throughout the week!

You might integrate this one into daily life by inviting someone over for a snack and letting the child make and serve Ants on a Log. Give the child the responsibility of buttering the whole family's toast for breakfast or a soup-and-bread dinner this week – they'll be so proud to use their skill to help!

Extension Recipes to Apply this Skill:

Recipes in *Recipes for Kids Cook Real Food*:
- Homemade Guacamole is great on veggies

Find these recipes online at
www.kidscookrealfood.com/recipes:
- Apple Squares (or use your favorite quick bread recipe)
- Yogurt Cheese Frosting
- Homemade Hummus
- Fruit Pizza

If you don't have the KCRF recipe books visit *www.kidscookrealfood.com/recipes* to get access

Next Week's Grocery List:
- Bananas
- Melon (cantaloupe and honeydew are great)
- Cheese (softer cheese better than an aged sharp cheddar)

Following a Recipe: Intermediate

How We Apply the Skill Today:
- Making homemade salad dressings

Skills That Loop into this Lesson:
- Measuring (Foundations 101)
- Pouring (Beg. Lesson 6)

Time Needed:
- Hands on Time: 15-30 minutes

Tools Needed:
- Liquid measuring cup
- Measuring spoons
- Glass jar or salad dressing container(s)
- Spoon
- Whisk, optional
- *Recipes for Kids Cook Real Food*

Today's Recipes:
Homemade Ranch Dressing and Italian Dressing

Food Needed:
- Extra virgin olive oil
- Red or white wine vinegar
- Dijon mustard
- Garlic powder
- Italian seasoning
- Salt and pepper
- Sour cream (or alternatives)
- Ranch mix (from Beg. Lesson 4) or herbs to make it (see KCRF recipe book)
- Something to taste the ranch dip with (cut carrots are great; if you have an Advanced child, they'll be cutting some today.)

Adults Should Prepare:
- Have the KCRF recipe book nearby
- May need veggies to test dip with

Extensions: how else could this basic skill be used?
- Reading ANY recipe needs this skill! We'll really use it again in Lesson 4 when the kids make a recipe by themselves.

Allergy Notes and Substitutions:
- **Dairy-free:** Use homemade mayo and/or thick canned coconut milk for the ranch.

"Olive Oil is so Cool"

Olive oil has the most nutrients when cold. It doesn't stand up to heat really well, so it's best to use it cold – like salad dressings! Also, don't store it near heat or in the light (clear containers aren't great).

Adults may want to understand: Most commercial salad dressings are made with soybean, corn or canola oils. These are called industrial oils because they are rather new in an historical perspective. They are high in omega-6 oils which are inflammatory (and Americans generally eat way too much of them).

Notes:

_____

_____

_____

_____

_____

_____

_____

_____

_____

_____

Lesson Overview: Reading a Recipe Well

Every style of reading has its own literacy, in a sense. We have to learn to read fiction differently than nonfiction, and as adults we read blogs differently than we would a daily devotional. Reading a recipe is the same – simply knowing "how to read" doesn't mean that reading a recipe comes easily.

We lay out quite a few steps for reading a recipe well. Coach your kids to:

- Read the whole recipe from top to bottom first. Make sure you understand the process and ask the adult questions if you're unsure.
- Collect the ingredients. Put them all to the *left* of the workspace.
- As you carefully measure each ingredient, move it to the *right* side.
- Stir a *uniform* mixture every time.

They can use the flash card from this Lesson and Class 4 to remind them of the steps to follow.

Catch Phrases to Remember:

Catch phrases help kids to remember the principles and the skills that they are learning. Try to incorporate these phrases into your lesson to help these ideas stick in your kids' minds. Additionally, be sure to cut out or photocopy the flash cards (page 363) and keep them handy throughout the week.

- Read the Whole Recipe First
- Move Ingredients from Left to Right
- Stir a Uniform Mixture Every Time

How to Demonstrate

Hopefully you've demonstrated this skill many times while working in the kitchen over the years.

If your child is a very early reader who might get fatigued reading the

> "If your child is a very early reader who might get fatigued reading the whole recipe, do it for them."

whole recipe, do it for them. The goal of learning the skill isn't to practice reading, it's to be prepared for the recipe and make sure all the ingredients are collected.

Adult guides should check that kids read from top to bottom, left to right and make sure they understand all the words. We quickly learned that for this age group, there's enough to learn already without trying to remember the difference between "tsp." and "Tbs." and how to read unfamiliar fractions.

All the recipes in the *Kids Cook Real Food* recipe book avoid abbreviations, and fractions are written out in words but also in numerical form in parentheses to help children bridge their knowledge. They'll be more ready for fractions in school because of "cooking class!"

How To Guide

"You'll help the kids find the right ingredients and measure correctly but you want them to do the majority of the work."

I'd call this entire activity the "guide" portion of your teaching.

As the adult, try to keep your hands out of the mix as much as possible. You'll help the kids find the right ingredients and measure correctly but you want them to do the majority of the work. Review the names of the measuring spoons: Dad, Mom, Kid, Baby and also explain the real names. Having both is helpful as you try to instruct without interfering too much.

I recommend starting with the ranch first, and remind your kids that this is one of those recipes where it's not important to measure perfectly. They can guess at the amount of sour cream, and you can taste the ranch and add more seasoning if necessary.

I like to tell kids: "You can always add more, but you can't take it out!" Sometimes mixes need to sit a bit for the flavors to blend before you really taste it, so encourage them to go a bit light if they are adding additional seasoning.

"Fidgeting with the flavors is a great chance to learn how to balance the ingredients– if it's too spicy, add more sour cream; too bland, add more seasoning."

Fidgeting with the flavors is a great chance to learn how to balance the ingredients – if it's too spicy, add more sour cream; too bland, add more seasoning.

I suggest using two styles of stirring: Pogo Stick (up and down) and Merry-Go-Round (around and around). For both, be sure to hold the jar firmly with the other hand. Kids can look through the sides of the jar to make sure there aren't any clumps of seasoning – remind them of the term "uniform mixture."

When you move onto the Italian dressing, kids get a chance to practice their pouring skills as well as their measuring, both dry and liquid (Remember: "Get Level with Liquids"). Plus, there's a cool science integration with the oil and vinegar separating and the Dijon mustard acting to *emulsify* them.

You should guide your kids through making their own decision about how much vinegar to use. Ask them to smell the vinegar and use more for tangier dressing and less for a tamer mix.

How to Coach to Independence

Since today's lesson is guided, the coaching to independence happens organically over the next few weeks. Continue to invite the children to make simple recipes with you, and in Class 4 we'll actually cut the apron strings and challenge them to make a recipe without the adult helping them at all.

Challenges You Might Encounter

Stirring in Jars. The ranch stirring spoon will just be messy. Be ready for it!

Forgetful Frank. It can be difficult for kids to remember where they left off in the recipe. Some may need to physically mark each ingredient with a small check mark, or if you're still working together, just remind them.

Heavy Handed Pouring. When kids are measuring spices, if they need to pour them out of the spice jar, having a little "spill bowl" to pour over is a helpful strategy. Any overflow can be scooped back into the spice jar. We did pour vinegar right over the jar because for this recipe, a bit too much won't hurt.

Don't forget to create opportunities to practice this skill throughout the week!

You might integrate this one into daily life by delegating homemade dressings to your kids, but in the immediate future you won't need any more. You could have a party and put the kids in charge of the dip, make a gift for a friend, or use extension recipes for more dip variety this week.

Extension Recipes to Apply this Skill:

Practicing any salad dressing recipe loved by your family will bring your child closer to being able to use this skill independently.

Experiment with basic dressings – use the ratio of olive oil and vinegar used in the recipe in this lesson and add other seasonings from the cupboard or other vinegars.

Recipes in *Recipes for Kids Cook Real Food*:
- Homemade Guacamole seasoning mix

Find these recipes online at *www.kidscookrealfood.com/recipes*:
- Pasta salads and cold grain salads are delicious with homemade dressings.
- Mrs. Kimball's Favorite Greek Dressing
- Create wraps or sandwiches with the ranch dip.
- Fruit Pizza (the "frosting" is easy, and if you have beginners they can spread it!)

If you don't have the KCRF recipe books visit *www.kidscookrealfood.com/recipes* to get access.

Next Week's Grocery List:
- Pineapple
- Strawberries
- Mushrooms
- If one of those is not in season or difficult/ expensive to source, just skip it.

Sharp Knife Skills, Level 1: Advanced

How We Apply the Skill Today:
- Cutting carrots into wheels and sticks, cucumbers into wheels and sticks, and dicing celery

Skills That Loop into this Lesson:
- Peeling straight vegetables (Beg. Lesson 1)
- How to wash produce (All-Kid Lesson 7)
- How to hold a knife (All-Kid Lesson 2)
- Dull knife slicing (Beg. Lesson 2)
- Intro to sharp knife skills (Int. Lesson 2)

Tools Needed:
- Vegetable brush
- Cutting board(s)
- Chef's knife or Santoku knife
- Bowl or container for food

Time Needed:
- Hands on Time: 20-30 minutes + guided practice time

Food Needed:
- Carrots
- Cucumbers
- Celery

Today's Recipes:
Crudités platter (a fancy word for raw veggies) or Simple Chicken Rice Soup

Adults Should Prepare:
- Consider making chicken soup with the cut veggies; have ingredients ready

Extensions: how else could this basic skill be used?
- With these basic sharp knife skills, you should be able to easily cut other straight-cut foods like green onions, lettuce, parsnips, and zucchini.

"Fermented Foods Feed our Guts"

Fermented foods add healthy bacteria to your diet (think yogurt, but with vegetables). With your sharp knife skills, you could make lacto-fermented veggies, like real pickles, Dilly Beans, Kimchi, etc.

Eating fermented foods adds probiotics to your meals and feeds the ONE TRILLION bacteria in your gut! Wow! You can also eat a yogurt dip with your raw veggies to get probiotics.

Notes:

_____

_____

_____

_____

_____

_____

_____

_____

_____

_____

Lesson Overview: Sharp Knife Skills, Level 1

Giving your child a big chef's knife for the first time can be a harrowing experience. You'll want to initially stick close and allow for time to practice, make mistakes, and go slowly – so that the mistakes are minor and quickly corrected.

I'll show you and your kids 3 safe ways to hold food and 4 ways to cut with a knife in this lesson.

Be sure to set the scene: your child needs to be comfortably above the surface on which s/he is working. You might need to allow them to use a stool at the kitchen counter or stand on the floor and work at a table. Provide one cutting board and one knife per child, plus a bowl for the cut food.

Remind your kids of the importance of washing produce. If you already went through the Intermediate level of *Kids Cook Real Food*, you learned that in Class 7. Review the need for both water and scrubbing to get the dirt (and other things) off your food. Allow your child to wash the necessary produce for the lesson or guide them in the process if they don't have much experience.

If your cucumbers or carrots should be peeled, ask the child to do it to loop that skill back in. Peeling is taught in the Beginner Class 1.

Catch Phrases to Remember:

Catch phrases help kids to remember the principles and the skills that they are learning. Try to incorporate these phrases into your lesson to help these ideas stick in your kids' minds. Additionally, be sure to cut out or photocopy the flash cards (page 363) and keep them handy throughout the week.

General Knife Skills:

- Always Carry Knives Point Down
- Hold the Knife Firmly – Be the Boss!
- Choke Up if You Need More Power (No finger!)
- Knife Moves, Eyes Down
- Food Moves, Knife Down
- Never Set the Knife Down with the Sharp Side Up

Safe ways to hold food:

- Top Chop
- Up and Over Soldier
- Hey, Hey, Outta the Way!
- (Never "Pick Me! Pick Me!")

Ways to cut:

- Rock-a-bye Knife (knife tip touches the board)
- Drive it Like a Vacuum (knife stays on the board)
- Saw Blade (soft foods and big items)
- Tug-o-War Pull (slicing)

How to Demonstrate

Demonstrating skills is particularly key when there is a risk of injury – but also because we want to establish incredibly good habits. Knife skills may be used daily for food prep, and with improper holds, the risk of hand fatigue or pain increases.

Ask your kids to pay close attention to the knife holds and food holds and make sure they have a good idea of the following principles:

- **Knife Safety.** Always carry a knife point down and set it down flat in a safe place, away from the edge of the counter.

- **Be the Boss of the Knife.** Hold the knife firmly in the fist of your dominant hand, with all your fingers wrapped around it. Your hand is on top and the palm of your hand is applying pressure downward.

- **Point the Tip Down.** Except in some "saw blade" motions, the tip of the knife should always point down toward the cutting board. This will cause the elbow to go up a bit, but it shouldn't be uncomfortable. If it is, your child might need to have more height above the cutting board (taller stool or chair).

- **Stand fingers up like a soldier.** Impressing the importance of keeping fingers out of the way is vital in this first phase of knife skills! Use the "Pick me! Pick me!" strategy to gently remind them if some fingers start looking unsafe. We say that if your fingers are horizontal and pointing toward the knife, it's like they're volunteering to go under the blade - "Pick me! Pick me!" Once that's been demonstrated and laughed at, all you have to do is squeak, "Pick me!" and your child will know to stand his or her fingers straight up and down. That creates a laugh instead of an uncomfortable correction.

- **Choke up if you need more power.** (No finger down the blade.) When it's hard to get the knife through the food, move your hand up the knife toward the tip – you can even put your fingers on either side of the actual blade of the knife. This is called "choking up" and will add

> "Demonstrating skills is particularly key when there is a risk of injury – but also because we want to establish incredibly good habits."

strength for you. Putting your index finger along the top of the knife is tempting but really won't add stability.

- **Knife moves, eyes down.** When your knife is moving and cutting food, you need to be looking at what you're doing.

- **Food moves, knife down.** When it's time to pick up food and move it to a bowl or into a pot, set the knife down flat along the side edge of your cutting board.

You'll also demonstrate our 3 safe ways to hold food while cutting and 4 styles of making the cuts.

Safe Ways to Hold Food:

1. **Top Chop**
   - The non-dominant hand goes on top of the knife (flat!) to both add pressure and stability and stay out of the way of the blade.
2. **Up and Over Soldier**
   - The thumb and fingers hold the food on either side, forming a tunnel that the knife goes through to make the cut. Fingers are straight up and down.
3. **Hey, Hey, Outta the Way!**
   - The basic hold – as far away from the knife as possible on the other end of the food, fingers standing straight up and down like a soldier.
4. **Never "Pick Me! Pick Me!"**
   - If the fingers get close to the knife, they're volunteering to be cut! "Pick Me!" We don't want that.

4 Ways to Cut:

1. **Rock-A-Bye Knife**
   - The knife tip touches the board and the knife rocks up and down, up and down. For dicing and some slicing with large chef's knives with a rounded edge; also works with Santoku.
2. **Drive it Like a Vacuum**
   - The knife tip also stays on the board but the knife moves back and forth and up and down, dicing or slicing on the way forward. For large chef's knives with rounded edges. It's a little easier to get through hard foods like carrots with this technique vs. Rock-a-Bye Knife, because the knife is moving forward through the food instead of simply trying to power straight down.

3. **Saw Blade**
   - Sawing back and forth – for soft foods and big items. All knife sizes.
4. **Tug-o-War Pull**
   - Pull the knife backward through the food toward you. For slicing, usually long pieces of food, all knife sizes.

Practice those phrases before working with your kids and definitely have the flash cards (from page 363) ready for today. Remind them to go slowly, because you can't uncut a finger...

How To Guide

Just as young children want to hold a pencil in awkward, inefficient ways because their hands are little and lacking in dexterity, rookies to sharp knives – especially the first time with a great big chef's knife – will typically need a lot of redirection to form good habits.

> "Don't be afraid to put your hand right on top of the child's and cut together for a while..."

Don't be afraid to put your hand right on top of the child's and cut together for a while, or if they are younger and don't have much experience with sharp knives, let them put their hand on top of yours instead. (That way you're more in control.) Help them to adjust their hands to a strong, hand-over-knife hold and use the phrases from the flash cards.

Don't feel like you have to be the bad guy. Try "Mrs. Kimball says..." as your lead in to correction.

After a few cuts, you should be able to gauge whether the child has the technique solidly enough to use the knife without you.

How to Coach to Independence

An easy vegetable to start with is definitely the cucumber. The holding hand can be "Hey, Hey, Outta the Way," on the other end, quite farrrr from the knife. Invite your child to practice making wheels/circles of cucumber using the Rock-a-Bye Knife or Drive it Like a Vacuum technique. Remind them to stand those fingers up like a soldier!

Move on to carrot wheels. It's more solid, so slightly more challenging. In this first round, you might not want the child to continue cutting close to their hand – so let them leave a rather long piece uncut. One helpful hint is to first cut the carrot lengthwise so that your child has a flat side to keep the carrot from rolling around.

Cutting celery into sticks for an Ants on a Log snack is a very easy, low-risk cut to practice. Top Chop is appropriate, as is Rock-a-Bye Knife. Some guidance may be needed on how to cut the large end off the celery, because the mass may be a challenge. Instruct kids to rock the knife gently back and forth while it's buried in the celery end (and demonstrate if you have enough celery on hand). Also show kids how to cut the leafy parts off the celery (save them in the freezer for making stock/bone broth).

Note: If you have Beginner level kids doing the course, have your Advanced kids cut enough celery sticks for the little ones' spreading lesson.

> "One helpful hint is to have you first cut the carrot lengthwise so that your child has a flat side to keep the carrot from rolling around."

Celery will allow some practice with the Tug-O-War Pull technique, because kids can pull the knife through two times the long way before dicing. This will create little square dices instead of half moons, and there's a little "leveling up" from the cucumber/carrot because now they'll be doing the Rock-a-Bye Knife dicing on three items at once instead of one.

If you're worried about cutting too much celery with nothing to do with it, you can freeze the dices and half moon slices, no blanching necessary. Use them in any soup, stir fry/sauté, or casserole recipe.

"If you're worried about cutting too much celery with nothing to do with it, you can freeze the dices and half moon slices, no blanching necessary."

If your child has any stamina left, they can learn to make carrot and cucumber *sticks* using the Up and Over Soldier hold. Have them cut 3-to-4-inch chunks first, then Tug-O-War pull lengthwise, and then turn the veggie over on its flat side to make the sticks.

Note: If you have kids in the Intermediate Level, they'll make a ranch dip for veggies today. If not, you might want to have your Advanced child make a ranch dip the day before.

There's a LOT to learn today if you count up all the different techniques! Be sure to gauge your learner's energy, motivation and attitude during the lesson and adapt to leave some of the work for another time if necessary. These skills allow for a lifetime of practice and refinement, so no need to cram every cutting technique into one day. DO make time to practice the skills throughout the week – I highly recommend hiring your new "sous chef" to help with a raw veggie platter for dinner this week – and from now on.

What's coming? This class only focuses on straight vegetables, but in the next few classes the kids will learn onions, peppers, garlic, and large fruits. They should already be familiar with the "cross-hatch" technique, which is the way you might cube potatoes (Beginner Lesson 3 and Intermediate Lesson 2). Consider creating opportunities to practice that on raw potatoes and other hard veggies over the next month(s).

"These skills allow for a lifetime of practice and refinement, so no need to cram every cutting technique into one day."

Challenges You Might Encounter

Time and energy. This can be a long lesson because there are so many foods to choose from. Keep it to an appropriate length for your child's age, experience, and motivation by only using some of the veggies and teaching some of the cuts. We want success and positive feelings for this first class!

Overconfidence. Kids may think, "This is too easy!" and not take it seriously. Big knives are serious business, so set the tone in your household to fit the way you wish kids to behave.

Fear. On the other hand, a child may be downright afraid of the "big knife." Downgrading to a medium sized knife works for this lesson and some of the following lessons, and guiding with your hand on the bottom first and theirs on top (then switching) may be a helpful bridge. Discussing hand placement of the food-holding hand can help too – if a child feels like the stand-up-like-a-soldier hold doesn't get a good enough grip, point out that as long as you're "Hey, Hey, Outta the Way" you can grasp the food tighter. The Up and Over Soldier hold also gives a firmer grip.

Floating knives. The tip of the knife should be touching the cutting board for all the dicing of carrots and celery. If the knife is dull, this can become a bit unsafe when making carrot sticks. You might need to demonstrate how to draw the knife through the carrot with the Tug-O-War pull technique – but for the initial entering, it stabilizes things if the knife is touching the board rather than floating in the air. Top Chop is another way to circumvent floating knives.

Sliding cutting boards. If your cutting board slides all over the place when the child is cutting, try putting a damp washcloth flat under the cutting board to keep it in place on the counter.

Anticlimactic Results. For kids who have the skills to begin right at the Advanced Level and don't have siblings at the other levels, having the "product" of the first lesson be just a tray of veggies might not be very exciting or rewarding for them. Plan ahead – have your Advanced kids make the ranch dip anyway or the guacamole from the KCRF recipe book, or plan a simple chicken rice soup (also in the recipe book) that enables them to cut all the veggies for it. Check out the extension recipes on the next page for more ideas.

Don't forget to create opportunities to practice this skill throughout the week!

You might integrate this one into daily life by setting the expectation that the child has the responsibility of creating a dipping platter each night for dinner with raw veggies. If you can plan a simple soup dinner, the child can teamwork with you and be in charge of the carrots and celery slicing.

Extension Recipes to Apply this Skill:

Recipes in *Recipes for Kids Cook Real Food*:
- Simple Chicken Rice Soup

Find these recipes online at *www.kidscookrealfood.com/recipes*:
- Six delicious cucumber recipes
- Lacto-fermented radishes
- Lacto-fermented pickles
- Lots of soup recipes allow for knife practice, especially after the next class (onions)
- How to make your own ferments

If you don't have the KCRF recipe books visit *www.kidscookrealfood.com/recipes* to get access.

Next Week's Grocery List:
- Bell peppers (green or colored)
- Onions (put them in the fridge the day before your lesson)

Class 2

Kids Cook Real Food
Class 2: Adult Information

The classes today will help you, the adult guides, teach children in your life basic cooking skills. Remember that great teaching and learning includes demonstrating, guiding, and finally coaching to independence. You are a vital part of that process!

You should demonstrate each step of today's skills for your child learner(s). Nothing can replace the guidance you will provide as your child first attempts today's new skills. Be sure to help them on each step - and then step back.

As the child begins to be comfortable with the skills, use your voice to redirect them or refocus them if necessary, but the ultimate goal is for you to fade into the background. Let's dive into today's skill so you feel prepared to work with the children.

What Adult Guides Need to Know

Everyone will be learning knife skills today!

The Advanced group was introduced to many of these terms in Class 1, but that's okay – practice and repetition are how we learn. The All-Kid Lesson also goes more in detail on all the ways to cut.

Practice is the name of the game today – and *you* might actually want to practice before you teach the lesson(s) to your child(ren) too! We adults do fall into some bad habits with knives, so I recommend going over the All-Kid Lesson and practicing on a few fruits and veggies to make sure you really know what you're doing once you slow down and demonstrate to kids.

When you start the kitchen lesson with the kids, you'll begin by demonstrating how to cut each of the fruits or vegetables your age groups are working with today. Remind the kids to watch closely as you show them, then allow their hand to be on the knife *with* yours, either over or under depending on how trustworthy they are.

Remember that demonstrating means you'll need at least one extra for each item so you have one to show. Best to have multiple extras on hand.

Although I suggest demonstrating with specific fruits and vegetables, that doesn't mean you must use exactly those foods or all of the options. Consider what is in season, available, and fits your family's needs. Your goal isn't to cut a specific food necessarily but to practice a skill. Each module has suggestions for alternate foods.

Big Knife or Little Knife?

Huge question! Most people say that sharper knives are actually safer because you're not trying to force the not-so-sharp blade through the produce, increasing the risk of it literally going sideways. I like to extrapolate that philosophy onto knife size.

Once a child is comfortable with a paring knife and feels confident in *themselves* with a bigger knife – and if their hand can easily hold it – you may feel ready to let them have at it with your big chef's knife. Also – do sharpen your knives.

What Kind of Knives do I Need?

If you have only two knives, get a paring knife and a chef's knife. Round out your collection with a medium-length kitchen utility knife (not serrated in my opinion) and a serrated bread knife. Step up your game a little more by adding a Santoku knife and a long boning knife.

I use a chef's knife often, and it is my personal favorite, the true workhorse in my kitchen. It spends more time out of the drawer than in for sure. It's a Wusthof brand, which is very good (but pricey), but you may not need to spend a lot on knives to make them work for you. It's not difficult to find 5- or 6-inch chef's knives that would be a better fit for little hands.

My Santoku knife, the one with the very flat blade edge, was $3 at a garage sale, and it's quite a nice knife when I keep it sharp. Santoku knives are supposed to release the food better because of those little divots on the side (although the jury's out for me whether that works or not). They're good for chopping, dicing onions, slicing large things.

Paring knives can range from little plastic-handled dollar store things, which are actually pretty great for children cutting soft foods, to $40 brand name sturdy knives.

They all have their place in the kitchen, and the more you work with fresh produce, the more you'll get a feel for what knife you like to choose for a given task.

I think there's no single perfect use for every knife. I use a boning knife to cut apples and love my Santoku for cabbage, but I'm sure not everyone feels that way. Make interesting conversation with your kids discussing how they might choose a knife for a given situation.

Challenges You Might Encounter

The Pointer. Children sometimes put their pointer finger down the knife to try to get more control or strength. Tell them to choke up instead, even potentially putting two fingers on either side of the blade of the knife (pinching the blade between their thumb and the side of their forefinger).

That Looks Awkward. Children will throw all sorts of other weird holds at you! Tell them "Mrs. Kimball says" to hold it properly, with the hand/palm on top, thumb and finger on either side of the hilt in a comfortable fashion.

Dangerous Fingers. Are your child's fingers pointing out too close to the blade? Say, "Pick Me! Pick Me!" to remind them that their fingers might be volunteering to go under the knife.

The Tipper. Is your child using the tip of knife for everything? Direct them to pull the knife downward and more flat. Demonstrate why the tip isn't as effective.

The Angler. If your child starts angling the knife sideways toward the hand holding the food, just straighten it up for them and show them how it's dangerous.

Too Low. Little ones may drift low in relation to their board – remind them to "Be the Boss of the Knife" and get up higher. If they're working at the kitchen table, get them up on their knees. Make sure they have a tall enough stool or chair to work at the kitchen counter.

Fat Slice. Littles are also famous for making "slices" as thick as their hand. :) Help them peek over the top of their knife to see where the end of the food is and continue to redirect them and challenge them to make slices as thin as possible.

Developmental Readiness and Kid-friendly Reminders

It's hard for us adults to remember sometimes how difficult learning a new skill can be, especially with small hands and far less small motor control than an adult is used to.

Knife skills will quickly remind you of that truth as soon as you watch your child give it a go!

Tap into your deepest well of patience for this one, and keep in mind that it will take lots of time for a child to look and feel comfortable with a knife. (That's why we always start with dull knives, yet teach knife safety and strategy as if the child is using a sharp knife so they're ready to transition.)

Knife skills are awesome to learn – there are lots of tools to make cutting go faster, but nothing beats a simple knife and cutting board and knowledge of how to use it. There are benefits beyond just knowing how to cut:

> **Beginner** – Knife work is excellent fine motor practice and gets their hands ready for writing with a pencil, so this can even help them be successful in school.

> **Intermediate** – Knife work helps this age group learn care and responsibility and gives them a chance to feel older and grown-up, without having to wear makeup or listen to teenage music.

> **Advanced** – This age group can revel in a real life skill and seriously help you in the kitchen now, which is great for both their sense of satisfaction and self-esteem and your stress load in the kitchen.

All-Kid Lesson

In the All-Kid Lesson today, we'll start with knife safety. You'll definitely want to ask your child to repeat the phrases on the flash cards for you so you can feel confident that they'll respect the dangerous nature of knives.

Teach:

- Always carry knives point down.
- Be the boss of the knife!
  - This means to get up over the cutting board to get the best visual and downward pressure, to hold onto the knife with the hand/palm on top, and to remain in control.
- Choke up it you need more power. (No finger!)
  - To get more control or pressure for cutting, children should move their cutting hand closer to the blade rather than trying to put their pointer finger down the knife.
- Knife moves, eyes down. // Food moves, knife down.
  - An important safety reminder – always look at what you're doing, and always set the knife down in a safe place when you are moving food around or off the cutting board. You'd be amazed at how often kids glance around at something else and continue cutting with a sharp knife!

You'll also learn our 3 safe ways to hold food while cutting and 4 styles of making the cuts.

Safe Ways to Hold Food:

1. **Top Chop**
   - The non-dominant hand goes on top of the knife (flat!) to both add pressure and stability and stay out of the way of the blade.
2. **Up and Over Soldier**
   - The thumb and fingers hold the food on either side, forming a tunnel that the knife goes through to make the cut. Fingers are straight up and down.
3. **Hey, Hey, Outta the Way!**
   - The basic hold – as far away from the knife as possible on the other end of the food, fingers standing straight up and down like a soldier.

4. **Never "Pick Me! Pick Me!"**
   - If the fingers get close to the knife, they're volunteering to be cut! "Pick Me!" We don't want that.

4 Ways to Cut:

1. **Rock-A-Bye Knife**
   - The knife tip touches the board and the knife rocks up and down, up and down. For dicing and some slicing with large chef's knives with a rounded edge; also works with Santoku.
2. **Drive it Like a Vacuum**
   - The knife tip also stays on the board but the knife moves back and forth and up and down, dicing or slicing on the way forward. For large chef's knives with rounded edges. It's a little easier to get through hard foods like carrots with this technique vs. Rock-a-Bye Knife, because the knife is moving forward through the food instead of simply trying to power straight down.
3. **Saw Blade**
   - Sawing back and forth – for soft foods and big items. All knife sizes.
4. **Tug-o-War Pull**
   - Pull the knife backward through the food toward you. For slicing, usually long pieces of food, all knife sizes.

Practice those phrases before working with your kids and definitely have the flash cards cut out or photocopied (from page 363) for today. Remind them to go slowly, because you can't uncut a finger...

Tips for Teaching Multiple Age Groups

I loved teaching this lesson to all the kids at once.

I gathered them all around the kitchen table and talked about the basic knife safety and how to hold knives correctly, and then I cut up some stuff while they all watched together.

I cut a cantaloupe and asked the Advanced kids to watch carefully because they'd be doing that in a few weeks, and then the Beginner kids got to take my half moon pieces and slice them into bite-sized chunks.

They all watched me core a pineapple, and then the Intermediate group cut that into smaller pieces.

Once I got all the groups going on cutting something, it wasn't that hard to walk around the table, redirect, remind, and demo the next item for them.

The Beginners will be finished first, most likely, but that's good because they're the youngest (we actually cut our cheese on another day because their focus ran dry). The little ones can and should put their fruit on a plate and offer it to anyone around (same with the Intermediate kids). If you have small tongs, invite the Beginner kids to use them to serve their fruit.

Likely your Advanced kids will be working the longest because (a) you'll probably get them started last and (b) their skill is just harder and takes longer. Hopefully they can enjoy some of the other groups' fruit when they need a little break.

The Beginner and Intermediate groups will end up with a great snack for everyone (cut fruit and cheese) and the Advanced group will generate veggies for the freezer for future food prep. Making a recipe for dinner using onions, peppers, and mushrooms (chili, a soup, a casserole, a stir fry) is an awesome way to utilize the prep work your new little sous chefs have done for you!

Dull Knife Skills, Level 1: Beginner

Don't forget to create opportunities to practice last week's skill:

- Spreading and peeling

How We Apply the Skill Today:

- Slicing bananas and melons for snack and making cheese cubes.

Skills That Loop into this Lesson:

- Holding a knife properly

Time Needed:

- Hands on Time: 20-30 minutes

Tools Needed:

- Dinner knife (butter knife)
- Crinkle cutter (optional but fun)
- Cutting board
- Plates or bowls for each food you'll cut
- Small tongs (optional)
- Toothpicks (optional)

Food Needed:

- Bananas, at least one per child plus one to demonstrate
- Melon, like a cantaloupe or honeydew
- 8 oz. block of soft cheese (like mozzarella, not aged sharp cheddar)

Adults Should Prepare:

- Either pre-wash and cut the melon into half-moon shapes OR plan to do both with the kids watching. (They like helping to scoop out the seeds, but remember to explain how to know how deep to go.)
- If your cheese is large, cut it down to a size the child's knife can handle.

Today's Recipe: Feel free to make a fun fruit salad!

Extensions: how else could this basic skill be used?

- Basic cutting skills can extend onto any soft fruit or vegetable and cooked vegetables too. The children probably won't be able to magically cut up their own dinners quite yet, but it's an important stepping stone to be comfortable with a knife.

Allergy Notes and Substitutions:

- Instead of cantaloupe and bananas, you could consider: anything soft and long, like a cooked carrot, slices of peach, pear or soft apple (for them to cut into dices), even a piece of bread pre-sliced into strips.
- Dairy-free: use any soft foods, or even make a favorite bar recipe and allow the child to cut them into bite-sized pieces.

Daily Nugget:

"Cut Your Own Cheese"

If your cheese comes all wrapped up in slices that someone else cut, it's probably fake cheese with weird ingredients. Cut your own so you know it's real cheese.

Notes:

_____

_____

_____

_____

_____

_____

_____

_____

_____

_____

Lesson Overview: Dull Knife Slicing

In this lesson, laying the foundation for knife safety is key. Even though we're "only" cutting with a dull knife, we want to teach all the skills – pointing the tip of the knife down, holding the knife with the hand on top, setting the knife down to move food – with utmost precision and care. Make it almost reverent to follow the pattern of knife safety.

I like to work at the table with my beginner group, because I want them to be able to get up on their knees to really see what they're doing and be high enough above the food to get the downward pressure they need for cutting. I don't want to be worrying that someone will fall off a chair at the counter while they're first learning knife skills. Working at the table allows them to be more independent as well, since they can set up their own supplies and don't need a space and a chair in the kitchen.

Catch Phrases to Remember:

Catch phrases help kids to remember the principles and the skills that they are learning. Try to incorporate these phrases into your lesson to help these ideas stick in your kids' minds. Additionally, be sure to cut out or photocopy the flash cards (page 363) and keep them handy throughout the week.

- Always carry knives point down.
- Be the boss of the knife!
- Hand over teeth.
- Choke up! (No finger)
- Knife moves, eyes down.
- Food moves, knife down.

How to Demonstrate: Bananas and Melon

Kids will likely be eager to pick up their knives and cut, and it is tempting to just let them do it. Resist the temptation! Here are all the steps you can break this simple process into:

- Show how to pick up the knife properly ("Hand on Top, Teeth on Bottom")
- Situate the banana or melon half-moon slice (no rind!) horizontal to your body
- Get up high above the cutting board
- Hold the food with your hand far away from the knife
- Slowly cut slices
- Set the knife down to move the food to a bowl

Remember that you'll need an extra banana for you to cut to demonstrate, so be sure to have enough on hand.

You can choose to use the term "saw blade" or "top chop" for bananas and melon.

Discuss the words "thicker" and "thinner" meaning bigger and smaller (those words may be new to very young children).

Talk about how you decide how wide to make the slice. You might remind that they need to be high enough up above the food to look over their knife so they can see with their eyes the thickness of the slice. Shoot for nice, thin banana slices and bite-sized melon chunks.

Note: With this age group, I like to call the dominant hand the "crayon hand," the hand they would pick up a crayon with to color. Certainly use the words right and left as well, but "crayon hand" is a quick way to get them holding the knife with the correct hand.

> "Discuss the words *thicker* and *thinner* meaning bigger and smaller (those words may be new to very young children)."

How To Guide

Invite your child to put their hand on top of yours for your last few cuts so they get a feel for the movements.

When it's time for your child to pick up the knife, remind them to use their crayon hand and to hold "Hand Over Teeth." You could allow the child to independently peel the banana (an important skill to know in itself!) and scoop the melon seeds if you use a cantaloupe or similar.

As they try the first few cuts, you may need to have your hand over the knife as well or adjust the child's hand. Don't be afraid to keep the bar high and continue to make sure the child's hand is on top of the knife, comfortably "in charge" of what they're doing. You're laying the foundation for sharp knives too and don't want to allow bad habits to happen when you're standing right there!

Similarly, be consistent and a bit strict about the rule: "Knife Moves, Eyes Down; Food Moves, Knife Down." It's a key skill not only to follow directions and take care with their work, but we also want to instill a respect for knives and a good habit of keeping the knife out of the way when we're removing food from a cutting board into a bowl. Remind your child not to let the cutting board get too cluttered up with pieces of food.

How to Demonstrate: Cheese

When it's time to try slicing cheese, you'll have to experiment a little bit to find the best tool for your child's hand size and strength using the options you have in your house. If you don't have something that works well for cheese for small hands, a butter knife really won't cut it (ha!).

Whatever cheese slicer you use is fine for the task (even though this is technically knife skills, it's so nice for kids to be able to cut their own cheese regardless of the tool). We love our crinkle cutter for this job, and we also have a great cheese slicer by Fox Run that is very kid-friendly and easy to use (find the KCRF resources page at www.KitchenStewardship.com/kcrfresources).

> "...you may want to slice long sticks of cheese and simply allow the child to make those into 1-centimeter chunks with their butter knife."

Cutting a thin slice of cheese is very tricky for young children, especially if you don't have a crinkle cutter. You may want to slice long sticks of cheese and simply allow the child to make those into 1-centimeter chunks with their butter knife. Top Chop is a good strategy.

Remember to get a clean cutting board (or flip yours over) so the cheese isn't in the moist fruit mess. For some children, cutting a third item might be too much for their attention span for the day (especially if you are working with multiple age groups and the beginner has had some wait time). Feel free to put off teaching the cheese slicing until another time when it's more convenient.

How to Coach to Independence

Cutting the banana and melon will likely be fairly easy for every age group, and you'll move into the independent phase rather quickly, as long as the child has been listening and following directions. Cheese can be more challenging, and very tiny hands simply might not have the strength to be able to do the job on their own at all. In that case, simply allow "guided cheese cutting" to be the end of the lesson today.

"Remember that beauty and perfect uniformity ought not be your goal at this age."

Be sure to include removing to the plate as part of the lesson. Providing small tongs makes that job fun, and it also promotes small motor control and helps develop the child's muscles that are used to hold a pencil, setting them up for success in school. It's worth investing in dollar store ice tongs or some small set that kids can get their hands around.

Remember that beauty and perfect uniformity ought not be your goal at this age. You'll likely have a lot of funny shaped cheese for a while, but it will be cut with love and pride, and that's what matters. On the other hand, DO redirect a child who is cutting 2-inch chunks of bananas to slim those up a lot – they should be capable of making bite-sized slices as long as you keep your expectations high.

Encourage the child to practice hospitality as well and serve their snack to others in the house (or just you). They might have fun putting toothpicks in the banana slices or cheese cubes for that purpose.

Challenges You Might Encounter

Paying attention. At this age, keeping one's focus might be the toughest challenge. Remind the child to do each step of the process without rushing, to take a lot of care with the knives, and to carefully move their food with the knife down on the cutting board. Help them know when they are "done" so you don't end up with a pile of mushy bananas because cutting was too much fun!

Bad knife habits. Some children may also allow the tip of the knife to point up into the air while cutting or hold the food with their hand much too close to the knife. Others want to hold the knife like a hammer. Try to see and nip these habits during the guided phase.

Don't forget to create opportunities to practice this skill throughout the week!

You might integrate this one into daily life by inviting the child to help prepare snacks of cheese and fruit or slice bananas for breakfast.

Extension Recipes to Apply this Skill:
Find these recipes online at
www.kidscookrealfood.com/recipes:
- Cheese and crackers
- Help make an appetizer platter
- Homemade pizza
- Sausage Zucchini Bake or any casserole with cheese on top

If you don't have the KCRF recipe books visit www.kidscookrealfood.com/recipes to get access.

Next Week's Grocery List:
- Cucumbers
- Zucchini
- Potatoes
- Whole mushrooms
- A variety of spices

Intro to Sharp Knife Skills: Intermediate

Don't forget to create opportunities to practice last week's skill:
- Following a recipe (making salad dressings)

How We Apply the Skill Today:
- Slicing pineapple, strawberries, and mushrooms (or any similar soft-ish foods)

Skills That Loop into this Lesson:
- How to hold a knife (Beg. Class 1 and 2)
- Washing fruits and veggies (All-Kid Class 7)
- Basic knife cutting practice with a dull knife (Beg. Classes 2 and 3)

Time Needed:
- Hands on Time: 20-30 minutes

Food Needed:
- Strawberries
- Mushrooms
- Pineapple
- (or other soft fruits or veggies)

Tools Needed:
- Small to medium-sized sharp paring knives (or other sort of small-ish knife appropriate for kid hands)
- Cutting boards
- Colander

Today's Recipe:

Fruit Salad

Adults Should Prepare:
- Cut the pineapple so that it's ready for kids to slice OR let them watch you work.

Extensions: how else could this basic skill be used?
- Basic cutting skills can extend onto any soft fruit or vegetable and cooked vegetables too. The children probably won't be able to magically cut up their own dinners quite yet, but it's an important stepping stone to be comfortable with a knife.

Allergy Notes and Substitutions:

- Alternate ideas instead of the strawberries, mushrooms and pineapple: grapes, melons (pre-cut somewhat for them), apple slices to cut into dices (have the kids lay the slice on its side so the skin is standing up; easier to cut through), cooked vegetables.

Daily Nugget:

"Raw Foods Have Workers Inside"

Raw food has enzymes, things that DO actions in our bodies – important jobs like digestion. You don't have to eat everything raw, but it's a good idea to eat something raw at every meal, like the fruit we're cutting today, raw veggies, or salad.

Notes:

_____

_____

_____

_____

_____

_____

_____

_____

_____

Lesson Overview: Intro to Sharp Knife Skills

This introduction to sharp knives is a pivotal lesson, one that the child must be ready for both in skill and responsibility. Do make sure that you trust the child to follow the knife safety rules and that they have had some dull knife practice already.

How to Demonstrate

Start with washing the produce – good practice from Class 7 if your child already completed the Beginner module. (Feel free to skip ahead to Beginner Class 7 on page 245.)

- Strawberries are usually washed in a colander.
- Pineapples need to be washed on the outside because it will touch our cutting board and knife and we don't want the dirt or chemicals from the outside to get onto the inside or into the food we eat.
- Mushrooms are a unique food to wash – use a damp washcloth and wipe the outside of each mushroom individually rather than running under water. Water makes them slimy. This task is rather time consuming and it's *wonderful* to have children who know how to do it to help out at dinnertime!

Catch Phrases to Remember:

Catch phrases help kids to remember the principles and the skills that they are learning. Try to incorporate these phrases into your lesson to help these ideas stick in your kids' minds. Additionally, be sure to cut out or photocopy the flash cards (page 363) and keep them handy throughout the week.

General Knife Skills:

- Always Carry Knives Point Down
- Hold the Knife Firmly – Be the Boss!
- Choke Up if You Need More Power (No finger!)
- Knife Moves, Eyes Down
- Food Moves, Knife Down
- Never Set the Knife Down with the Sharp Side Up

Safe ways to hold food:

- Top Chop
- Up and Over Soldier
- Hey, Hey, Outta the Way!
- (Never "Pick Me! Pick Me!")

Ways to cut:

- Rock-a-bye Knife (knife tip touches the board)
- Drive it Like a Vacuum (knife stays on the board)
- Saw Blade (soft foods and big items)
- Tug-o-War Pull (slicing)

Allow your kids to help with each part of the washing, especially having a mushroom or two to themselves.

Now it's time to cut!

Remind your children that they must watch you first before they pick up the knives. Have bowls or containers ready for each food you're cutting.

If you are working with a pineapple, that's the easiest to start with. You should have already quartered and cored it so there are four long slices. Demonstrate the "Hey, Hey, Outta The Way!" hold on the far end of the pineapple, and use a smaller knife (although perhaps larger than a small paring knife) to cut very thin slices off the end. You can use Saw Blade or Tug-o-War Pull for this. Demonstrate about five slices.

Then show another way to cut a pineapple, into chunks. Use the Up and Over Soldier hold and make two long Tug-o-War Pull cuts down the length of the pineapple to make three long sticks.

Top Chop one of them into 1-inch chunks (leaving the others for the kids). You can use other holds/cuts to accomplish this too.

Practice before moving to the next food.

> "Remind your children that they must watch you first before they pick up the knives."

> "If you are working with mushrooms, demonstrate slicing using pretty much the same strategy as with strawberries."

If you are working with strawberries, talk about how we want to cut off only the green and save as much of the red as possible. This is great practice in fine motor and being precise (good life skill!). Putting the fingertips on the pointy end of the strawberry and trimming the green with a small paring knife is a good strategy. Up and Over Solider is a good hold for slicing with a Tug-o-War Pull slicing motion. Demonstrate how you set the knife down to move each slice to a bowl.

Practice before moving on to the next food.

If you are working with mushrooms, demonstrate slicing using pretty much the same strategy as with strawberries. Sometimes it's easier to cut the mushroom in half, then lay it down on the flat side to make more slices. Include the cross-hatch pattern for dicing IF you'd like, but for some children that may be too much for day one with a sharp knife.

How To Guide

Allow your child to try cutting each food themselves immediately after you demonstrate. Remember that this is the first time with a sharp knife, so practice all the knife safety reminders and stay very close.

If your child is quite young and inexperienced, allow them to put their hand either on top of yours or under yours for a few slices to help them get a sense of direction and pressure.

Talk through each step and each hold. Try to let them figure out their own mistakes as long as there is no safety issue.

If the child is cutting off too much red strawberry with the green leaves, point to the discard pile and ask them, "Do you see anything here that you might like to eat?"

How to Coach to Independence

You'll want to continue to allow the child to use a sharp knife on soft foods over the coming weeks. Be sure to be nearby or fully engaged in the early practices to keep the child safe. You'll know when the child is ready to be more independent with you farther away, and you'll also likely get a sense of when the child is ready for more difficult knife skills.

There are four sharp knife lessons in the Advanced module.

Challenges You Might Encounter

The Pointer. Children sometimes put their pointer finger down the knife to try to get more control or strength. Tell them to choke up instead, even potentially putting two fingers on either side of the blade of the knife.

Rolling Food. Just because strawberries and mushrooms are round doesn't mean they should be rolling around. Have your child use the Up and Over Soldier hold OR if that's not working, cut everything in half for them to give them a flat edge.

That Looks Awkward. Children will throw all sorts of other weird holds at you! Tell them "Mrs. Kimball says" to hold it properly, with the hand/palm on top, thumb and finger on either side of the hilt in a comfortable fashion.

Dangerous Fingers. Are your child's fingers pointing out too close to the blade? Say, "Pick me! Pick me!" to remind them that their fingers might be volunteering to go under the knife.

The Tipper. Is your child using the tip of knife for everything? Direct them to pull the knife downward and more flat. Demonstrate why the tip isn't as effective.

Don't forget to create opportunities to practice this skill throughout the week!

You might integrate this one into daily life by having soft fruits on hand for kids to cut for snack, or better yet, inviting people over and asking the children to make a fruit salad (then praise them in front of the company).

Extension Recipes to Apply this Skill:
- Stir fry, omelet, or anything else with mushrooms
- Strawberry shortcake
- Fruit kebobs

Find these recipes online at www.kidscookrealfood.com/recipes:
- Veggie Bean Burritos
- Chicken Leek Barley Soup
- Hamburger casserole

If you don't have the KCRF recipe books visit www.kidscookrealfood.com/recipes to get access.

Next Week's Grocery List:
- 1-2 dozen eggs
- A variety of spices

Sharp Knife Skills, Level 2: Advanced

Don't forget to create opportunities to practice last week's skills:
- Washing vegetables and cutting carrots, cucumbers and celery.

How We Apply the Skill Today:
- Slicing and dicing onions and peppers

Skills That Loop into this Lesson:
- Washing veggies (All-Kid Class 7)
- Previous knife safety and skills

Time Needed:
- Hands on Time: 20 minutes

Tools Needed:
- Variety of sharp knives, especially a chef's knife
- Cutting boards
- Bowls to put the cut food in
- Plastic bags to freeze (optional)
- Swimming goggles

Food Needed:
- Onions (sweet are optimal)
- Bell peppers

Today's Recipe: Prep peppers and onions for the freezer or for future recipes

Adults Should Prepare:
- Chill the onions.

Extensions: how else could this basic skill be used?
- So many recipes are now open to you once you can cut an onion! Plus, other round vegetables -- like potatoes and maybe even tomatoes -- will be easier to handle once you understand these skills. (Tomatoes are a saw blade veg!)

Allergy Notes and Substitutions:
- If either onions or peppers aren't a good fit for your family, simply consider what you DO cut often when you cook. We'll cover garlic, apples and melons in future lessons, but anything other than that is fair game.

"Onions are Powerhouses"

Onions are good for your heart, for your immunity, for preventing cancer, are anti-inflammatory, AND the good parts don't go away when cooked or boiled – they go into the water.

Notes:

_____

_____

_____

_____

_____

_____

_____

_____

_____

_____

_____

_____

Lesson Overview: Cutting Onions and Peppers

Time to make the kids cry in the kitchen!

Cutting onions is not a favorite job for kids – you might want to grab the swim goggles for this one, or use my tip about chilling the onions in the refrigerator overnight. It's worth it though, because once someone has knife skills to cut these tough items, they'll be able to make just about any recipe they come across.

Because of the crying thing, I recommend starting with peppers so they can run away after completing the onions.

Catch Phrases to Remember:

Catch phrases help kids to remember the principles and the skills that they are learning. Try to incorporate these phrases into your lesson to help these ideas stick in your kids' minds. Additionally, be sure to cut out or photocopy the flash cards (page 363) and keep them handy throughout the week.

- Cut the ends off the onion.
- Flat side down, cut it in half.
- Tear off the peels.
- Slice rainbows and dice around the rainbow.
- See Class 1 for all the knife safety and holds.

How to Demonstrate

Peppers

To cut a bell pepper, you basically need to get the seeds out, then slice the outside. You can cut it in half first and then go around the end in a half moon to get the seeds out, or you can stand it upright and cut down the sides four times, leaving you with a "core" of seeds to get rid of.

Either way, you can then slice the pepper, and if you're dicing, use the slices and Rock-a-Bye knife or Drive it Like a Vacuum to dice. Help your child decide how many slices they can manage at once when dicing. For rookies, one might be plenty. Usually three at a time is a good goal. As you demonstrate, talk through each step you take and how you're keeping your fingers safe. You might discuss uniformity as well – the fact that it's important to keep the slices the same width for even cooking.

Onions

Here are some key strategies for cutting onions:

1. Slicing off both ends
2. Cutting in half
3. Taking the peels off (easier to do after halved)
4. Cutting from the side edge (instead of the half moon flat edge) for slices (supposedly makes you cry less because you're going "with the grain" so to speak and not cutting the cells of the onion so much).
5. Flipping the onion halfway through to keep fingers farther away from the knife
6. Using a rainbow cut "around the clock" for dices

However, I know there are lots of ways to cut onions, especially when it comes to dicing. Go ahead and demonstrate whatever system you like to use, but I encourage you to be open to allowing the child to try your way, my way, or another safe, effective strategy to tackle this challenging vegetable.

> "Go ahead and demonstrate whatever system you like to use, but I encourage you to be open to allowing the child to try your way, my way, or another safe, effective strategy to tackle this challenging vegetable."

Note: A lot of people, my former self included, use a "chopper" of some sort to dice onions. It's still good to know the skill with a knife, since there's not always a chopper available – adults and kids will have to discuss merits and make decisions on how they want to learn and practice day to day.

How To Guide

You've already had some great practice with sharp knives in Class 1, so hopefully the child is getting the hang of safe holds, but they still might need some redirection since peppers and onions can be so much harder to control than long skinny vegetables that sit there nicely on the cutting board.

> "Don't be afraid to hold the knife with the child, and certainly move at a pace at which you're *both* comfortable."

Don't be afraid to hold the knife with the child, and certainly move at a pace at which you're *both* comfortable. You need to feel certain that the child will cut the onion, not their fingers! If you need to cut the onion in half to make a stable, flat edge and your child can finish it up, that's a great way to bridge the gap for a temporary time.

You might suggest that the child try different methods for the pepper to see what they like best, including testing how it feels to cut the slices with the pepper skin side up or skin side down. I feel there are advantages to each.

How to Coach to Independence

Since peppers and onions can be frozen (without blanching) for any cooked recipe, you can practice as long as the child's eyes can handle it! (I wasn't joking about the swim goggles, by the way. They can be really helpful.) Refrigerating your onions may help eliminate tears, and using milder sweet onions is a huge help as well.

Keep a close eye on progress, especially if the child is still quite new to using a big sharp knife.

Big Sharp Knife?? Yes – peppers and onions really do need a large knife to be effective, so be sure to find a knife that is

> "Yes – peppers and onions really do need a large knife to be effective, so be sure to find a knife that is comfortable for the child's hands but also big enough to do the job right..."

comfortable for the child's hands but also big enough to do the job right. My son definitely preferred a chef's knife to any other style. Keep it sharp – accidents can happen too easily because someone is trying to jam a dull knife through resistant, round, rolling food.

When the child seems to be independent with this skill, rejoice! You can really teamwork in the kitchen to make dinner, and you're well on your way to having a child who can cook entire recipes/meals on their own.

Challenges You Might Encounter

Smooth movements. The "Drive it Like a Vacuum" strategy is very good for dicing, but it doesn't come naturally. I highly recommend holding the child's hand and knife and practicing that fluid movement together. Remind them to cut the food on the way *through*, going forward, not on the way back toward your body.

Floating knives. Some kids will have trouble getting the knife to stay touching the food, so you may need to adjust their hold or help them get the appropriate part of the knife (the front half) in on the action. When the back half of the knife is cutting the food – in other words, the blade too close to the hilt – it really makes things awkward.

Construction worker? Some kids will want to hold the knife more like a hammer – just help them readjust. I recommend trying to hold the knife *yourself* exactly how they are holding it to best explain how they need to adjust to be more comfortable/safe.

Crying eyes. Try putting the onions in the refrigerator the day before your lesson. It's supposed to reduce the tears that come when cutting onions. But the most foolproof way to avoid the tears is to lock them out entirely with a good pair of swim goggles!

Don't forget to create opportunities to practice this skill throughout the week!

You might integrate this one into daily life by inviting your child into the kitchen while you're preparing any recipe that includes peppers and onions. Avoid the stress of the dinnertime rush by having them do some prep work at off times, like right after school, or even after dinner for the next day. Maybe they want to make a special dip for the family with raw pepper slices or learn to caramelize onions (there's a French Onion Dip in my eBook, Better Than a Box, that is divine).

Extension Recipes to Apply this Skill:

Find these recipes online at
www.kidscookrealfood.com/recipes:

- Black Bean Avocado Dip
- Pizza Breakfast Hash
- Slow Cooker Freezer Meals
- Salsa Soup Starter
- Steak Fajita Soup
- Fresh Salsa
- Avocado Dip

If you don't have the KCRF recipe books visit www.kidscookrealfood.com/recipes to get access.

Next Week's Grocery List:

- Garlic
- Onions and peppers (or use this week's, frozen)
- Zucchini
- Other stir fry vegetables to your liking (green beans, broccoli, pea pods, etc.)
- White or brown rice
- Olive or sesame oil
- Rice vinegar
- Soy sauce (optional)
- A variety of spices, including some stir fry spices like curry, ginger, turmeric, cayenne pepper, cumin
- If you don't have Intermediate Level kids, you'll also need eggs.

Class 3

Kids Cook Real Food
Class 3: Adult Information

The classes today will help you, the adult guides, teach children in your life basic cooking skills. Remember that great teaching and learning includes demonstrating, guiding, and finally coaching to independence. You are a vital part of that process!

You should demonstrate each step of today's skills for your child learner(s). Nothing can replace the guidance you will provide as your child first attempts today's new skills. Be sure to help them on each step - and then step back.

As the child begins to be comfortable with the skills, use your voice to redirect them or refocus them if necessary, but the ultimate goal is for you to fade into the background. Let's dive into today's skill so you feel prepared to work with the children.

What Adult Guides Need to Know

Today we're getting the Advanced group to the stove to make a real meal for the first time, and if you have multiple age groups, everyone's new skill will work together to make dinner.

Besides that joyful experience, you'll also get a chance to organize your spices! *(Read that with an ominous undertone, mwahahaha!)*

The All-Kid Lesson today, a sensory spice exploration, is a little more involved than some, so you may choose to put it on a different day from the module lessons.

Your Beginner kids are doing some more complicated and difficult slicing with a dull knife today. To integrate the spice exploration lesson, you could invite your little one(s) to choose the seasoning for a veggie sauté. They'll cut the veggies and you sauté them. Even for kids who don't love veggies, a cubed potato sauté (with a few mushrooms and zucchini sneaking in there) will likely be a hit.

The Intermediate skill is very targeted – just cracking eggs. Use them in Egg Fried Rice, or invite the kids to choose some herbs to add to scrambled eggs. (Their eggs can be stored in a container in the refrigerator overnight so you can have breakfast partially prepared when you wake up.)

If you've got Advanced kids, they're really stepping up their game today. They'll be crushing garlic AND sautéing veggies to make a stir fry with the spices they'll choose after the opening lesson.

Plan to teach cooking class before a meal – but remember to leave double the time you'd expect if you were making the stir fry by yourself. If you only have Advanced kids, they can have some extra sharp knife practice cutting some more vegetables for their stir fry (and you can use last class's peppers and onions if you stored them in the freezer!)

Challenges You Might Encounter

Veggies are Too Hard. Cucumbers, zucchini and mushrooms may each be too hard physically (and thus too difficult!) for the Beginner kids. For cukes and zukes especially, a crinkle cutter is a magical tool. I highly recommend getting one (or putting it on a stocking stuffer list or something). They are very inexpensive (find the KCRF resource page at *www.KitchenStewardship.com/kcrfresources*).

Eggs are Too Easy. For kids who have been helping in the kitchen for a long time, cracking eggs might be old hat. Many found that kids who DID know how to crack eggs actually still learned some new tips from the Intermediate Lesson, but it's pretty short regardless. If you want a bit more challenge, go ahead to Class 5 and teach how to cook rice. If you have Advanced kids, they'll use it in the dinner today anyway, and then when Class 5 comes around, your Intermediate kids won't be bored because they can do the extension of making Mexican rice that day.

Egg Allergies. If you can't or don't use eggs in your household, you need a completely different skill for the Intermediate Level today. See that section for some ideas.

Stove Confusion. When adults cook, we just GO. When working with kids at the stove, you'll want to take a few extra minutes to organize your space. Have everything ready (cut and prepped) and in the area before turning on the heat. Show the child exactly where they can set lids and utensils before they're dealing with something hot. The best antidote to this one is prevention! (Some kids will be too nervous to even work at the stove – we address that in the Advanced Level section.)

Developmental Readiness and Kid-friendly Reminders

Beginner
Let your kids explore the spices as long as they want, since using the five senses is a key skill for this age group. Try to make cutting a cross-hatch pattern like a game or challenge, so that they stay motivated throughout the lesson.

Intermediate
The Intermediate kids get wonderful practice in self-control to crack eggs gently but will need lots of guidance and practice. Some will be more motivated than others and that will make all the difference.

Advanced
We talk a lot about the need for self-esteem in our culture and how its absence causes all sorts of problems in the tween and teen age groups. Sometimes we overcompensate, though, and praise kids for everything, which ends up meaning nothing. Cooking is a real skill, a difficult skill, an adult skill, one worthy of praise. Take this opportunity to build up your Advanced kid(s) for their maturity and responsibility on this occasion of their first time making a meal.

All-Kid Lesson

Today we're doing a full lesson for all the kids, one that will be an ongoing conversation for years to come as you work in the kitchen.

Cooking is all about the flavors. Whole foods, fresh veggies, and fruits have awesome flavors all on their own – but we'll explain to kids that certain plants also provide additional seasoning power – herbs and spices to really add flavor to our food. Our goal for this "spice exploration lesson" is to get to know some spices, think about what you like, and predict what you think might go together. This lesson should be part of your cooking and eating all the time from here on out – talk about what spices are in foods, talk about what goes together, test things out.

You'll get a few chances to officially practice "making it up as you go along" during the classes, including today for the Advanced kids and the final lesson for everyone.

To prepare, get out most of the herbs and spices in your cupboard and set them out on your table or counter. Make signs that say "Pleasant" and "Unpleasant" and put them on the table. Group the spices a bit by category (see below), grab a bit of something sweet (we used maple syrup) and something savory (we used shredded cheese) and invite your child(ren) to bring their noses and tongues to cooking class!

Explain to your learner(s):

The difference between herbs and spices: When people talk about all the little jars in your spice cupboard, you'll hear both "herbs" and "spices." They are somewhat interchangeable but generally herbs come from the leaves of a plant (so they're usually green-ish) and spices come from all sorts of parts (seeds, bark, roots).

The difference between sweet and savory: Cooking and baking can be rudimentarily divided into sweet and savory recipes. Things like cookies and cake are obviously sweet, but something like a muffin, biscuit or quick bread could be either depending on the seasonings used. For example, a basic muffin recipe could be made sweet like a pumpkin pie for snack or breakfast, or savory with basil and cheese and intended to be eaten with soup.

If you don't have many seasonings in your home, now is a great time to branch out! You can find herbs and spices inexpensively at health food stores in the bulk foods section. You can get as much (or as little!) as you want for a fraction of the price.

You can invite friends over for this activity even if you're only teaching the cooking class to your own children. More kids make it more fun, and there's a definite potential for positive peer pressure.

On my table, I tried to organize my spices based on how we use them and ethnic style of meal:

- **Sweet: Pumpkin pie spices:**
  - Cinnamon
  - Cloves
  - Nutmeg
  - Ginger
  - *Note: ginger also shows up in Asian cooking as savory...and actually the occasional savory recipe will have all the other three as well, which is interesting! If you use a recipe that your kids would recognize that does that, discuss.*

- **Super basic everyday cooking:**
  - Onion powder
  - Garlic powder
  - Parsley
  - Turmeric

- **Italian seasoning spices:**
  - Italian seasoning blend
  - Pizza seasoning
  - Sausage seasoning (Fennel)
  - Other herbs:
  - Marjoram
  - Thyme
  - Rosemary
  - Oregano (pizza)
  - Basil

- **Mexican spices:**
  - Chili powder (also used outside Mexican food)
  - Mexican oregano
  - Cilantro
  - Coriander
  - Cumin (Mexican OR Asian)

- **Asian:**
  - Cumin
  - Turmeric
  - Curry (Indian)
  - Red pepper flakes
  - Cilantro (again)
  - Lemongrass (Thai)
  - Cinnamon, Ginger

You should organize based on what you have, what your family already likes, and maybe what you'd like to try to like!

If you have children who struggle with liking herbs and spices, this is a great way to introduce them to flavor! Sometimes, however, your kids may *need* bland food because of sensory processing issues.

For now, just gently encourage your kids to smell something new, even if it's outside their comfort zone.

Your kids will probably love getting a little taste of syrup or honey to help them experience "sweet" and cheese or an herby cracker to experience "savory." Ask them if they can think of recipes they like that would fit into each category or others that can go both ways, like spiced nuts. Talk about some of your family favorites and how you use herbs and spices to make their food delicious and varied.

The seasoning exploration is a true sensory experience – and fun! Give your child(ren) the chance to smell one herb or spice at a time, and ask questions like:

1. Does it smell pleasant or unpleasant to you? (Kids can organize their choices using the signs; you might omit that part if you have multiple children who would argue!)
2. What other spices do you think would fit with this one well?
3. What foods can you think of that you'd like to taste this spice on?

Invite each child to choose some seasoning that they can use in their class today and set those aside so you'll have an immediate application and taste testing opportunity. Be sure to evaluate how you like the end result as you enjoy a meal together!

You may not necessarily remember the ones you liked best, but it gives a foundation and jumping off point for conversation. Every time you cook, you should talk about the smells and flavors, and eventually your kids will begin to recognize them and figure out what goes together nicely.

Extension activity idea: If you have fresh herbs around, do a side-by-side smell test of fresh vs. dried herbs (taste too!). I can see super conversations ensuing, and for Advanced kids who are getting ready to start experimenting more with their own flavors in cooking, you can explain that even though fresh herbs smell stronger, dried herbs are stronger in cooking. Usually you need about three times more fresh herbs than dried!

Tips for Teaching Multiple Age Groups

You'll love seeing how all the kids' skills work together today to make an awesome stir fry for lunch or dinner. Even though everyone will contribute to the stir fry, you'll still have potatoes from the Beginner group and likely some eggs leftover from the Intermediate group for breakfast.

If you're juggling all three module levels, here's the order I recommend:

1. During the spice exploration, each level can choose some seasoning: Beginners for a potato hash, Intermediate for some scrambled eggs, and Advanced for the stir fry.
2. For the module lessons, start with the Beginner group and do the cucumber and zucchini slicing (if they're old enough for it). Set the zucchini slices aside for the stir fry later. You should stay close to them during this part to monitor difficulty and safety – many kids may not be ready yet so you can simply move on to the next skill.
3. If you'd like your Intermediate or Advanced kids involved, they could wash the produce for the little ones.
4. Teach the cross-hatch pattern to your Beginner kids. Particularly for cooked potatoes, many will be able to practice the skill on their own once they understand the technique.
5. Then you can move on to your Intermediate kids. Most likely, the egg cracking lesson won't take a very long time.
6. Intermediate kids can practice their measuring skill by measuring the spices for the Fried Rice. That's one less thing your busy Advanced kids won't have to worry about!
7. I recommend teaching the Advanced kids on their own once everyone else is finished, since it's the first time at the stove. Keep littler ones busy outside the kitchen or give them some dinner-related tasks like setting the table or preparing raw veggies and dip.
8. If you need to, the Advanced kids can be taught on a different day than the others. Eggs, zucchini and mushrooms from the other levels will all last a few days in the refrigerator if need be.

If you don't have Advanced kids, you could either make the stir fry meal yourself OR use only the Beginner and Intermediate foods in a delicious egg scramble or "hash.

Slicing with a Dull Knife, Level 2: Beginner

Don't forget to create opportunities to practice last week's skill:

- Slicing bananas, melon, and cheese

How We Apply the Skill Today:
- Slicing cucumbers and zucchini
- Cross-hatch pattern dicing mushrooms and cooked potatoes

Skills That Loop into this Lesson:
- Dull Knife Skills, Level 1 (Beginner Lesson 2)
- Peeling (Beginner Lesson 1 – optional)

Time Needed:
- Hands on Time: 20-30 minutes

Tools Needed:
- Butter knives or spreaders
- Cutting boards
- Crinkle cutter if you have one
- Bowl or container for each cut food

Food Needed:
- Cooked, peeled potatoes
- Whole mushrooms
- Cucumbers
- Zucchini
- Remember to have at least one extra of each for the demonstration step.

Today's Recipes:
Stir Fry
or
Potato Hash

Adults Should Prepare:
- Cook whole potatoes in advance and peel them.
- Consider washing produce or plan to work together with the kids.

Extensions: how else could this basic skill be used?
- The cross-hatch pattern is very common for dicing and will return in Intermediate and Advanced Levels.

Allergy Notes and Substitutions:

- This lesson can be taught with absolutely any cooked vegetable you want, from cooked carrots to gently roasted butternut squash. If you can make it into a manageable and not-totally-mushy block for kids, they can do the cross-hatch pattern. That's the goal here. Also soft fruit cut into slices for them can be diced: kiwi, pear, peach. Even an apple slice can be diced with a dull knife if it's standing up so that the knife can go through the skin vertically.

- If you have a crinkle cutter, some children are even strong enough to slice wheels of hard vegetables like raw carrots.

Daily Nugget:

"Don't Slip on the Skins"

There are lots of nutrients in and near the edible skins of many fruits and veggies – so if you don't have to peel something, don't do it!

Notes:

_____

_____

_____

_____

_____

_____

_____

_____

Lesson Overview: Dull Knife Skills

Prepare for this lesson by cooking whole potatoes. Baking is easy and can be done for dinner the day before or in a toaster oven the night before (and just leave them in there overnight). Or you can boil them whole, then get them out of the cooking water quickly and rinse them off so they're not slimy or sticky.

For today, you should probably peel the potatoes so the kids don't have to deal with one more step, but it is possible for kids on the older end of the Beginner level to peel baked potatoes with just their fingers and a dull peeler. It's difficult though and takes some serious time.

You'll be demonstrating how to cut these cooked potatoes and raw mushrooms into small cubes using the "cross-hatch pattern," and for those kids who are old enough, we're going to try slicing cukes and zukes today as well.

Not all of these dull knife skills are appropriate for the younger crowd — cucumbers and zucchinis may take too much strength – but they all should be able to accomplish cutting cooked potatoes.

Loop the peeling skill from Lesson 1 back in and invite kids to peel their cucumbers. Alternately, use small salad or pickling cucumbers or long English style cukes with thin skins which are often easier to cut anyway.

Catch Phrases to Remember:

Catch phrases help kids to remember the principles and the skills that they are learning. Try to incorporate these phrases into your lesson to help these ideas stick in your kids' minds. Additionally, be sure to cut out or photocopy the flash cards (page 363) and keep them handy throughout the week.

- Tip of the Knife is Down (when cutting)
- Cross Hatch =
  1. Lay Flat.
  2. Cut into Sticks like String Cheese.
  3. Turn Like a Clock.
  4. Cut into Cubes.
- Make Room for the Knife – Choo, Choo!
- Like a Train Going Through a Tunnel!

How to Demonstrate

You'll start with slicing cucumbers, which utilizes the same motion as last class's banana slicing, but on a much more solid piece of produce. If you don't have a cheese slicer or semi-sharp spreader, ask if your child wants to try with a butter knife.

The saw blade motion is necessary, and be ready to abort the mission if it's just too hard for your child. Show them how you keep the point of your knife *down* toward the cutting board, which keeps you safe, lays a foundation for sharp knife skills, and, I think, makes the cutting easier because of the angle. (See the Challenges section below for some other ideas.)

> "Show them how you keep the point of your knife *down* toward the cutting board, which keeps you safe, lays a foundation for sharp knife skills, and, I think, makes the cutting easier because of the angle."

The crinkle cutter is much easier for all age levels with cukes and zukes! It's worth the tiny investment.

Also remind how you set the knife down to move the food: "Food Moves, Knife Down."

If your child can slice the cucumber, then the zucchini uses the exact same technique and may even be a little bit easier because the zukes are a little softer.

Next you'll demonstrate the cross-hatch pattern on the cooked potatoes. Here's how it goes:

- Use the *Up and Over* hold to cut the potato in half (Or into ~4 flat, fat slices)
- Remind kids to *Make Room for the Knife* when it's their turn – Choo, Choo! Like a Train Going Through a Tunnel!
- *Lay Flat* like a deck of cards
- Cut into Sticks – Like String Cheese
- Turn halfway – *Like a Clock*
- Cut each stick into cubes – 1-2 sticks at a time.

Some children will latch right onto the idea of the cross-hatch pattern being like a Tic-Tac-Toe grid, if they're familiar with that game.

Class 3: Beginner

"Don't forget to have your Flash Cards handy to help remind everyone about the proper steps."

Depending on the age of the child, size of your potatoes, and the tool you have available to use, you might need to cut the potato in half or even into the "deck of card" slices so your child has a flat surface to work with instead of a round potato.

You'll use the same process to dice mushrooms. If using a butter knife, the Saw Blade motion is necessary to get through mushrooms. Again, you may need to facilitate with a sharp knife and just let your child complete the final (dicing) step. You'll know during the guide process.

How To Guide

I recommend the hand-on-hand technique when first attempting cucumbers and zucchini. Many little hands will have trouble getting through the dense foods, but feeling how you angle the knife down and in what direction to apply pressure will help them a lot.

Be diligent about reminding your child of safe holds, preferably "Hey, Hey, Outta the Way." Remember that you can delay this skill application if it isn't going well.

"Be diligent about reminding your child of safe holds, preferably 'Hey, Hey, Outta the Way.'"

Once you're ready to move on to potatoes, you should still do a set together as you assess whether your child can start with a whole potato or not. The more organized you keep the cutting board as you present it, the easier time they'll have remembering the steps and making actual dices instead of a chopped mess – although your fried potatoes will still be yummy no matter the shapes!

Don't forget to have your Flash Cards handy to help remind everyone about the proper steps.

Stick close by when switching to mushrooms, since they take a different motion than the potatoes. Remember that you might need to slice them in order for your child to dice them. Choking up on a long butter knife can make a huge difference in success rate, so be sure to try allowing your child's hand to get right up past the halfway point of the knife.

Once the vegetables are cut, there are lots of ways you can use them that day for meals:

- *Potatoes:* Make potato salad, make soup, mashed potatoes, sauté with butter for American fries, add to eggs.
- *Cucumbers:* Use with a dip as an appetizer, make a cucumber salad
- *Zucchini and Mushrooms:* Sauté with potatoes to make a hash (add eggs and it's a whole breakfast), check out the extension recipes OR if you have Advanced Level kids, set them aside for their stir fry.

How to Coach to Independence

I feel pretty comfortable allowing even quite young children to work on cooked potatoes with a butter knife, so I allow a lot of exploration and discovery with this skill. We also provide many opportunities to practice on cucumbers for our dinner veggies.

The main goal of the child working toward independence is to master the cross-hatch pattern and remember the steps needed to make cubes.

Challenges You Might Encounter

When Dull Isn't Enough. It really does require a semi sharp knife, something stronger than a butter knife, for cukes and zukes. If you can find something like our magic cheese knife or a crinkle cutter, you'll open up possibilities for your 3-5-year-olds that can't be done with truly dull knives.

When Muscles Just Aren't Enough. Also the child needs some muscle strength, so for the 2-3-year-old crowd this lesson is better kept to the truly soft things like cooked potatoes, cooked carrots, maybe mushrooms if they can handle the roly poly-ness of those.

Gettin' Chunky. Their pieces will probably be bigger than ideal. Just expect it because of motor control but try to encourage them to keep things thin. You can encourage your learners to peek OVER their knives to actually see how big the slices are, which is something they don't actually think of on their own. Go back to the banana if need be!

Don't forget to create opportunities to practice this skill throughout the week!

You might integrate this one into daily life by baking extra potatoes for dinner and asking your child to dice them up for breakfast or planning a mushroom or zucchini recipe (or both) this week and enlisting your little sous chef.

Extension Recipes to Apply this Skill:

- Fried potatoes (made from leftover baked taters)
- Omelets
- Crudités platter

Recipes in *Recipes for Kids Cook Real Food*:
- Potato Salad

Find these recipes online at *www.kidscookrealfood.com/recipes*:
- Mushroom recipes, soups and casseroles
- Sausage Zucchini Bake
- Blended Green Soup
- Creamy Cucumber Salad
- Six Cucumber Dishes

If you don't have the KCRF recipe books visit www.kidscookrealfood.com/recipes to get access.

Next Week's Grocery List:

Lots of spices, including:
- Paprika
- Cumin
- Onion powder
- Garlic powder
- Cayenne pepper
- Dried dill
- Dried parsley
- Dried chives
- Black pepper
- Salt
- Dry oats, flour, rice – a few of those for measuring practice

Cracking Eggs: Intermediate

Don't forget to create opportunities to practice last week's skill:

- Using sharp knives on soft foods

How We Apply the Skill Today:

- Cracking eggs – without mess!

Skills That Loop into this Lesson:

- Teamwork baking is a good habit to have done before this lesson so the child has some guided practice opportunities with cracking eggs.

Time Needed:

- Hands on Time: 5-10 minutes

Food Needed:

- Eggs (lots)

Tools Needed:

- Whisk
- Bowl

Today's Recipes:
Omelets or
Scrambled Eggs
and
Fried Rice

Adults Should Prepare:

- Think ahead about how you want to use the eggs. Extra ideas are at the end of the lesson.

Extensions: how else could this basic skill be used?

- A lot opens up when a child knows how to crack eggs independently – baking, breakfast, easy dinners – all of which save Mom and Dad time.

Allergy Notes and Substitutions:

- You'll actually need a totally different skill if you can't have eggs. This is one of the rare classes for which there's no easy substitute or adaptation. If you're familiar with flax egg substitute, you might teach your Intermediate kids how to grind flax seed and mix up the sub; gelatin eggs also could be a skill to learn.

- There's an extension idea in the Lesson Overview about teaching basic rice cooking today instead of eggs, and then in Class 5 when we teach rice, your Intermediate kids can make Mexican rice.

- Otherwise simply examine your week – what is something that you do often in the kitchen that isn't on the Curriculum Map for the eCourse but you'd love your Intermediate Level child to know how to do? Break it down using the 3-step teaching process and make it a new lesson.

"Eggs have God's Packaging"

A lot of food is packaged by humans – sometimes with lots of ingredients and weird stuff that's icky for your body. The way the egg comes – one ingredient, two parts, lots of nutrition – is just perfect.

Notes:

_____

_____

_____

_____

_____

_____

_____

_____

_____

_____

_____

_____

Lesson Overview: Cracking Eggs

Today's lesson is extremely singular, but it's such an important skill that I thought it deserved its own class. In Lesson 4, we'll be asking our Intermediate kids to make a recipe by themselves, completely without an adult stepping in to help. They're going to need to know how to crack eggs!

In our family, my daughter loved cracking eggs, and she was so motivated that she mastered the skill at age 4 or 5. She often cracks a dozen for me as I'm making a recipe, and that saves me a ton of time! Plus, she is very proud of her skill. I do think motivation is important for this one, so do whatever you can to make egg cracking seem like a pinnacle of achievement, something that everyone wants to know how to do but most people aren't very good at. Hopefully that will motivate your children to desire to master the skill.

One the other hand, if cracking eggs is too simple or your child has already learned the skill, there is a little extension you could use, especially if you also have Advanced Module kids. In Class 5, the Intermediate group will be learning to cook rice. But today's Advanced Lesson needs already-cooked rice as a side. So if you'd like, you could teach the Intermediate kids to cook basic rice today, and then for Class 5 they can level up that skill and make a Mexican rice dish. Just an option for you!

Catch Phrases to Remember:

Catch phrases help kids to remember the principles and the skills that they are learning. Try to incorporate these phrases into your lesson to help these ideas stick in your kids' minds. Additionally, be sure to cut out or photocopy the flash cards (page 363) and keep them handy throughout the week.

- Crack on a Flat Surface
- Bullseye!
- Can't Unbreak an Egg
- Thumbs In, Then Out

How to Demonstrate

When I demonstrate how to crack an egg, I slow down the process immensely:

1. Hold the egg firmly.
2. Crack on a flat surface.
3. Crack right in the center of the long side of the egg.
4. Find the right pressure – better to start off too gently than the reverse, since you can always crack twice, but you Can't Unbreak an Egg!
5. Look for the Bullseye. This is a circular break in the center of the eggshell that shows you where to put your thumbs.
6. Put both *thumbs* on the bullseye.
7. Slowly press IN, then pull OUT.

How To Guide

Hopefully you've had some opportunities to bake side-by-side with your child before, and they've gotten to see you crack eggs and even perhaps have their hand on yours. I feel that this guide step is supremely important for eggs.

Crack over a bowl, never over the hot stove for rookies.

"Ask the child to put their hand on top of yours to feel the amount of pressure you apply to crack the eggs."

Ask the child to put their hand on top of yours to feel the amount of pressure you apply to crack the eggs.

Then say, "Put your thumbs on my thumb*nails*," so they get in exactly the right spot to mirror/help you on the "press in, then out" portion.

Depending on the age and impulse control of the child, I might have my hand over theirs for their first crack at the skill. (Oh, so punny!) That way I can curtail an overzealous crack and resulting mess.

If your child makes a mistake, like cracking the wrong part of the eggshell or exploding it over the bowl, feel free to help them out at this point.

Remember that you're a team and they're just learning. Work to ensure that they don't feel like mistakes are a big problem.

For those who do crack too hard and end up with a sloppy mess on the counter, be ready with a thin-sided cup or bowl to scoop up what you can and put it in the bowl anyway. You can also talk about how if they realize they over-cracked, they can move really quickly over the bowl and still save most of the egg before it comes out all over.

What About Shells?

You're probably going to have some shells in the bowl when little ones are learning. But I get shells in my eggs, too. It's a great habit to allow kids to see your own faults and mistakes as an adult, so be sure to tell them about your "oopses" when they happen.

We have a little trick that is almost like magic to get eggshells out of the bowl:

Use the empty half shell of the egg to scoop the little piece out. It will almost jump right into the eggshell! This doesn't work if your eggs are too terribly deep, so you might use two bowls, one little bowl for each individual egg, and then a larger bowl that you pour the egg into one at a time after you check for shells. Using a little "egg shell bowl" is a good habit for all egg cracking for kids so that they have a chance to get shells out before the eggs go into the batter or a hot pan.

> "Use the empty half shell of the egg to scoop the little piece out. It will almost jump right into the eggshell!"

Whisking

Whisking without spilling the eggs over the side of the bowl is another very helpful skill, and for some reason I've noticed that a whisk is one of my children's favorite tool. Demonstrate proper strokes, quick but *small* so that there's no sloshing- like a Hula Hoop.

Recommend that the children start slowly and break each egg yolk individually so they don't feel like they have to stir too hard. Show them how to use quick flicks of the wrist only, and guide them for a while until they feel comfortable doing it on their own. (Once you're whisking, make a note of how many eggs are in the bowl so you know how to use them later!)

How to Coach to Independence

Talk your child through each step while they practice on their own. Give them as many eggs as they feel they need to be comfortable with the process. You'll probably be able to see when they hit their stride, and they'll feel it, too.

There are plenty of ways to use all these cracked eggs! They'll be fine in the refrigerator for a day or two if you need to store them.

If you have Advanced Level kids, you can use 4-6 of the eggs for a big batch of fried rice (with about 5 cups of rice). Other ideas are in the Extensions below.

Note to parents: Of course we want to remind our new egg crackers that washing hands is very important after cooking, but especially with raw eggs or meat. If you're concerned about bacteria, washing the outside of the egg before using might give you more peace of mind.

Challenges You Might Encounter

The OverSmash. Egg on the counter is no fun, but it's also not a disaster. Have that thin-sided cup nearby to scoop up and save most of the egg. Don't make a big deal of it.

Wave the White Flag. If your child ends up smashing many eggs on the counter and your patience runs out, it's ok to postpone the independent part of the skill. Plan to work with them the guided way and try to make scrambled eggs a lot this week to practice until they're ready to do it on their own.

Don't forget to create opportunities to practice this skill throughout the week!

You might integrate this one into daily life by making scrambled eggs for breakfast, baking something throughout the week, or planning to have a quiche for dinner one night.

Extension Recipes to Apply this Skill:

- Omelets (use veggies from the Beginner Level if you have them)

Recipes in *Recipes for Kids Cook Real Food*:
- Grain-free pancakes

Find these recipes online at www.kidscookrealfood.com/recipes:
- Grain-free muffins
- Egg Drop Soup
- Coconut Macaroon Cookies

If you don't have the KCRF recipe books visit www.kidscookrealfood.com/recipes to get access.

Next Week's Grocery List:

- Whole wheat or GF flour (GF blend)
- Pumpkin or pureed squash
- Cinnamon, nutmeg, cloves
- Baking powder, baking soda
- Salt
- Sucanat (or cane sugar)
- 2 eggs
- Butter or coconut oil
- Muffin liners

Sharp Knife Skills, Level 3: Advanced

Don't forget to create opportunities to practice last week's skill:

- Cutting onions and peppers

How We Apply the Skill Today:

- Crushing garlic
- Sautéing veggies for stir fry

Skills That Loop into this Lesson:

- Measuring (Foundations 101)
- Slicing Veggies (Adv. Lesson 1)
- Cutting Onions and Peppers (Adv. Lesson 2)
- Following a Recipe (Int. Lesson 1 & 4)
- Stovetop Safety & Cooking Rice (Int. Lesson 5)

Tools Needed:

- Skillet or frying pan
- Tongs
- Measuring spoons
- Chef's knife
- Cutting board
- Garlic press
- Large pot for rice
- *Recipes for Kids Cook Real Food*

Time Needed:

- Hands on Time: 5-10 minutes

Food Needed:

- Cooked rice
- Eggs, if no Intermediate Level
- Garlic
- Onions and peppers (or use last week's, frozen), including ½ c. red pepper
- Zucchini
- Other stir fry vegetables to your liking (green beans, broccoli, pea pods, etc.)
- Olive or sesame oil
- Rice vinegar
- Soy sauce (optional)
- A variety of spices, including some stir fry spices like curry, ginger, turmeric, cayenne pepper, and cumin

Today's Recipes: Basic Veggie Stir-Fry and Egg Fried Rice

Adults Should Prepare:

- Cook rice for the stir fry (or if the Advanced kids have gone through the Intermediate level already, they should know how and can start it before the stir fry).
- You might need to prep veggies for the stir fry if you want the kids to focus only on one skill (but they should have the skills to cut them if you can provide time).
- During the All-Kid Lesson, the Advanced kids should have chosen spices they want to use for the stir fry. If not, pull some Asian spices out, like curry or ginger.

Extensions: how else could this basic skill be used?

- Crushed garlic is wonderful in salad dressings (Int. Class 1), dips, salsa, and lots and lots of dinner meals.

- Sautéing extends to any vegetable, and knowing what vegetables look like when they're cooked is a first step toward being able to create one's own recipe and fiddle with things in the kitchen creatively. Kids can now caramelize onions to add flavor to a dip or taco night, be responsible for the side veg at dinner, or head up the toppings for burgers or brats by sautéing mushrooms, onions, and peppers.

Allergy Notes and Substitutions:

- Feel free to use ANY vegetables you have in your stir fry! In the video we used a mix of veggies. Some we cut and froze the previous week, some were cut by our Beginner kids, and some were purchased frozen veggies. It all works out!

- Egg free? Just skip the eggs in the rice altogether. Add beans or meat if you want protein.

- No grains? Add more veggies! Or make zoodles or cauli rice.

Daily Nugget:

"Free Nutrition Inside Garlic"

Did you know that garlic gets healthier 7 minutes after it's crushed – and then better yet in another 7 minutes? When you first start cooking, crush your garlic and let it sit and wait.

Garlic can fight sick bugs and infections, is good for your heart, helps prevent cancer, is anti-inflammatory, and is good for digestion, blood pressure, and blood sugar. Wow!

Notes:

_____

_____

Lesson Overview: Garlic and Sautéing

I know our Advanced kids are antsy to make something real and get cooking. Stir fry is one of the easiest and most flexible meals to have in one's repertoire, and I'm excited to teach your kids how to do it today.

If you have multiple age groups, Beginner kids can slice or dice mushrooms and zucchini for the stir fry, the Intermediate group can crack eggs and measure the spices for the fried rice, and maybe even cook the rice if you choose. This means that Advanced kids should work last so your attention won't be divided and you can focus on them.

Catch Phrases to Remember:

Catch phrases help kids to remember the principles and the skills that they are learning. Try to incorporate these phrases into your lesson to help these ideas stick in your kids' minds. Additionally, be sure to cut out or photocopy the flash cards (page 363) and keep them handy throughout the week.

- Crush Garlic First; Add Garlic Last
- Pac Man the Lid
- Sauté Long Cooking Veggies First

If you have only Advanced kids, you can extend the lesson and loop their sharp knife skills back in by having them prep all the veggies for the stir fry before jumping into the main event of the lesson today.

Depending on how much experience your child has had in the kitchen and how adventurous their personality, you may not want to tackle everything in one day. We are teaching two skills but with the potential of four major parts: crushing garlic, preparing other vegetables, stir frying veggies, and making an optional rice dish we feel makes the meal complete.

Some families made both recipes in one day while others preferred to make the rice for one lesson and follow up with the veggie sauté another time. Both recipes do include the skill of sautéing.

To teach the whole lesson in one day (totally doable!), I recommend splitting the lesson up and work it into 3 or 4 parts:

1. Crush garlic.
2. Prepare your veggies.
3. Cook both recipes. Or make one recipe at a time. The rice can hold better than the vegetable sauté, so make the rice first.

How to Demonstrate

Crushing Garlic

Show your kids the difference between a bulb of garlic and a clove and how to separate one clove. Lay the clove on your cutting board. With a large, flat knife – pointing the sharp edge away from yourself – use your flat hand or fist to hit or press the knife down firmly. Once the clove cracks open, the papery part is easy to peel off.

"To mince garlic, use the Rock-a-Bye Knife technique and a Top Chop hold and simply go back and forth over the clove until it's all very tiny."

If you have a garlic press, you as the adult guide should demo your own – each works differently.

Also demonstrate how to mince garlic with a knife, which is a good skill to have in case one is ever caught without a garlic press. (*Vocabulary check: mince is smaller than dice.*) To mince garlic, use the Rock-a-Bye Knife technique and a Top Chop hold and simply go back and forth over the clove until it's all very tiny.

Put the Daily Nugget into practice by setting your garlic aside while you work on everything else – free nutrition!

Give your child time to practice on a few cloves, guiding and coaching them just like last class with the sharp knife skills.

How To Guide

Sautéing

The entire stir fry process is a "co-working" guided project for you and your child (so no demonstrating as a separate event). You'll work together, discuss what's happening, and build their skills for another day entirely when they might be able to take over by themselves while you observe.

You can provide the vegetables or work together on the choosing and/or preparing. Frozen green beans and broccoli are very easy, sliced onions and peppers are classic, and pea pods are a fun one for kids, too – and easy to prepare simply by washing them in a colander.

Onions and peppers need the longest time to cook, so start with those. Ask kids to observe and describe the properties of the raw onion and pepper, both visually and physically.

Sauté Process

1. Get your pan hot and "sizzle test" it with a few drops of water. I think that's some kids' favorite part of cooking!
2. Pour in about 2 tablespoons of oil. (Kids may practice attempting about a tablespoon "glug" into a bowl, then pouring in the pan.)
3. Add onions and peppers. Talk about the balance between getting your hand too close (and getting burned with the oil) and dropping things from too high and splashing hot oil on yourself.
4. Stir the vegetables around, scrape the bottom, move food from the bottom to top, inside to out.
5. Covering the pan shortens the time, but keep the heat on medium if you cover. Check often.
6. Discuss how to tell if onions are done and use your scientific powers of observation:

   - Raw = crunchy, breaks when bent, white
   - Partly cooked "al dente" = bendable, translucent, might have some brown parts
   - All the way cooked = nearly transparent, much smaller, browning

Making Fried Rice

This is a good side-by-side cooking process for making the fried rice:

1. Heat a medium or large pot over medium heat. (child)
2. Add oil. (adult or child)
3. Add diced peppers from Lesson 2. (optional, can be used frozen)
4. Stir around until browning. (teamwork)
5. Garlic only needs about a minute to cook – add and stir constantly. We used 4 cloves for a double batch and saved some for later. (child)
6. Add spices. (child)
7. Optional: 1-2 Tbs. rice vinegar
8. Stir in rice. (we used 5 cups, teamwork)
9. Cook over medium heat for a minute or two while stirring rice to coat with spices, then turn to low while you work on the sauté. (adult)
10. When the rice is hot, turn the burner to medium and make a well in the center. Add 4-6 eggs (could be from the Intermediate group) and stir until the eggs are cooked.

Stovetop Skills Review

Please start with stovetop safety reminders (in Intermediate Lesson 5, page 191) and make sure your child is high enough to see into the pan you're using. Get a stool or chair as necessary.

Clear a space for the lid. This is really important when working with kids at the stove. Kids should always know where lids and utensils can go safely before they begin.

Demonstrate the steam coming out of the pan when you lift the lid. We teach a safe way to pick up the lid called "Pac Man," which means you angle the lid away from yourself, making the lid/pan look like Pac Man opening his mouth. Also point out that hot water will drip from the lid as you move it, so remind your child to keep the lid over the stove/counter. If your lid is all metal and very hot, provide oven mitts for a safe and easy way to pick it up.

How to Tell when Veggies are Cooked

When the onions are halfway done, add the next longest cooking veggie. Feel free to include an optional science lesson: Discuss the length of time different foods need to cook and hypothesize some reasons why. Predict/hypothesize which veggie will cook faster (just put two out on the cutting board, like zucchini and something else).

Example: Green Bean is a longer cook because it's denser/sturdier and has less water content. The zucchini is already closer to "soft" is one way to think about it.

Show your child how green vegetables change as they cook and ask what they notice. When they are done they should look bright like spring grass.

Add chosen spices from the All-Kid Lesson and stir well. Remind your child that they can always add more seasoning but they can't take it out. So start light, then smell and taste, and add more if needed. Be sure they have stirred thoroughly first!

> "Feel free to include an optional science lesson: Discuss the length of time different foods need to cook and hypothesize some reasons why. Predict/hypothesize which veggie will cook faster..."

Class 3: Advanced

Continue to demonstrate and guide your child on thorough stirring, using tongs to pick up and turn over all the food or a wide spatula. If your pan is quite full, different vegetables might have trouble cooking all at the same time. Add a splash of water and turn the heat to high to steam them – reminding your kids of the importance of pac-manning the lid!! Check progress after just 2-3 minutes.

> "Have the children serve the family with pride and offer soy sauce at the table if you choose."

When all the vegetables are just a breath from done, add a clove or two of the fresh garlic your child minced and stir around for a minute.

When the veggies are done, turn the heat off and move the pan (if on an electric stove). Have the children serve the family with pride and offer soy sauce at the table if you choose.

How to Coach to Independence

Independence will be obtained in future practice times on future days. Use the Flash Cards to remind your child about the finer points of sautéing and do your best to make opportunities to practice as often as possible in the coming days/weeks.

If you have extra garlic from the crushing practice, hang onto it in the fridge in an airtight container overnight if you know you can use it in a meal the next day. Or pour some olive oil over it to preserve it longer, either refrigerated or frozen. You can dip some garlic out of the oil to sauté anything or to add to homemade salad dressings or dips.

Challenges You Might Encounter

Stove Rookie? If this is your child's first time at a stove, please be sure to review the stove safety from Lesson 5, Intermediate on page 191. Here's a review:

1. Show what is hot and what is not.
2. Give your child a safe place to put their hands – we use the towel bar on the oven as ground zero.
3. Clear your space.
4. Know where they'll set tools and lids.
5. Have everything prepped before turning stove on – this is not like adult cooking.

If you can go back to Intermediate 5, you'll learn to cook rice, too, which is handy for this lesson.

Do it Myself! Remember that you're tandem cooking and hang close to help this first time – I'd like to see the kids do most of the sautéing (but you may help a lot on the rice so they're not overwhelmed).

You Want Me to What? If hitting a knife seems way too scary for your child, they can also press hard and sort of rock their hand on top of the knife. Some garlic presses also can smash an unpeeled clove without a problem.

Not Popeye? If your child can't smash the garlic hard enough to really get it open, have them try grabbing the tip and pulling down. They can also smash it again or cut off the end and use a paring knife to catch hold of the papery part (might be an adult job since we haven't used a paring knife in that fashion yet). If your child is not strong enough to press the whole garlic clove, they can cut it in half and press or simply mince with a chef's knife.

Stinky Hands! To get garlic smell out of your hands, rub them on stainless steel. This might be your sink, a spoon, or a bowl or pot. I've heard rubbing on yellow mustard or coffee grinds may also help.

Super Sensors. Garlic smells can be simply overwhelming for folks with keen noses. Don't worry about skipping the garlic altogether – that's what garlic powder and dried minced garlic are for!

Slow to Fast Vegetable Timing Chart

Vegetables might take longer or shorter times depending on how high your heat is and whether you have a lid on or not. But relative to one another, they stay pretty standardized. Here's the order you should add vegetables to your pot in a mixed-veggie sauté (assuming they are sliced thinly; chunks will always take longer):

1. Onions
2. Peppers
3. Raw Potatoes
4. Mushrooms
5. Thinly Sliced Carrots
6. Celery
7. Cauliflower
8. Water Chestnuts
9. Leeks
10. Brussels Sprouts*
11. Cabbage
12. Stems of Greens, like woody Bok Choy or Swiss Chard Ribs
13. Broccoli Florets*
14. Asparagus*
15. Green Beans*
16. Peas*
17. Radishes
18. Eggplant
19. Zucchini/Summer Squash

Veggies can always be cooked "al dente" (a little bit crisp) or really soft; the longer you sauté them, the softer they'll get. I prefer to stop when they are at their brightest color and only lightly cooked because I don't like them mushy, but when you're the chef, you get to choose! In other words, pretty much anything on this chart can be moved around according to preference.

* In my opinion, these vegetables are best when cooked JUST RIGHT. I don't like them overcooked, so I might actually wait until last to add them because other veggies can cook a long time and still taste more or less the same, and I want to be in charge of just when to finish/serve the more sensitive ones.

Don't forget to create opportunities to practice this skill throughout the week!

You might integrate this one into daily life by simply cooking with your child, asking them to make a side veggie or crush garlic for a recipe for you.

Extension Recipes to Apply this Skill:

Recipes in *Recipes for Kids Cook Real Food*:
- Homemade Chicken Rice-a-Roni

Find these recipes online at
www.kidscookrealfood.com/recipes:
- Caramelized Banana Apple Dessert Topping
- Tastes Like Pizza Breakfast Hash
- Meatless Veggie Hash
- Sausage Spinach Pasta Toss

If you don't have the KCRF recipe books visit *www.kidscookrealfood.com/recipes* to get access.

Next Week's Grocery List:
- Cantaloupe or honeydew
- Watermelon
- Apples

Class 4

Kids Cook Real Food:
Class 4: Adult Information

The classes today will help you, the adult guides, teach children in your life basic cooking skills. Remember that great teaching and learning includes demonstrating, guiding, and finally coaching to independence. You are a vital part of that process!

You should demonstrate each step of today's skills for your child learner(s). Nothing can replace the guidance you will provide as your child first attempts today's new skills. Be sure to help them on each step - and then step back.

As the child begins to be comfortable with the skills, use your voice to redirect them or refocus them if necessary, but the ultimate goal is for you to fade into the background. Let's dive into today's skill so you feel prepared to work with the children.

What Adult Guides Need to Know

Independence is the name of the game for our Beginner and Intermediate groups today. The littlest ones get to dive into measuring (hopefully not quite literally) with their own tactile practice that can double as a free time activity AND they get some special seasoning measurement cards that will enable even non-readers to follow a recipe all by themselves. They'll be your seasoning blend masters!

The Intermediate goal today is to make an entire recipe without you, the adult, touching anything. "Look Ma, no hands!" They'll be so proud of themselves. Try hard not to help, but make sure they're ready first. If you're a bit apprehensive, you can prep for the lesson by baking a recipe together first, then allowing them to go it alone again few days later (if you're making muffins, you can always freeze them).

The big kids in the Advanced group are tackling big fruits with their sharp knives plus oven safety. If you don't have Intermediate kids, you'll have to make a recipe to bake in order to really learn the oven skills in context. You could use the delicious pumpkin muffins from the KCRF recipe book if you like or make an apple crisp with the apples they cut. If you don't have time you can always practice with a cold oven and look for a chance to practice for real any time throughout the week.

There is no official All-Kid Lesson because I wanted to create a dedicated time for you to going through the Foundations 101 materials if you haven't already. The measuring modules are essential for the Beginner work today, and all of them are very helpful (if not essential) for all ages.

Challenges You Might Encounter

These challenges refer to the Foundations 101 lessons.

The Eyes Don't Have It. For adults, it's easy to "eye it up" and see if something is level, full, heaping, etc. For your Beginner kids, they sometimes just don't have the estimation ability to measure very accurately. Don't expect perfection on day one. Keep reminding, demonstrating, guiding, and practicing – both your patience and their measuring! That's what the measuring activity is for. There's no risk since they're not actually making anything, and they can keep practicing as much as they like. Give them times where they can just "play" and others where you're hovering and "checking their work."

Fudge? Even the big kids might want to be sloppy with measuring sometimes. Remind them that sometimes we can "fudge it" and other times we really have to be precise for the recipe to work out. (See the Measuring Mastery notes and the Bonus Mini Lesson "Season Like a TV Chef" for more.) If it's one of those precise times, give them a "spill bowl" to measure over and make sure it's accurate before adding to the recipe.

Multiple Fractions. Kids who aren't all that familiar with fractions will likely be stymied by something like "3/4," which won't match any of the cups they have available. Head this off at the pass by asking your child during the "reading the recipe" step how they anticipate measuring something like "three-fourths cup" or "one and one-half cup." Show them how to break it down into "three FOURTH cups" and use the fourth cup three times, or how ONE and ONE-HALF need to be in two parts, the whole cup and the half cup. Use both the family terms for the cups and the real fraction names

Developmental Readiness and Kid-friendly Reminders

One major goal for most parents is to help their children develop independence and skills so that they become competent adults. Today's lessons all give those gifts to your children! The kids will truly have something to be proud of after class – and they will glow.

Beginner

The measuring exploration uses the senses and is so tactile and hands on. There is no risk and it allows them to truly explore their world without an adult guiding every move.

When they are practicing measuring, leveling with a knife is great bilateral coordination practice, meaning that your child is using both hands together to do a task. It's important for them to integrate one hand with the other at this age.

The spice cards have loads of academic connections: counting, identifying numerals, ordering sizes, remembering symbols, and even pre-reading practice by matching the letters on the card to the letters on the side of the jar. For those who are ready, you can also practice beginning sounds or even learn to read whole words.

We even have large motor skills today with the jar shaking dance.

Intermediate

The challenge today may be as much for you as for them. It's not easy for some parents to let their children do something real all by themselves! You may need to push yourself to let them go a little...they will rise to the challenge. Wait until you see their pride in a job well done.

Advanced

Our oldest group should have the small and large motor control and responsibility to use the oven – but you know your child better than any developmental chart. If they aren't strong enough or careful enough to take something potentially heavy out of the oven, pull the plug on that part of the lesson. They need to feel comfortable too. Definitely practice with a cold oven even if you don't plan on moving to working with a hot oven – that exposure can do wonders for their own confidence and skill as well as your trust in them.

Beyond responsibility, we also get to introduce a little creativity in today's lesson if you'd like. There are lots of ways to cut a watermelon and lots of shapes kids might want to try. What have you got to lose? Encourage a little experimentation if you like (as long as they are still safe with the knife).

All-Kid Lesson: Choose Your Own Adventure

During your regular "All-Kid Lesson" time you can choose from any or all of the Foundations 101 lessons if you haven't already gone over them with your kids (see pages 33-41).

Measuring and stirring skills are a good reminder for the Advanced and Intermediate groups and really important for the little ones – in fact it's their entire lesson today.

Foundations 101 covers four topics:

1. Language to use for little ones
2. Two elements of great mixing and 5 ways to stir
3. Dry measuring strategies including flour
4. Measuring fat and basic liquid measuring skills

The Beginner group should definitely go over the "KCRF Language for Measuring for Young Children" and "Measuring Mastery, Part 1" lessons. Before you tackle Class 6, you'll want to integrate the second Measuring Mastery lesson for them.

If you have Intermediate or Advanced kids, you'll want to be sure to go over both measuring lessons and the stirring lesson. Also find some time for the bonus section "Season Like a TV Chef" at some point if you haven't already. It's a short (3 minute) strategy to learn to estimate measuring herbs and spices.

Tips for Teaching Multiple Age Groups

Everyone has a lot of independent time today, so you can really get any group started, let them roll onward, and get another group started. Because we don't want to fatigue our youngest group, you may want to start the Intermediate group with the "on my own" recipe, then show the Advanced kids how to cut a melon (it will take quite a while for them to finish), and then get the Beginner group started on exploring measuring.

You should be close enough to monitor everyone – keep an eye on your Advanced kid's knife, help the Beginner measure nice and flat, and be there if the Intermediate has any questions or is about to make a major error – like putting 1/3 cup baking powder in their muffins. Ask me how I know to watch for that mistake.

Likely your Advanced kids can start their second melon or their apples while the Beginners are exploring measuring, and then you can get the Beginner kids started with their seasoning blends. They'll likely need you pretty close for the first attempt.

Make sure the Intermediate group knows they're allowed (and encouraged) to ask you questions. When they are finished with their recipe and ready for the oven, have them ask the Advanced group for help so older kids can get their oven practice (demonstrate and guide with a *cold* oven first, whenever that fits in the lesson).

You might end up splitting some of these lessons into two days. For example, the Beginner Level might do their seasoning blends on a second day and the Advanced Level might make a recipe to bake on day two if you don't have Intermediate kids. There are some integrations possible on the extension recipes, especially if you choose one with apples. If the Advanced kids quarter and slice apples, Beginners can dice them if you lay each slice on its side. Intermediate kids could get some sharp knife practice by taking the quartered apples and slicing them and/or dicing them.

As you continue to work through the eCourse, I encourage you to look at recipes in this way: What skills do my kids have that apply to this recipe? How can they all have a hand in it?

Measuring Ingredients: Beginner

Don't forget to create opportunities to practice last week's skill:
- Dull knife slicing and the cross-hatch pattern

How We Apply the Skill Today:
- Making homemade seasoning blends like taco seasoning and ranch dressing mix

Skills That Loop into this Lesson:
- Foundations 101 - measuring

Time Needed:
- Hands on Time: 30-45 minutes

Tools Needed:
- Measuring cups and spoons
- Butter knives
- Little bowls
- Jars with lids
- *Recipes for Kids Cook Real Food*
- Seasoning blend measuring cards (page 337-345)
- Tape
- 9x13 glass casserole dish (or any container that is wide and could be used for the child to scoop and pour flour)
- Scoops (optional)

Today's Recipes:
Taco Seasoning & Ranch Salad Dressing Mix

Food Needed:
- Lots of spices, including:
  - Paprika
  - Cumin
  - Onion powder
  - Garlic powder
  - Cayenne pepper
  - Arrowroot starch or corn starch
  - Dried dill
  - Dried parsley
  - Dried chives
  - Black pepper
  - Salt
  - Bulk salt, sugar, cornmeal, or something granulated for measuring spoon practice
  - Dry oats, flour, rice – a few of those for measuring cup practice

Adults Should Prepare:
- Cut apart the seasoning blend measuring cards from pages 339-345. Tape them to the jars. Note that you should choose the "boy" or "girl" cards for the half teaspoon, not both.
- Fill containers with oats and/or flour for measuring practice.

Extensions: how else could this basic skill be used?

- Obviously good measuring skills are a foundation for nearly any recipe you'll encounter. Once your child understands how to measure carefully, they could pre-measure herbs for something you're cooking at the stove, be a bigger help than ever when you co-bake something delicious, and even make homemade flour blends or mixes without much help.

Allergy Notes and Substitutions:

- If your family doesn't do gluten or grains, of course anything can be used to measure with measuring cups. I'd be nervous allowing children to manipulate expensive ingredients like coconut flour, so I might recommend buying a cheap bag of rice just for this purpose.

Daily Nugget:

"Swim the Salty Oceans"

Too many spice blends have lots of white salt in them. REAL salt in nature has lots of colors, and white salt needs to be processed. The natural is healthier with more minerals, so we use that.

Notes:

_____

_____

_____

_____

_____

_____

Lesson Overview: Measuring Skills

Not only is this skill vital to almost everything you can do with a recipe, but it gives the kids a great gift in the immediate present: Something they usually can't do – reading – is made accessible to them to be totally independent making something for their family.

I love so many parts of this lesson – the fact that you can set up the measuring practice as a tactile exercise for free time, the fun kids have manipulating the tools, and the joy on their faces when they see the seasoning cards made just for them. Plus, as a teacher, integrating the counting and the bridges to reading created by matching the names of spices on the cards to the labels on the jars is priceless.

My best two tips for adults are these:

1. Set the tone when you demonstrate: move slowly, speak calmly, and show your children how to take care with their work.
2. Have a broom nearby.

Catch Phrases to Remember:

Catch phrases help kids to remember the principles and the skills that they are learning. Try to incorporate these phrases into your lesson to help these ideas stick in your kids' minds. Additionally, be sure to cut out or photocopy the flash cards (page 363) and keep them handy throughout the week.

- Dad = 1 Tbs.
- Mom = 1 tsp.
- Kid = 1/2 tsp.
- Baby = 1/4 tsp.
- Flat: No Holes, No Hills
- Flour Falls Like Snow (No Sandcastles!)
- Snowplow it Flat
- Get Level with Liquids

5 Ways to Stir:
- Merry-Go-Round
- Pogo Stick
- Roller Coaster (toward the center)
- Lawnmower
- Hula Hoop (whisk)

Mix it Well!
- Hold the Bowl
- Uniform Mixture

More details on all these phrases in the Foundations 101 on pages 33-39. You can find the spice cards on pages 337-347.

How to Demonstrate

Part 1: Dry Measuring Spoons

Supplies on the table: Bowl of salt, sugar, or something granulated; empty small "practice bowl;" measuring spoons; butter knife.

If you haven't yet gone over the Foundations 101 materials for the beginners that covers the Dad, Mom, Kid, Baby language that we use in the eCourse, find it on page 35 before you teach this lesson to your Beginner group.

Ask your little ones to line up the measuring spoons biggest to smallest (or stack them up if yours nest nicely) and then identify the players: Dad, Mom, Kid, Baby. For very young children who are still working on understanding sizes, you may want to have two sets of measuring spoons.

> "Ask your little ones to line up the measuring spoons biggest to smallest (or stack them up if yours nest nicely) and then identify the players: Dad, Mom, Kid, Baby."

You organize your set correctly and ask them to match theirs up. *Note: If your measuring spoons are all connected on a ring, it may be more effective to separate them, although the activity still works if they're all together.*

Show them how you can either scoop or use another spoon to fill your measuring spoon with salt or sugar. Ask, "Do I have hills or holes?" or "Is that perfectly flat?" (especially when it's not). Demonstrate how to "Snowplow it Flat" with the flat edge of the butter knife, holding the spoon over the bowl. Pour it into the practice bowl.

You might demonstrate a hole as well as a hill and how to fix the problem, and it's also good to demonstrate what happens if you don't use the flat side of your tool by making a dent in your spoon. Remind your child of the importance of keeping everything very flat, and then let them have a try with some guided practice.

Part 2: Dry Measuring Cups

Supplies on the table: 9x13 or similar pan of oats or rice, another with flour; standard measuring cups; scoops (if you have them), butter knife.

Begin with asking your child to organize and identify the measuring cups again. Be sure to help them clarify "biggest" and "smallest" and "bigger than" and "smaller than." Those are great preschool concepts!

> "Remind your child of the importance of keeping everything very flat, and then let them have a try with some guided practice."

Demonstrate how the oats (and especially the flour) "Fall Like Snow" when you scoop it into your measuring cup and then "Snowplow it Flat" with the straight edge of your scoop or a butter knife. Make a mistake and create a dent in your flour and show how to fix the problem. Remind them, "No sandcastles!" (You could demonstrate the difference between a packed half cup of flour and a properly measured "Fall Like Snow" half cup if you like.)

How To Guide

You'll quite quickly be able to move into guided practice and then independent practice with the dry measuring spoons and cups. I recommend letting kids practice with dry oats or rice first, then flour. *Skip the flour for the youngest children to keep it simple.* Invite them to feel the difference with their fingers to get the senses really involved.

"Skip the flour for the youngest children to keep it simple."

With multiple kids, they can work from the same salt/sugar bowl but should have their own practice bowls. More than one should be able to work from a 9x13 dish. Give them time and space to explore the textures too and touch the flour especially.

Extensions:
- To help kids get ready to measure spices out of the jars, since they can't pour/shake them into spoons without overdoing it yet, you could fill an empty spice jar with sugar or salt and teach them how to tilt it to get the spoon full instead of half full.
- Have fun practicing measuring skills in the sandbox (with a dedicated set of measuring cups).

Part 3: Making Seasoning Blends

Note: Feel free to postpone to another day if your little ones are getting tired or would rather continue exploring with measuring today. Omit or heavily guide for very young children.

Supplies on the table: Seasoning cards, cut apart, appropriate spices, measuring spoons, butter knife, empty jar, empty "spill bowl." I've provided a handful of seasoning blend recipes to choose from. I recommend no more than two for this first day of practice.

Because the measuring exploration is so independent, the real guidance on the skill comes when it's time to make the seasoning blends. Introduce the cards to your child and see if they can remember who all the players are. Help them identify and count the spoons on the cards.

> "Demonstrate how you scoop a spice by tilting the jar a bit, or use another small spoon to fill your measuring spoon over the "spill bowl" and scrape it flat with a measuring spoon or butter knife."

You can tape the cards to your spices or simply put them in a line on the table. If they are a beginning reader or interested in letters and sounds, show your child how they can match up the name of the spice on the card with the word on the jar. Be sure to take all the lids and shaker tops off the jars before the child needs to use them.

Demonstrate how you scoop a spice by tilting the jar a bit, or use another small spoon to fill your measuring spoon over the "spill bowl" and scrape it flat with a measuring spoon or butter knife. Resting the spoon on the bowl can help steady it for young children.

Pour it into the empty jar and count: "One." Remind them to tap-tap it so all the spices get emptied out. If they have to measure more than one spoonful and they have a lot in their dump bowl, they can measure right from there. Continue until you're finished with that herb or spice and then enlist your child's help scooping your spills back into the jar. Use a small funnel if you have one.

Teach a system to help your child keep track of what they've used. As you finish each jar, show how you mark "done" by moving the herb or spice to the other side of the bowl, taking the sticky note off, or turning the card over if it's sitting on the table. This gets a little confusing with multiple kids if they're all making their own mix. It's best to have them make different

> "Teach a system to help your child keep track of what they've used. As you finish each jar, show how you mark "done" by moving the herb or spice to the other side of the bowl, taking the sticky note off, or turning the card over if it's sitting on the table."

mixes at the same time so they're not sharing jars.

I recommend working together on a few spoonfuls, especially because it can be very hard for young children to get their spoons into a jar. Your ultimate goal is to allow them to be completely independent making a seasoning blend with the special cards, so work together to troubleshoot any problems that pop up that make this task difficult for young children.

How to Coach to Independence

You'll have to figure out how long you'll need to stay close when your child is measuring spices – it might only be through the first whole recipe and then they can do it independently, and it might not be for another year or two when they develop counting and organizational skills. For most kids this age, they'll need to keep all four spoons in front of them for comparison.

> "For most kids this age, they'll need to keep all four spoons in front of them for comparison."

Once they have completed the whole recipe, help them get the lid on their mix jar tight and let them do the fun part – shake it like crazy! You might want to have a soft surface like carpet or grass underneath in case of drops.

When you get to make recipes using the seasoning blends, it's a great opportunity to build up your little ones and praise their good work. It's also a good chance to bring back the seasoning conversations from Class 3. Ask questions to the whole family about what seasonings they think are in the meal, how they go together, and whether they like the amount or would prefer more or less.

See the KCRF recipe book for instructions to use each seasoning blend.

Use the seasoning blend measuring cards regularly to give your child that independent or guided practice, whatever they're ready for. Feel free to create seasoning blend measuring cards for some of your favorite recipes as well.

Storage Note: Tape or glue the cards to an index card to store them. For those who can read or at least match up the names of the seasonings, the cards won't have to be taped to the jars.

As I mentioned above, the salt/sugar and oat/rice/flour practice is a great tactile activity to make available anytime you're willing to put up with the mess (maybe when an older sibling is having cooking class!). Remind them of good habits and the catch phrases we use.

> "Feel free to create seasoning blend measuring cards for some of your favorite recipes as well. "

You'll get another chance to practice large-scale dry measuring next class when we work with dry beans, and we're doing liquid measures the class after that.

I recommend that you do try to bake with your little ones as often as possible – you'll get opportunities to practice all these skills and determine how quickly you can release various tasks to them. Integrate a "spill bowl" for them even if it's not something you would usually use in your own baking – they need a safe way to overmeasure without getting too much into the recipe.

Challenges You Might Encounter

Magical Thinking. "Oh yeah, that's flat." Call it an inability to estimate, call it "magical thinking" where the child wants the world to react how they expect and make it true by their thoughts – but little ones at this age group sometimes think that half a spoonful is completely full and flat, no matter what you tell them. I recommend gently using a "baby" teaspoon to demonstrate that more will fit in. You can also coach them to make a hill every single time because it's fun to Snowplow it Flat – and then they'll almost always get enough in the spoon.

The Finger Snowplow. Kids would much rather use their finger to Snowplow it Flat than grab another utensil, and for adults, that usually works. But kids' fingers are often so short or simply uncoordinated that they struggle to make a flat line, and they end up creating a divot in their measurement. Insist that they use a spoon or knife. It is worth demonstrating what happens when you do it (wrong) and asking, "Do I have hills or holes?"

The Scoop Stopper. For little hands, it can be really hard to scoop a full measure from a jar of herbs or spices. Every spoonful will come out with holes, and kids can get very frustrated. If filling the holes with another spoon also isn't working because of the depth of the jar, some parents choose to allow their child to be totally independent by dumping the contents of each jar into its own little prep bowl. Hopefully they can scoop each one back into the jar for you so it doesn't become a lost-time activity instead of saving you time!

Transition Worry. Some parents worry that their child will be calling measuring spoons Dads and Moms forever, but it's not hard to transition. To do this, I use the family names until about age 5 or 6, and I'll start saying something like, "We need 1 teaspoon salt - can you find the teaspoon?" Give them a beat, and then help: "That's the Mommy. So Mommy is the teaspoon..."

In our Intermediate Level when the kids are reading their own recipes, the amounts are written out like "one-fourth teaspoon" and also the numerical fraction so they have a bridge to the proper digits. At that age if they're having trouble finding the right spoon, it's nice because you don't have to go show them but can say "the Daddy" from across the room. They won't likely be fluent in the proper lingo until they start becoming comfortable with fractions in school.

Don't forget to create opportunities to practice this skill throughout the week!

You might integrate this one into daily life by brainstorming all the ways you can invite your child to help you measure in the upcoming week and month!

Extension Recipes to Apply this Skill:
Recipes in *Recipes for Kids Cook Real Food*:
- Any of the seasoning blends
- Fried Rice - the child can measure the spices for you

Find these recipes online at www.kidscookrealfood.com/recipes:
- Gluten-free Flour Blend
- Mild Curry Powder Blend
- Homemade Playdough
- Homemade Whole Grain Pancake Mix
- Homemade Gluten-free Pancake Mix

If you don't have the KCRF recipe books visit www.kidscookrealfood.com/recipes to get access.

Next Week's Grocery List:
- Dry beans (any kind you can use in a recipe)

Making a Whole Recipe Without Help: Intermediate

Don't forget to create opportunities to practice last week's skill:

- Cracking Eggs

How We Apply the Skill Today:

- Making muffins

Skills That Loop into this Lesson:

- Measuring ingredients (Beg. Lesson 4)
- Careful Pouring (Beg. Lesson 6)
- Following a Recipe (Int. Lesson 1)
- Cracking Eggs (Int. Lesson 3)

Tools Needed:

- Mixing bowl
- Measuring cups and spoons
- Spoon or whisk
- Muffin tin(s)
- Muffin liners
- *Recipes for Kids Cook Real Food* (or choose a favorite recipe for your family)

Time Needed:

- Hands on Time: 60-90 minutes

Food Needed:

- Whole wheat or GF flour (GF blend)
- Pumpkin or pureed squash
- Cinnamon, nutmeg, cloves
- Baking powder, baking soda, salt
- Sucanat (or cane sugar)
- 2 eggs
- Butter or coconut oil

Today's Recipes:
GF or Whole Wheat Pumpkin Muffins

Adults Should Prepare:

- Melt the butter or coconut oil
- If not using cans, bake and puree the squash/pumpkin

Extensions: how else could this basic skill be used?

- We're really moving our Intermediate kids toward independence in the kitchen. For now, recipes that are fairly simple and don't involve much cooking, especially one-bowl "dump" recipes, are great for this group. Pancake ability coming soon!

Allergy Notes and Substitutions:

- Any recipe, from a new salad dressing to a favorite muffin or quick bread, can be used for this lesson. The goal is to be independent, so do choose a recipe that (a) the child has helped with before and/or (b) is very simple -- preferably a one-bowl dump.

- The recipe we used is gluten-free already (but can be whole wheat as well), and although it includes eggs, a flax-egg substitute (1 Tbs. flax in 3 Tbs. warm water for each egg) has been tested and works great. Use coconut oil for dairy-free. And homemade baking powder works for corn-free -- or you can just skip it!

Daily Nugget:

"Sugar is a "Sometimes" Food"

Recipes that have as much sugar as flour are always desserts – we try to cut down the sweetener whenever we can and only it eat "sometimes" – if at all. Natural sweeteners like honey, maple syrup, and sucanat are better, but still should be eaten in moderation.

Notes:

_____

_____

_____

_____

_____

_____

_____

Lesson Overview:
Making a Whole Recipe Independently

Our kids took such triumphant joy in this activity because I emphasized, with a twinkle in my eye, that *I wouldn't touch anything.* Believe me, that will be the "catch phrase" from this one since it's so rare for an early elementary aged child to be able to do things on their own, especially real skills like this!

But prepare yourself – it may also take an entire hour to make muffins, not including the baking time! Just remember that it's time well spent, and you can certainly do other things while your kids are working.

Catch Phrases to Remember:

Catch phrases help kids to remember the principles and the skills that they are learning. Try to incorporate these phrases into your lesson to help these ideas stick in your kids' minds. Additionally, be sure to cut out or photocopy the flash cards (page 363) and keep them handy throughout the week.

- Read the recipe all the way through first. Ask questions about anything you don't understand.
- Get out all the ingredients.
- Organize your ingredients on the left (and move to the right after using).
- Level measuring! (Use a little bowl for spices and/or eggs to help your confidence.)
- Hold the bowl to stir.
- Proper stirring. (Scraping the bottom, around like a Merry-Go-Round and also some up and down like a Pogo Stick, some flipping over like a Roller Coaster, etc.)
- Look for a uniform mixture.
- Ask an adult (or an Advanced class member) for help with the oven when it's time.

How to Demonstrate

Your demonstrating has been done!

In past classes, you've talked about good measuring, stirring, and egg cracking, and now it's time to let them loose...

How To Guide

Before your child gets started, set the tone with a few reminders from the Catch Phrases list.

Kids should read all the way through the ingredients with the adult guide and make sure everything is out and to the left of the bowl.

Give them a little bowl to measure spices over/into – that way if they get too much (and they will!) they have the opportunity to put it back in the container. You might do this for eggs as well to avoid shell fragments in the batter.

"Have them ask an adult (or an Advanced class member) for help with the oven when it's time."

They can use a large dinner spoon to get the batter into the muffin cups. You might demonstrate the amount needed by filling one (or "approving" their first fill so you don't actually touch anything), and they can match the rest. Have them ask an adult (or an Advanced class member) for help with the oven when it's time.

Tips for Making a Recipe Kid-Friendly

If you are choosing to use your own recipe instead of one from the KCRF recipe book, I recommend writing or typing it in a kid-friendly format:

1. Use a larger font.
2. Make sure the ingredients are in the order they are used.
3. Write simple instructions (For example, list out the ingredients to add to the bowl if your recipe just says "Mix dry ingredients.")
4. Write out the fractions ("three-fourths") and abbreviations ("teaspoon").
5. Change stylized fractions (¾) to plain (3/4) so it is easier to read.
6. Number the instructions – not using bullets or paragraph form.
7. Be sure to print it out!

How to Coach to Independence

As with all skills, this one will take practice. Reading and following a recipe is certainly a skill that comes with experience. Try to incorporate the actual reading of the recipe – whether that's you reading it out loud instead of just directing traffic or them reading it themselves – whenever you cook with this age group.

Be ready and prepare yourself for spills and messes. It's an investment! Have a glass of wine with dinner.

Remind kids about clean-up, to fit your expectations. For example, I made mine put ingredients back where they belonged and get all the dishes into the sink, but not actually "do" the dishes.

Challenges You Might Encounter

Rookies. If you haven't spent much time baking or cooking with your Intermediate group, it may quickly show. If frustration sets in because the child's skills simply aren't well practiced enough to do this on their own, don't hesitate to pull the plug and switch to a side-by-side co-baking opportunity. Explain to the child that they need more practice and that you'll work to make sure they can do as much as possible on their own, and then set another practice time and try to release a little bit more into their sphere.

Fraction Trouble. Most kids don't have exposure to fractions in school until at least second grade. If yours isn't sure what 3/4 cup would look like, you can direct them to the words "three-fourths" to help them remember that they'll need to use the "fourth cup, three times for three fourths."

#fail. I'm hoping that no one has to experience flat cookies or muffins that didn't rise and only burned, but I know it's possible. You may want to brainstorm some funny, light-hearted responses that fit your personality and your child's to take the edge off. It hurts to fail, and it will be important for the adult guide to set the tone of the learning process: that everyone makes mistakes and has failures, but it's a chance to learn and try again.

Don't forget to create opportunities to practice this skill throughout the week!

You might integrate this one into daily life by choosing another recipe or two that your child will be able to handle and scheduling time for them to work on it once or twice this week.

Extension Recipes to Apply this Skill:

Find these recipes online at www.kidscookrealfood.com/recipes:

- Grain-free Coconut Flour Muffins
- Granola Bars
- Gluten-free Bacon and Green Onion Savory Dinner Muffins
- Apple Squares
- Gluten-free Pumpkin Cookies

If you don't have the KCRF recipe books visit www.kidscookrealfood.com/recipes to get access.

Next Week's Grocery List:

- Rice – white or brown

There are optional recipes in the next lesson. If you already taught your Intermediate kids to make rice, you'll also need tomato sauce and taco seasoning.

Sharp Knife Skills, Level 4: Advanced

Don't forget to create opportunities to practice last week's skills:

- Knife skills with garlic and sautéing

How We Apply the Skill Today:

- Slicing apples, cantaloupes and watermelons
- Baking muffins (or apple crisp)

Skills That Loop into this Lesson:

- Sharp Knife Skills (Adv. Lessons 1-2)
- Washing Produce (All-Kid Class 7)

Time Needed:

- Hands on Time: 60+ minutes

Tools Needed:

- Sharp knives
- Cutting boards
- Spoon
- Bowls to hold cut foods
- Oven mitts
- Cookie sheet and other baking dishes

Food Needed:

- Cantaloupe or honeydew
- Watermelon
- Apples

Today's Recipes:
Pumpkin Muffins (if Intermediate kids) or Oven Baked Apple Crisp

Adults Should Prepare:

- Remember to wash the produce with the children first.
- If no Intermediate kids, choose a recipe to bake this week.

Extensions: how else could this basic skill be used?

- Oven safety, as long as your child is strong enough and careful enough, will open up a host of recipes that can now be completely independent for them. From casseroles to quick breads, baked mac and cheese to pies, oven recipes are lots of fun!

- Apple skills can be generalized for pears and persimmons, and it's only a small leap to pitted fruits like peaches, plums and nectarines. Wrangling big things like a watermelon will give your Advanced kids the confidence to try a pineapple, cauliflower, cabbage, and more.

Allergy Notes and Substitutions:

- This lesson is definitely "Choose Your Own Adventure." Do as little or as much as you like depending on what is in season and what your family will eat. Be sure to choose oven recipes that everyone loves!

- **Seasonal Substitutions:** If melons aren't in season, either skip them or cut one of these other "large item" options: pineapple, cauliflower, broccoli, or cabbage. Although winter squash seems like an equivalent skill, they're so solid that the difficulty level nears impossibility for a child.

Daily Nugget:

"Eat the Whole Fruit, Skip the Juice"

God made a whole package in each fruit with a balance of nutrients. Juice doesn't have the fiber to balance out the sugars. Did you know that fresh fruit even gives your body water for your daily needs?

Notes:

_____

_____

_____

_____

_____

_____

_____

Lesson Overview: Oven Safety

My kids have always had a healthy fear of the oven, even as one-year-olds when we signed "Hot! Hot! Hot!" and made them be across the room when we opened it. So it's no surprise to me that it's intimidating for them to reach into it and get something heavy or awkward out!

That's one reason I'm going to ask you to practice oven safety skills with the oven OFF first. Your kids will be so much more comfortable (and so will you).

Catch Phrases to Remember:

Catch phrases help kids to remember the principles and the skills that they are learning. Try to incorporate these phrases into your lesson to help these ideas stick in your kids' minds. Additionally, be sure to cut out or photocopy the flash cards (page 363) and keep them handy throughout the week.

- Quick but Slow.
- Like a Hotel Key in a Slot
- 100% OUT then UP.

I also want to help your kids get comfortable with big, gangly, uncomfortable pieces of fruit. Melons are such wonderful fuel for the family, but they always need to be cut and they're not the easiest things to handle. I cannot tell you how awesome it was to have my oldest cut watermelon while I was making dinner this summer – everyone was happy with the result!

If you have Intermediate Level kids in your home, your Advanced group can put their muffins in the oven. If you don't have Intermediates, teach the apple cutting first and then make some baked apple crisp (or simple baked apples with cinnamon and butter on top).

How to Demonstrate

With the oven off, open it and show your Advanced kids the inside, the hot parts, where the food needs to go, and the risks:

1. You could get blasted by heat when you first open the door.
2. You could bump your forearm on the top edge.
3. You could touch the top grate while getting something out of the bottom shelf.
4. Your food could bump the top if you lift it too soon.
5. You could tilt the food too much and spill it.

Give a quick lesson about baking in general:

- Use the middle rack for even-heating from the top and bottom.
- Be quick with the door open to try to keep as much heat in as possible – the oven temp can change when you open the door.
- Emphasize the important habit of turning the oven off when you're finished.

With oven mitts on, demonstrate picking up a cookie sheet (and possibly other trays or pans). They'll need to practice this as well.

I have to tell you – I did this wrong the first time. I discussed the dangers and then asked the boys to put a tray of potato skin crispies into the oven. Total. Disaster. They couldn't even pick up the tray! So believe me when I say you'll need to demonstrate how to slide a cookie sheet a few inches off the counter so that there's an edge to grab – especially since the puffy oven mitts kill all your dexterity!

Some ovens really send a wall of heat at your face – you know if yours does this, so be sure to add an extra "catch phrase" for your kids called, "Wait For It." They should count to two or three before they put anything in or out after opening the door, and of course keep their face far away as they pull the door down.

> "Some ovens really send a wall of heat at your face – you know if yours does this, so be sure to add an extra 'catch phrase' for your kids called, 'Wait For It.'"

> "With children, it's also really important for them to know exactly where they're going to set the hot item down so there's no fumbling as the heat soaks through the pads to their hands."

Talk about moving slowly enough to be careful with what you're putting in the oven, but also being mindful of the heat escaping from the oven and the need to hurry up and get the door closed. It's a "Quick but Slow" conundrum that you simply need to demonstrate! Talk about how you bend with your knees and look where you're going.

As for keeping trays level, you can use any analogy you like with your kids, but the one I use is "Like a Hotel Key in a Slot" – that you have to put the cookie sheet (or whatever) into the oven completely flat, just like those credit-card-style hotel keys sometimes need to go straight in, straight out.

Also demonstrate taking something out and the importance of clearing the oven completely so you don't bump and spill whatever you're holding. You can also demonstrate pulling out the rack a bit to get what you need more easily.

With children, it's also really important for them to know exactly where they're going to set the hot item down so there's no fumbling as the heat soaks through the pads to their hands. Be sure to not only clear an appropriate space, but also make sure your child knows right where it is.

How To Guide

It's practice time! Practice both in and out of the oven, picking up a variety of dishes with oven mitts on, and knowing right where to put what you're removing.

Later on you can invite your child to practice putting something in a hot oven. Keep your voice calm and guide your child's first attempt with reminders only if they need them once the oven door is open.

How to Coach to Independence

Work to include your child as much as possible in putting things in and out of the oven in the coming months. I have a feeling it may take some children quite a while to feel completely comfortable with a hot oven, and that's totally okay. But it's up to us adult guides to provide opportunities to practice the skill.

Lesson Overview:
Sharp Knife Skills, Level 4 (Whole Fruits)

It was like a melon fiesta when we were teaching this lesson! You may need to invite some company over just to help eat all the cut melon you'll have, since you'll really need one for yourself to demonstrate with and a new one for your child.

There are really 4 different skills taught today, and some kids simply won't be able to do it all. Melons take kids a *longggg* time for kids to cut, so brace yourself. If you need to do part of this class on one day and part on another, that will work just great (we actually did apples on a completely different day ourselves).

Think ahead and plan it out – if you need apples for your oven practice, teach apples first, then oven safety, and then melons if you can swing it.

Remember to wash all your produce – even melons where you're not going to eat the rind.

How to Demonstrate

When a big knife disappears into a huge melon, the worst fear is that the tip of knife shows up somewhere unexpected.

It's a good time to strongly emphasize the importance of the "Tip Down" habit with knives. If the tip of the knife is pointing down, you won't surprise yourself with it coming out of the melon in a bad place.

To cut watermelon slices:
Use a saw blade cut to halve a watermelon, then lay it on the flat side and halve it again (always with the knife tip pointing downward). You'll see a rainbow of melon available, and you can simply slice off 1-inch rainbows, then lay each one down the cut the classic watermelon triangles.

> "It's a good time to strongly emphasize the importance of the 'Tip Down' habit with knives."

To cut cantaloupe cubes:

Saw blade a cantaloupe (or honeydew or honeyrock) from end to end so that the center cut is oblong, not round. Using a large spoon, scoop out the seeds and discard.

Show your children how to slice half moon shapes through the rind. Then you have some options to offer.

3 ways to get the rind off a cantaloupe:

1. Lay flat, cut straight lines.
2. Lay flat, knife standing up (like a dagger).
3. Stand up half moon, cut top to bottom.

To quarter apples:

1. After washing, stand the apple up, stem on top.
2. Cut in half with the Up and Over Soldier hold.
3. Lay each half down on the flat edge and halve again so that you have 4 pieces of apple. This is "quartering."

Coring apples:

Now you need to get the core out. Hopefully you have some strategies that you're personally comfortable with for coring already.

I do it by holding the apple quarter in my hand and sliding the knife toward my thumb, and some people prefer to stand up the piece, keeping fingers right up top, and cut downward toward the cutting board.

How to Demonstrate

You're probably getting pretty good at guiding with sharp knives by now – this is your last knife skills lesson, so you know not to hesitate to put your hand on the child's if need be. They'll be applying quite a bit of pressure to power through a watermelon, so really watch for errant fingers getting too low and potentially in harm's way.

Challenges You Might Encounter

Nervous Nellie. Hot things are scary. I guarantee there will be some kids who are really afraid of using the oven, and I think we should respect that. It's not really losing much independence if an adult has to put something in the oven for you. Postpone oven safety until whenever your child is ready.

Roly Poly. Melons are not stable things! If your child seems to really be struggling to keep control of the round melons, there's no shame in you making the initial cut to create a flat surface for your child to be more stable.

Stuck Knife. Sometimes the knife will get stuck in a melon, especially a big watermelon. Help your child wiggle the knife gently up and down to pull it back out and start over, and be sure that the other hand is NOT below the blade in any way. It should probably be right on top of the melon in fact.

Big Ball of Mess. Melons can be very, very tricky to cut. Do make sure your child can handle the melons or feel free to create a flat side for them by making the first cut. You might also get a lovely puddle of watermelon juice on the floor where your Advanced child cuts a watermelon. Wet Sock City. Be ready for it! ;)

Core Challenges. Getting the core out of the apple is a harder skill than I realized and might not be appropriate for kids until they are older. However, a motivated young person will figure it out.

Bore Challenges. Cutting fruit may be anticlimactic after last week's pride in making an entire meal. Please encourage your kids to make a recipe with their apples or melons (baked apple crisp or choose from the list below) and remind them how much independence they're gaining with oven skills.

Don't forget to create opportunities to practice this skill throughout the week!

You might integrate this one into daily life by assigning snacks of fruit to your Advanced child and asking them to help you whenever you use the oven.

Extension Recipes to Apply this Skill:

- Extra melon can go into smoothies
- Any casserole or baking recipe - ask your Advanced kids to practice their oven skills when you cook

Recipes in *More Recipes for Kids Cook Real Food*:

- Watermelon Agua Fresca
- Potato Skin Crsipies

Find these recipes online at *www.kidscookrealfood.com/recipes*:

- Apple Squares
- Grain-free Coconut Flour Muffins
- Fail-Proof Fruit Custard
- Roasted Vegetables
- Blossom Cheese (to dip apples in)

If you don't have the KCRF recipe books visit *www.kidscookrealfood.com/recipes* to get access.

Next Week's Grocery List:

- Dry pinto or black beans
- Olive oil or lard
- Onions
- Ground cumin
- Garlic
- Mexican oregano (or regular oregano)
- Salt
- Cheddar or jalapeño jack cheese block

Class 5

Kids Cook Real Food
Class 5: Adult Information

The classes today will help you, the adult guides, teach children in your life basic cooking skills. Remember that great teaching and learning includes demonstrating, guiding, and finally coaching to independence. You are a vital part of that process!

You should demonstrate each step of today's skills for your child learner(s). Nothing can replace the guidance you will provide as your child first attempts today's new skills. Be sure to help them on each step - and then step back.

As the child begins to be comfortable with the skills, use your voice to redirect them or refocus them if necessary, but the ultimate goal is for you to fade into the background. Let's dive into today's skill so you feel prepared to work with the children.

What Adult Guides Need to Know

Two of the three groups are working with dry beans today, and if you've never used them before, you're in for a treat. Cooking with dry legumes is one of the most frugal practices I know, even compared to canned beans (which are already inexpensive compared to meat).

A lot of people get nervous about cooking dry beans, or perhaps they try it once, have a crunchy-bean dinner, and vow never to bother with them again.

But I promise – it's not that difficult, and there's nothing to be afraid of. You'll save so much money on your dinners. You can thank me later.

Cooking dry beans is a two-day event, so be sure to read ahead and plan appropriately. For example, before teaching the All-Kid Lesson, you'll want to soak some beans for comparison so your kids can see the difference between soaked and dry.

Your Intermediate kids are learning to make rice, so you can have plenty of "beans and rice" pauper meals coming up – but they'll taste so good you won't even miss anything.

I want to make sure adult guides know how to work with dry beans so they can better incorporate the Beginner and Advanced kids in the process. Please read and utilize the "Guidebook to Cooking Dry Beans" in the Resources section on page 321. Even if you're a pro with beans, there's lots of great info inside.

Challenges You Might Encounter

Planning. The hardest part about today's lesson is YOUR part – making sure the beans are soaked when they need to be soaked, cooked on time, ready for dinner, and without stressing out or rushing your kids. You can do it!

Overzealous Bean Counters. When picking over beans, it's tempting to pull every wrinkly bean and throw it away. That may end up in 50% of your beans in the toss pile, and you don't want that!

Stove Fears. You may discover that your Intermediate kids or Advanced kids are nervous or downright scared to be at the stove. That's one reason we start stove safety training with the heat source OFF. It's safe and not scary. (Advanced kids could return to stove training if they are nervous.) After working with a cold stove, if your child is still too apprehensive to turn the heat on, allow them to measure the rice or beans without approaching the heat (into a cold pot). They can let you know when they are ready. Some kids will gain confidence BY working with everything while cold, so be sure to do that even if your child thinks they don't want to learn stove safety yet. Give them the opportunity to change their mind.

Developmental Readiness and Kid-friendly Reminders

Beginner
This is a very tactile activity with their hands in the beans, plus sorting, which is a preschool skill. It's also a nice "no risk" activity because it doesn't really matter if they measure inaccurately, so you can give them *lots* of independence on this one. Little ones feel so happy to have a job they can do on their own!

Intermediate
Every child will go through developmental phases differently, and personality and experience also play a role in stovetop readiness. Both you and your child need to feel confident to work around heat, but by age 6 or 7 many children have enough self-discipline to be safe.

Advanced
Convenience food is such a fit for our culture of immediate gratification! If we want real food, sometimes we have to learn to wait. This two-day lesson with the long cooking time and process of preparing dry beans is important practice in delaying gratification, a habit that can apply well beyond the kitchen for our Advanced kids.

All- Kid Lesson

Today we put our science hats on and do a little exploration. Prepare by soaking some beans in water overnight, even if you just soak a dozen or so in a small bowl for show. You could also launch the lesson the day before with the Beginner and/or Advanced kids getting the beans soaking, and do the All-Kid Lesson on day two with everyone.

Hand all your kids a dry bean and ask them to describe its properties. Explain that you started with the same kind of beans the day before and soaked them in water overnight.

Hand a soaked bean to each child and ask them to compare with their dry bean, describing the different changes they notice.

Ask them, "Are these ready to eat now?" (No.) Then ask what they think will happen to the beans once you cook them.

Now you're ready to move on to phase two of your lesson and cook those beans!

Extension Ideas:

If your kids are eager for more kitchen science, you could add a few steps to the lesson:

- What happens if you soak beans even longer? (Change the water every 12 hours and you can soak for days.) Compare both cooked and uncooked-yet-soaked beans.
- Sprout beans (an exciting and fun science experiment that everyone should experience)
- Compare the taste, look and texture of canned beans to your cooked-from-dry beans at the end of the lesson.

Note: If you only have Intermediate kids, you could either make beans yourself to go with their rice or simply skip cooking the beans and just soak a few for exploration purposes. Rice reacts the same way – expanding and fluffing when soaked and/or cooked, but it's not as dramatic because the grains are so small. You could certainly sprout rice with your kids if they desire something more related to their lesson.

Tips for Teaching Multiple Age Groups

This lesson is very easy for adult guides with many age groups – but may be challenging if you're trying to teach kids in one session and they don't live in your house!

Because making dry beans is a two-day event, Beginner kids will have their short lesson on day one, with Advanced kids observing/helping/integrating into their lesson.

Advanced kids will need to help soak the beans on day one, then drain and begin cooking on the morning/lunchtime of day two, and then finish the job and make refried beans leading up to dinner.

Intermediate kids are at the stove for the first time, so it's not optimal to be balancing multiple levels, at least for the 10-15 minutes that they are really first working. If you're making refried beans and plain rice for dinner, you might want to have some Mexican seasoned meat in a crockpot or already prepared to go over the rice so it can all be ready at the same time. Use the taco seasoning your Beginner kids made last class! *(That's in the KCRF recipe book if you don't have Beginner kids.)*

Refried beans can hang out on warm for a while, so have your Advanced kids get the bean recipe started first, and while the onions are caramelizing on low, introduce your Intermediate kids to the stove. While their rice is cooking (No Peeking!) you can go back to the refried beans and finish them off, perhaps with your Beginners slicing some cucumbers for a salad.

Other related dinner ideas:

- Nachos with chips, refried beans and cheese (Beginners or Intermediates could potentially grate cheese)
- Sauté veggies with Mexican spices, add salsa, and serve over rice with a side of refried beans
- Quesadillas with refried beans and cheese with salsa mixed into the rice as a side and cubed avocado on top
- Mix some homemade enchilada sauce or something similar into the hot rice; it makes instant Mexican rice + refried beans. Add any seasoned meat in taco shells to complete the dinner.

Your children will be so proud to have all worked together to make dinner – yum!

Soaking Dry Beans: Beginner

Don't forget to create opportunities to practice last week's skill:

- Making homemade seasoning blends

How We Apply the Skill Today:

- Helping to prepare dry beans for a recipe

Skills That Loop into this Lesson:

- Measuring (Beg. Lesson 4)

Time Needed:

- Hands on Time: 10 minutes

Tools Needed:

- Measuring cups
- Colander
- Large pot with lid

Food Needed:

- Dry black or pinto beans (or any dry beans)

Today's Recipe:

Your choice of bean recipe

Adults Should Prepare:

- Look up how to cook the beans in the Guidebook to Cooking Dry Beans on page 321.
- Choose a recipe for your beans. For ideas check out my *Everything Beans eBook* (go to *www.kitchenstewardship.com/recipes* for a special discount or online recipe ideas.

Extensions: how else could this basic skill be used?

- Measuring and soaking rice, helping with crispy nuts, washing berries or small tomatoes in a colander, sorting through freshly picked produce, sprouting legumes

Allergy Notes and Substitutions:

- Paleo adaptation: If you don't eat legumes as a family, teach soaking crispy nuts. Find a link to instructions at *www.kidscookrealfood.com/recipes*

Daily Nugget:

"Balance Beam Beans"

Beans keep us balanced because they have protein and carbs.

Notes:

_____

_____

_____

_____

_____

_____

_____

_____

_____

_____

_____

_____

_____

_____

Class 5: Beginner

Lesson Overview: Soaking Dry Beans

Your littlest age group is perfect to help you get started on the multi-step process of soaking beans, and it's an easy task for you to give them to get a head start on the next day's dinner.

Beginners can measure, sort, and rinse the beans for the family, and then the adult will do all the heavy lifting in the pot.

Catch Phrases to Remember:

Catch phrases help kids to remember the principles and the skills that they are learning. Try to incorporate these phrases into your lesson to help these ideas stick in your kids' minds. Additionally, be sure to cut out or photocopy the flash cards (page 363) and keep them handy throughout the week.

- No Rocks in the Beans

How to Demonstrate

This step will go fast, because the skill is pretty easy today.

Explain to your kids that beans grow outside, so there could be dirt or rocks mixed in with them. Their job is to sift through the beans and pull out any clumps of dirt or rocks they can find. They can also pull out ugly, wrinkled beans, and that's where most of the demonstrating comes in – make sure they only pull problem-beans, not every bean with a wrinkle. Otherwise you'll throw away three-quarters of your bag!

Invite your child to practice their measuring skills by scooping out a few cups of the beans into a colander. If you're soaking one or two whole pound bags that you want to simply dump into the colander, they can practice just for kicks and "measure" right back into the colander.

To make it easier to pick out problem-beans or stones, you could have your child pour each cup onto a cookie sheet first, inspect, and then scoop into the colander. Or just inspect one cup at a time in the colander.

How To Guide

Watch your child as they sort for a few minutes, checking to see if they're learning to be thorough and making sure they only pull out problems.

Help them carry the colander to the sink and rinse together, swishing the beans around with your hands. This gives you one more chance to get a visual on any dirt or rocks that may have been missed.

> "Watch your child as they sort for a few minutes, checking to see if they're learning to be thorough and making sure they only pull out problems."

Allow your child to scoop the beans from the colander into a large pot, and then they can watch/help you fill the pot with water and put the lid on *(refer to the Guidebook To Cooking Dry Beans on page 321 for the how-to on cooking beans)*.

How to Coach to Independence

Try to choose a few more bean recipes for the coming weeks and invite your Beginner child to get you started. They should be able to be independent quite quickly with this skill!

If you have Advanced kids, they'll use the beans you soaked in this lesson in theirs. If you don't, you get to make something with beans for dinner on day two.

Challenges You Might Encounter

Quick and Dirty. About the only problem you might run into with this is if the child simply won't focus to sort more than the top layer of beans. Luckily, most beans won't have rocks or dirt at all, so you don't need to work too hard on that.

Too Quick. Particularly if you don't have other age groups, this lesson may seem too quick and easy for your Beginner kids. Feel free to keep going with them, to cook the beans, and then to invite them to help make a recipe with you (more ideas at the bottom of this page) or try:

- Sprout the beans – a really cool science experiment!
- Mixing the beans with cooked rice and Mexican seasonings – gives your child a chance to practice the seasoning lesson from last class and do some measuring with you.
- Make the Mexican rice from the KCRF recipe book and add 2 cups of beans. Your child may have already proudly made the taco seasoning needed (also in the recipe book); now they can measure it for you.

Don't forget to create opportunities to practice this skill throughout the week!

You might integrate this one into daily life by considering how your Beginner kids can help measure and do small parts of big tasks, especially soaking beans.

Extension Recipes to Apply this Skill:

Find these recipes online at *www.kidscookrealfood.com/recipes*:

- Black Bean and Avocado Salad
- Tex-Mex White Bean Dip
- Tuscan Beef and Bean Stew
- Veggie Bean Burrito
- Cold Spelt Salad
- Tuscan Bean Soup

If you don't have the KCRF recipe books visit *www.kidscookrealfood.com/recipes* to get access and grab a deal on *The Everything Beans Book* as well!

Next Week's Grocery List:

- Gelatin (grass-fed best; find the resources page at *www.KitchenStewardship.com/kcrfresources*)
- 100% juice (grape is great)

Stovetop Safety and Cooking Rice: Intermediate

Don't forget to create opportunities to practice last week's skill:
- Making a recipe independently

How We Apply the Skill Today:
- Making Basic Rice (or Mexican Rice)

Skills That Loop into this Lesson:
- Measuring (Foundations 101)
- Following a Recipe (Int. Lesson 1)

Time Needed:
- Hands on Time: 30 minutes

Tools Needed:
- Medium pot
- Heat-safe spoon
- Measuring cup
- "How to Cook Perfect White Rice" on page 327
- If trying Mexican Rice, you'll need the KCRF recipe book nearby

Food Needed:
- Rice – white or brown
- If trying Mexican Rice: tomato sauce, taco seasoning (recipe in *Recipes for Kids Cook Real Food*)

Today's Recipe:

Basic Rice

Adults Should Prepare:
- Plan how you want to use the rice today, whether to enjoy it plain, make fried rice, use in a rice pudding, make Mexican rice, etc. If you decide to use the rice in a recipe, gather the ingredients. Recipe ideas are at the end of this lesson.

Extensions: how else could this basic skill be used?
- Cooking any whole grain side dish (quinoa, for example) or hot porridge (like oatmeal); reheating soup or leftovers in a pot; cooking frozen veggies in a bit of water.

Allergy Notes and Substitutions:

- Even if you usually cook rice in a rice cooker, knowing how to cook rice on the stove is a great skill for your kids. It also serves as a gentle introduction to stove safety.
- Paleo adaptation possibility for a rice substitute: making zoodles or cauli-rice.
- Other substitution ideas: You can teach anything else you might cook at the stove: warming up leftovers or soup, cooking frozen veggies in a bit of water, even hard-boiled eggs. *(Note on hard-boiled eggs: Teach the children to scoop each egg out of the hot water and into a bowl of ice water with a slotted spoon, rather than messing with children trying to pour boiling water anywhere.)* See page 301 for more.

Daily Nugget:

"Rice is Nice"

Rice is an unprocessed food, whole grain or white. Brown and white are just different. Brown has a longer cook time and all the parts of the seed, but white is still ok – both have their strengths.

Notes:

_____

_____

_____

_____

_____

_____

_____

_____

Lesson Overview: Stovetop Safety

This first time at the stove is a big milestone for your Intermediate children, and you want to set the tone for safety and caution – but also confidence – as they grow in their cooking skills.

Take a moment to determine the safest way for your kids to approach the stove. Do they need a small stool or a tall chair? They should be high enough above the pot to see everything inside and be able to comfortably manage a spoon and the lid of the pot without their arm getting close to anything hot. Please remind girls to keep flowy dresses, aprons, or long hair away from open flames.

Catch Phrases to Remember:

Catch phrases help kids to remember the principles and the skills that they are learning. Try to incorporate these phrases into your lesson to help these ideas stick in your kids' minds. Additionally, be sure to cut out or photocopy the flash cards (page 363) and keep them handy throughout the week.

- Stay Away from the Heat
- Pot Center, Handle Side – Hold it!

How to Demonstrate

With the stove *off*, take some time to talk with your children about the heat, including:

- What parts of the *stove* are hot?
- What parts of the *pot* are hot?
- Where is a safe place they can put their hands if they feel the need to rest on something? *(We show that the handle for the oven is a safe place.)*
- If you have an electric stove, you'll want to explain to your kids that even when the burner is off, it can be hot for quite a long time. Talk about what it means when the light is on.

Talk about pot etiquette:

- Keep pots and pans centered on the burner.
- Turn the handle away from the edge and always hold it when you stir.
- What spoons do you use? Can you leave it in the pot, or not? What would happen if you left a metal or plastic spoon in a hot pot? Where do you put the spoon when you aren't using it?
- Where is a good place to set a hot lid? **(This question is really important to answer before you start working with heat.** The last thing

you want is for a child to pick up a hot lid and freak out because they don't know where to set it, or set it somewhere unsafe.)

- How do you open a lid on something that is hot? (We call it "Pac Man the Lid" and teach kids to vent the lid away from their bodies to let the steam out, then lift it carefully. It's a good idea to practice with a cold pot!)

Now it's time to turn the stove on! You as the adult guide should demonstrate first, likely more than once.

Special Notes for Gas Stove Users:
If you have a gas stove, you'll definitely want to break down the steps of turning the knob as detailed as possible. Show them how it goes on and off a few times and discuss the ramifications of leaving the gas on without flame for too long. What should they do if it doesn't light right away? (Typically it's best to turn it off and start over, in my opinion.)

> "If you have a gas stove, you'll definitely want to break down the steps of turning the knob as detailed as possible."

Example steps might be:

1. Push the knob in (show the child how to hold their hand on the dial)
2. Turn it toward the [sink/window/fridge/etc. – something they can remember in your house] and stop at the word "light."
3. When you see the flame light, turn the dial to medium.
4. If the flame doesn't light, turn it back all the way off. You can feel it is off when you can't turn it any further toward the [insert your house's landmark here] and you see "off" on top.

Also explain why it's important to keep the burner area clear of food (especially spill overs), for fire safety reasons. If your flame goes out but the burner is still on, your stovetop is still letting dangerous gas out. You might even make sure your children know what that gas smells like.

> "While it's intuitive to be cautious with gas stoves and open flame, an electric stove still needs to be treated with caution."

Special Notes for Electric Stove Users:
While it's intuitive to be cautious with gas stoves and open flame, an electric stove still needs to be treated with caution. Be sure to show your child how to tell they are turning on the correct burner (look for the icon). Because

there's no obvious flame (like a gas stove) to provide a quick visual, remind kids to double-check. Even experienced chefs can turn on the wrong burner!

How To Guide

Take a deep breath. Your child is about to make fire.

I recommend that you stay close, talk your child through the process, and even have them practice "air stove" (like playing "air guitar") by talking through it with their hand in the air and not yet on the dial.

"Let your child turn the stove on and off at least 3-5 times in a row and practice setting to low, medium and high."

Let your child turn the stove on and off at least 3-5 times in a row and practice setting to low, medium and high. You want them to get a good feel for the dial and be comfortable with directions for "off" especially. Coach them that if they're not sure if it's going correctly, turn it off (gas stoves). Practice setting to low, medium and high during this time.

Next, with the stove off, grab a pot and spoon and do some "quiz questions." For example, ask, "Where should the handle go?" or "What does careful stirring look like?" and have the child show you using the tools.

Once you've done the stove safety lesson, you'll definitely want to incorporate your kids into cooking regularly over the next few weeks and onward. Even if they're just stirring or helping you do minor things, a few minutes here and there to remember their skill is important.

Lesson Overview: Cooking Rice

Now that your child knows how to turn on the stove, let's give them something to cook.

Cooking rice is like a non-recipe kind of recipe, something that you can simply remember and might not have to look up.

Basic Rice Instructions

Type of Rice	How Much Rice?	How Much Water?	Cooking Time
Basic White (long grain)	1 cup	2 cups	15-18 minutes
Basic Brown (long grain)	1 cup	2 cups	40-45 minutes
Basmati and Jasmine	1 cup	1 1/2 cups	15-25 minutes
You really should check *your* rice package for the ratio of rice to water (it will range from 1 cup rice/1 cup water to 1 cup rice/3 cups water). You might ask the child to read it. Some folks rinse rice in a strainer before cooking. This can yield a better result (less sticky/starchy) but is not 100% necessary in my opinion.			
For troubleshooting information, check out the Challenges You May Encounter section at the end of this lesson.			

Once they've watched you demonstrate, you can coach your child on measuring the rice, then the water (Get Level with Liquids) into the pot. Give it a gentle stir.

Some people add butter/oil and salt into the pot as well. This is optional and depends how you're going to use the finished rice, but it won't hurt the cooking process like it does with beans.

Ask them to turn on the stove and set it to high. If your pot has a smaller diameter than the "high" burner on a gas stove, you'll want to explain that you need to turn the heat down to fit the pot.

Basic Rice Cooking Instructions:

1. Measure rice and water into pot (usually 1 cup rice, 2 cups water).
2. May add salt or oil at this point.
3. Gentle stir.
4. Bring to a boil over high heat, lid on.
5. Turn the heat to very low.
6. Keep the lid on the pot.
7. Set the timer (see chart for the kind of rice).
8. NO PEEKING!
9. The rice is done when you see little craters show up on the top surface.
10. Let it sit 5 minutes with the lid on, heat off, for best fluff.

Talk about how the lid helps the food get up to high heat faster. We always use a lid when we're getting something to a boil, personally. Talk about what a boil looks like: bubbles coming to the surface, etc. You might even get to demonstrate the difference between a gentle and rolling boil, which is pretty fun.

Once boil is achieved, coach your child to turn the heat to low and keep the lid on the pot. A gentle stir at this time won't hurt the rice cooking process. For those with an electric stove, you'll need to remove the rice to a different burner and set to low, because the original burner will stay on high for too long.

The trick to cooking perfect rice is to start with the proper ratio of rice to water and then to cover the pot with *no peeking* (and especially no stirring)! This was a step I didn't know years ago – we ate a lot of semi-crunchy rice.

"The trick to cooking perfect rice is to start with the proper ratio of rice to water and then to cover the pot with *no peeking* (and especially no stirring)!"

(For the science geeks among us: It has something to do with steam cooking the rice – as steam builds up under the rice, that's actually what cooks it and of course the rice is absorbing the water while it cooks. If you peek under the lid or stir the rice, you upset the balance and let all that steam out, and then it's boiling instead of steaming and doesn't always work out as well. Interesting, right?!)

Help your child set a timer (sometimes a skill in itself!) and feel free to tease them that you're just going to go check the rice. They'll enjoy accosting you with "No Peeking!" Remember that different kinds of rice require different cook times, typically from 15-45 minutes.

Start by setting a timer for the shorter time in the range given. When the time is up, remind your child to "Pac Man the Lid" to check the rice. If the rice is done (nice and soft) on the top, and you can see little pockets like craters on the moon starting to show up, you know it's done. Allow it to rest for a few minutes with the lid on before serving for best results.

If you see any water puddles or the rice looks/feels crunchy on top, get that lid back on and set the timer for more time, but don't stir.

Some people like to soak whole grain (brown) rice before cooking though some of the information about phytase is still up for debate. This process would make the All-Kid lesson from today more applicable to the Intermediate Level. You can see some expansion in rice, just like beans, but it's not as dramatic.

More on cooking basic rice at www.KidsCookRealFood.com/recipes

How to Coach to Independence

If your kids are just making basic rice today, be sure to incorporate it into a meal somehow (see other recipes below for ideas). If you've got Advanced kids, too, make a Mexican meal to go with their refried beans.

Some kids may have learned basic rice already (it was recommended in class 3 if egg cracking was too easy). If so, move on to Mexican Rice today, which goes well with the refried beans if you have kids at other levels. That's a nice way to practice both following a recipe and the technique of making rice (No Peeking!) since it still applies to flavored rice. You can also discuss the seasonings in the Mexican Rice recipe, see if people at the table can figure out what herbs and spices were used, and ask your children if they would use any different seasonings.

Challenges You Might Encounter

'Fraidy Cats. Some kids will simply be afraid to be at the stove. I recommend giving them an out: "You don't have to do this lesson today but let me know when you think you're ready." However, you can also have them be close but not helping and gently nudge them to do a little here and there. Maybe they won't turn on a gas burner or lift a hot lid today, but they could stir a little. Whatever they're comfortable with, roll with it.

Stove Boredom. If this lesson isn't inspiring for your kids (or you), I recommend making the Mexican Rice recipe even if it's the first introduction to rice. It's always more fun to have something ready to eat at the end of a lesson!

Crunchy Rice. Wouldn't that be sad!? I hope no one has crunchy rice, but if you do, resist the urge to stir! Just check the very top, and if it's crunchy, get that lid back on for 5-10 more minutes. Once the water is all absorbed, let it sit for another 5-10 minutes with the lid on, and only then should you stir. If all the water IS absorbed and it's still crunchy, you can add a little more, but it gets dicey because you need it to boil yet not scorch the rice on the bottom. For next time, double check your ratio of water and rice, and also extend the timing at least 5 minutes and be sure to allow for a "rest" after turning the heat off. Crunchy rice is usually caused by stirring before it's done or not enough time cooking with the lid on. In some circumstances it can be too much water though – rice is crazy like that!

Sticky or Creamy Rice. If your rice seems too mushy or creamy at the end, you probably had too much water. Cut 1/4 cup water per cup of rice next time. You can also include a few rinses until the water runs clear or nearly clear. This will help the rice separate after cooking and be less mashed together, because there's not extra starch in the water from the outside of the rice.

Don't forget to create opportunities to practice this skill throughout the week!

You might integrate this one into daily life by planning some rice dishes in the coming weeks and inviting your children to help at the stove as often as possible.

Extension Recipes to Apply this Skill:

- Fajita filling over rice
- Basic stir-fry

Recipes in *Recipes for Kids Cook Real Food*:

- Mexican Rice
- Chicken Rice-a-Roni
- Egg Fried Rice

Recipes in *More Recipes for Kids Cook Real Food*:

- Beef and Cabbage Over Rice
- Stovetop Rice Pudding
- Veggie Rice Muffins

Find these recipes online at *www.kidscookrealfood.com/recipes*:

- Baked Rice Rudding
- Mexican Stuffed Peppers
- Veggie Rice Muffins

If you don't have the KCRF recipe books visit *www.kidscookrealfood.com/recipes* to get access.

Next Week's Grocery List:

- 9 Eggs
- Can of pumpkin or homemade puree (squash or sweet potato is fine too)
- Cinnamon, cloves, ginger, nutmeg
- Salt, baking powder, vanilla
- Maple syrup
- Coconut flour (OR almond flour, whole wheat flour, GF flour blend)
- OR make your own favorite pancake recipe

Cooking Dry Beans: Advanced

Don't forget to create opportunities to practice last week's skills:

- Slicing whole fruits and oven safety

How We Apply the Skill Today:

- Making homemade refried beans from dry beans

Skills That Loop into this Lesson:

- Measuring (Foundations 101)
- Stove Safety (Int. Lesson 5)
- Dicing Onions (Adv. Lesson 2)
- Crushing Garlic (Adv. Lesson 3)
- Sautéing (Adv. Lesson 3)

Time Needed:

- Hands on Time: 10 + 5 + 60 minutes (spread out over 2 days)

Today's Recipe:

Homemade Refried Beans

Tools Needed:

- Measuring cups and spoons
- Large pot
- Knife and cutting board
- Colander
- Liquid measuring cup
- Immersion blender or potato masher
- Cheese grater or food processor (optional)
- *Recipes for Kids Cook Real Food*

Food Needed:

- Dry pinto or black beans
- Olive oil, lard, or coconut oil
- Onions
- Ground cumin
- Garlic
- Mexican oregano (or regular oregano)
- Salt
- Cheddar or jalapeño jack cheese block (optional)

Adults Should Prepare:

- Plan the rest of your Mexican meal

Extensions: how else could this basic skill be used?

- The bean cooking process involves heavy pots, long cook times, and straining the beans. All of these skills can be used in making bone broth, too, which leads into making homemade soups with your knife skills for vegetables.

Allergy Notes and Substitutions:

- Paleo adaptations: teach how to make a roast or pick a cooked chicken, or stick with the soaking idea and teach how to make crispy nuts (instructions at *www.KidsCookRealFood.com/recipes*).

- For bean haters: Try the *Pasta with White (Bean) Alfredo Sauce* recipe at *www.KidsCookRealFood.com/recipes* with pureed beans in a creamy, cheesy sauce – great over pasta, rice, veggies or meat, and no one ever guesses that it's full of beans.

Daily Nugget:

"Beans are Musical for a Reason"

Beans can help pull bad stuff out of your body, but they can be hard to digest. That's why we long-soak and long-cook them.

Notes:

_____

_____

_____

_____

_____

_____

_____

_____

_____

Lesson Overview: Cooking Dry Beans

You are basically going to work together with your Advanced kids to cook dry beans, which is a very multi-step process over two days. You won't demonstrate much or it would be a 4-day lesson.

Follow the detailed instructions in the Guidebook to Cooking Dry Beans on page 321 to guide and coach your child to success. The only big decisions to make are about heavy pots: Can your child lift the pot full of water from the sink to the stove, and can they safely pour the water out to drain the beans when they're finished?

We did not have our 10-year-old drain the beans, but he was strong enough to move the full pot on his own. Draining is more risky because everything is so hot.

Otherwise, this lesson is a super cooking practice with the refried bean recipe. Your kids get to practice sautéing some onions, and the rest of the recipe is pretty simple until the mashing part.

Catch Phrases to Remember:

Catch phrases help kids to remember the principles and the skills that they are learning. Try to incorporate these phrases into your lesson to help these ideas stick in your kids' minds. Additionally, be sure to cut out or photocopy the flash cards (page 363) and keep them handy throughout the week.

Steps to Cooking Dry Beans:

- Pick over for rocks or dirt.
- Rinse the beans.
- Cover the beans with LOTS of water to soak overnight.
- Drain the soak water off the beans.
- Fill the pot with new water – LOTS of it again.
- Boil and reduce heat to medium low - Looooong cook all day – 4-8 hours.
- Make sure they're done. (special baking soda trick)
- *(More detailed instructions in the Guidebook to Cooking Dry Beans on page 321.)*

If you have an immersion blender, be sure to coach very closely on its use because you want to avoid splashing hot beans or liquid out of your pot. Keep it down in the food whenever it's on! You might even choose a taller pot than necessary to facilitate immersion blender safety.

If you are using a potato masher, it's not difficult to mash the beans, just slightly more time-consuming and requires a fair amount of elbow grease.

When the meal is served, take the opportunity to have others in your family guess about the spices used in the refried beans. Ask if anyone would have used a different seasoning. *(A squeeze of lime juice at the end, some fresh jalapeño sautéed with the onion, dry cayenne or crushed red pepper for spice, or adding cheese all are great options.)*

If you make a big batch, you can freeze refried beans or extra cooked beans for an easy meal later. Use them as a basic side for tacos or other Mexican meals, in quesadillas with or without meat (Intermediate kids are making homemade tortillas in class 7 – yum!), or even cold in a layered chip dip or as a dip for carrots as an after-school snack.

How to Coach to Independence

I've said before that a new recipe should be tandem work to help your Advanced kids get comfortable. Some kids won't even need that anymore - but some will. No biggie! Next Mexican night, refried beans will be independent now that you've made them together.

Grab the Mexican Rice recipe from the Intermediate group and the Taco Seasoning from the Beginner level and make a whole taco meal: meat, beans, rice. Yum!

Challenges You Might Encounter

Splashing Beans. When you're mashing the refried beans, be sure to warn kids about getting too energetic with the potato masher or coming up too high with the immersion blender. No hot bean splatters, please!

Heavy Pot. Dry beans is a tandem job unless you have teenagers or very tall, strong pre-teens. The pot full of water is way too heavy for a child to manage, but they can still master the rest of the process.

Crunchy Beans. It happens. We can fix it. (See the Guidebook to Cooking Dry Beans on page 321 for details.)

**Don't forget to create opportunities to practice
this skill throughout the week!**

You might integrate this one into daily life by planning some beany recipes in the weeks to come.

Extension Recipes to Apply this Skill:

Recipes in *Recipes for Kids Cook Real Food*:
- Mexican Beans and Rice

Find these recipes online at
www.kidscookrealfood.com/recipes:
- Veggie Bean Burrito
- Cold Spelt Salad
- Tuscan Bean Soup
- Three Bean Soup
- Black Bean Soup
- Hearty Lentil Stew
- Southwestern Pot Pie
- White Bean Sauce over Rice with Chicken

If you don't have the KCRF recipe books visit *www.kidscookrealfood.com/recipes* to get access.

Next Week's Grocery List:
- 1-2 dozen eggs

Class 6

Kids Cook Real Food
Class 6: Adult Information

The classes today will help you, the adult guides, teach children in your life basic cooking skills. Remember that great teaching and learning includes demonstrating, guiding, and finally coaching to independence. You are a vital part of that process!

You should demonstrate each step of today's skills for your child learner(s). Nothing can replace the guidance you will provide as your child first attempts today's new skills. Be sure to help them on each step - and then step back.

As the child begins to be comfortable with the skills, use your voice to redirect them or refocus them if necessary, but the ultimate goal is for you to fade into the background. Let's dive into today's skill so you feel prepared to work with the children.

What Adult Guides Need to Know

Time for breakfast!

By the end of today's lesson, you will be able to turn breakfast over 100% to your Intermediate and Advanced kids. Using their stovetop safety skills and ability to follow a recipe completely without you, they'll rock out on eggs and pancakes, and you can sit back and watch your Beginners thoroughly enjoy pouring.

That pouring lesson is one of our favorites at the Beginner Level, because it's so much fun for the kids and has so many ways to adapt it. Practically, being able to pour their own milk or syrup will likely become an often-utilized and appreciated skill.

The biggest reason I hear for parents not cooking a hot breakfast is the time it takes, and pancakes have to be at the top of the list. No sooner have you put a batch on the serving plate than it's being returned to you, empty. And then you realize that you've been flipping pancakes for half an hour and will only have 7 1/2 of them for leftovers (who always eats half and leaves it, anyway?). Having a little teamwork for this task... it's priceless. And delicious.

Although scrambled and fried eggs may seem like a step back for some Advanced kids, it's a guaranteed "independent" skill without needing a parent around at all, unlike some other recipes where you might still need to hang close. If your kids have already mastered eggs, encourage them to be an artist and add cooked meat, sautéed vegetables, herbs, cheeses or raw toppings. In the kitchen, there's always something more you can learn or do!

Challenges You Might Encounter

Little Hands. Our youngest crowd, the 2- and 3-year-olds, likely won't have the dexterity and control (yet) to complete the stopping challenges and pour into smaller receptacles, but this lesson is so adaptable to any age. Simply use the parts they can handle and hold off on the others for another year. (If you want to know how much different a child's small motor control is from yours, have them brush your teeth while you're brushing theirs. You can't help but notice!)

Little Flippers. For the youngest crowd, it might be too tricky to flip onto the same plate. Although that's the ultimate goal, your 2-year-old won't be doing pancakes anytime soon, so adapt the flipping lesson by using two little plates, one for the starting point and the other for the target.

Fear of Stove. No biggie. Intermediate kids can make the pancake batter and you can flip the 'cakes, or Advanced kids can crack the eggs and watch you cook. Waiting even six months to try again can make a huge difference. Think of how much a child's handwriting changes in one year of school in the kindergarten through 3rd grade range! That's their motor control improving, and many other skills will increase just as quickly.

Flipping Cheaters. During practice, we might use our hands to scoot the bread onto the spatulas, BUT in real life – with eggs and pancakes – that will never work. Challenge your children to *not* use their other hand. Make sure your Intermediate and Advanced kids know that they'll need to do a quick *Scoop* and *Flip* in order to be successful with pancakes and fried eggs. If they're smart, they'll practice with the bread.

No Eggs? Think of something else you can do at the stove that would incorporate a specific stirring or flipping strategy. Examples include stir frying meats, making a soup, or a favorite family sauce recipe.

Developmental Readiness and Kid-friendly Reminders

Beginner
Your kids will develop the small motor skills and self-control needed to stop pouring before they overflow something. What a great gift that can translate into their life – to be able to stop doing something and slow down. Also a bonus: practice in patience, because it takes 4 hours or more for homemade gelatin to set!

Intermediate
Pancakes require both patience and efficiency. Your child will have to wait for each pancake to cook and watch for the signs using logical thinking, but they'll also need to move quickly when the time comes to get everything flipped or removed from the pan. Different personalities handle this in different ways, some of which are more well-adapted to flipping pancakes than others!

Some kids will get bored with the length of the task but be able to have grace under fire without a problem, and others will never say a word and be engaged the whole time but will have trouble turning on their rocket boosters when it's time to flip quickly. You might choose faster or slower cooking pancakes to fit your child's tendencies.

Advanced
This task being placed at this stage of the game is all about responsibility. In ages past, 8-10-year-olds would be helping the family on the farm or doing real jobs. My dad assisted on a milk truck and other jobs when he was just 8, so I think my son can take over a breakfast independently at his age. It's a mental hurdle to get over, however, because our culture is somewhat built around kids "having it easier than their parents" and not having to work so hard. Personally, I want to raise capable, conscientious adults, so I choose to teach them to share the family's workload.

All-Kid Lesson

It's a quickie today!

We're working on a very basic skill with all age levels – flipping. A cook needs solid flipping skills for fried eggs, pancakes, tortillas, sausage patties, hamburgers, chicken, fish and more.

Practice today away from the stove to polish the wrist motion of the flip without any risk of heat or time pressure. I gathered all the kids at the kitchen table, and each had a small plate or saucer, a slice of bread, and a spatula. Even a pie server will do! We used bread because it won't break apart and is a good size to be slightly challenging but not heavy. Pre-made pancakes from breakfast would be another option if you don't have bread on hand.

Demonstrate how to scoop the spatula under the bread, then flip it toward the inside of your body. I call it "giving yourself a high five" because whether you're right or left-handed, you always flip toward your other hand. Aiming the bread back onto the plate is good practice too, because usually if you have a full frying pan or griddle, your pancake or egg or whatever will need to get right back in the same spot.

For Advanced practice, you can challenge your kids to get the spatula under the bread with a quick, sharp motion and no help from hand number two. Using a very flat surface like a cookie sheet rather than a plate might be in order.

212

Tips for Teaching Multiple Age Groups

Breakfast for dinner, anyone?

If you're juggling all three module levels, you might consider splitting the Beginner group into two days. Do the pouring practice on one day and make gelatin the next, partly because you've already got two things going at the stove, so there might not be room for you to heat the juice.

I recommend this order as one possibility for maximum efficiency:

1. Teach the All-Kid lesson.
2. Do a quick flipping practice with the whole group.
3. Set the Intermediate level up with their recipe and ingredients and get them started mixing up the pancakes.
4. Teach the Beginner lesson (have a measuring cup handy to talk about the parts of a pitcher).
5. Demonstrate and guide with the Beginner kids, then let them explore and have some practice pouring back and forth while you check on the pancake batter.
6. Get your Intermediate kids started at the stove or griddle when they're ready.
7. Depending on how much space you have at the stove and how many kids, the Advanced group could make their eggs concurrently with the pancakes. If you have an electric griddle so there are two separate spaces to cook, all the better. Work with the Advanced kids on cooking eggs...
8. ...then check back with your Beginner kids and give them some fun challenges and new things to pour into.
9. If it would be too busy at the stove to have pancakes and eggs going all at once, you could either have the Advanced group make eggs while the Intermediate kids are mixing up their batter (you'd deal with cooled eggs to eat, though) or let the pancakes finish and then the eggs begin (keep the pancakes warm in a 250F oven on a cookie sheet).
10. Work with the Beginner group on gelatin either after the meal or the following day. It takes at least 4 hours to chill and set anyway. Alternately, you could make the gelatin earlier in the day (or the day before) and serve it with the pancakes and eggs.

Pouring Wet and Dry: Beginner

Don't forget to create opportunities to practice last week's skill:

- Sorting Dry Beans

How We Apply the Skill Today:

- Pouring practice and challenges
- Homemade gelatin

Skills That Loop into this Lesson:

- Dry Measuring (Foundations 101, Beg. Lesson 4)
- Liquid Measuring (Foundations 101, Measuring Mastery Part 2)
- Stirring (Foundations 101, Stirring Specialties)

Tools Needed:

- Liquid measuring cups (1, 2 and 4-cup size if you have one)
- Glass casserole dish
- Cookie sheets or trays with sides
- Creamer pitchers and/or gravy boats
- Large pitcher of water (optional) and hand towel
- A variety of receptacles – we use a shot glass, coffee mug, and wine glass
- Dry beans and/or rice to manipulate
- Measuring cups and spoons
- Small pot
- Whisk
- 8x8 or oval casserole dish
- Cookie cutters (optional)
- *Recipes for Kids Cook Real Food*

Time Needed:

- Hands on Time: 30-45 minutes

Food Needed:

- Gelatin
- 100% juice (grape is great)

Adults Should Prepare:

- Collect supplies and prepare the pouring activity
- Fill a pitcher with water to streamline things

Today's Recipe:
Homemade Gelatin or "Gellies"

Extensions: how else could this basic skill be used?

- Pouring maple syrup on pancakes, milk on oatmeal or cereal, measuring liquids and pouring into recipes to help a parent bake, pouring gravy, pouring salad dressing, making homemade mayo, pouring ingredients into a blender for smoothies and more.

Allergy Notes and Substitutions:

- If you are on the GAPS diet or can't/won't use juice, check the extension recipes for a few gelatin alternatives that work great for GAPS or try one of these substitutions:
  - Thaw frozen raspberries in a bowl and use the juice to create your own raspberry flavor. You may need to add a touch of honey for sweetness.
  - Use homemade kombucha, water kefir, fresh-pressed green juice (or any vegetable juice), or coconut milk and mint instead of juice.
  - Just use straight fruit, with a little lemon juice if you'd like. Go to *www.KidsCookRealFood.com/recipes* and I'll I show you how.

Daily Nugget:

"Start Your Day with a Glass of Water"

Every body needs water, so get a glass in as soon as you wake up – pour it yourself!

Notes:

_____

_____

_____

_____

_____

Lesson Overview: Pouring

Set up a pouring practice zone with small "pitchers" (like coffee creamers, gravy boats, liquid measuring cups), dry beans and/or rice, and a rimmed cookie sheet or 9x13 glass casserole dish underneath to catch spills.

Nearby, be ready with some other receptacles like a shot glass, taller drinking glass, wine glass, coffee mug, wide bowl – whatever you can think of in your house – to challenge those who are able to exercise their self-control.

Catch Phrases to Remember:

Catch phrases help kids to remember the principles and the skills that they are learning. Try to incorporate these phrases into your lesson to help these ideas stick in your kids' minds. Additionally, be sure to cut out or photocopy the flash cards (page 363) and keep them handy throughout the week.

- Pour with your Crayon Hand
- Up High, in the Center
- Pour with the Spout

Vocabulary:
- Spout
- Pour
- Center
- Pitcher
- Liquid measuring cup

How to Demonstrate

As usual, we'll use our 3-step process to break this skill down into more steps than you thought possible. Use the Flash Card Phrases on page 369 to help you explain the finer points of pouring as you demonstrate pouring dry beans or rice from one small pitcher to another:

1. What hand do you hold the handle with? *(Crayon Hand.)*
2. Where does your other hand go? *(It guides the pitcher.)*
3. Get up over the tray so you're the boss, you're in charge.
4. Make sure you can see what you're doing.
5. Pour up high, never resting on the other glass.
6. Aim for the center.
7. Pour with the spout, not the edge.
8. Pour slowly, stay in control.
9. Look at what you're doing so you know when to stop.

Then take a pause to talk vocabulary and make sure your child understands the five words on the flash cards (also in the catch phrases list on this page).

On the second pour, it's tempting for kids (and adults) to take the fast/ easy route and pour directly back into the first container using their non-dominant hand. And that's actually good bilateral practice for kids (doing things with both hands), but I prefer to let that happen in bathtubs and outside water play. In the kitchen, I want accuracy, so I insist on using the Crayon Hand for careful practice.

> "In the kitchen, I want accuracy, so I insist on using the Crayon Hand for careful practice."

Show your kids how to switch the pitchers and turn the handle so that the one being poured is always at your dominant hand. This one will take some reminders!

How To Guide

Allow your child to have a turn pouring the dry beans or rice, reminding them of where each hand should go and potentially guiding their non-dominant hand with yours to ensure that they don't rest the pouring pitcher on the receiving container (more on why in the Challenges section).

If finding the center is difficult, consider putting a small sticker on the outside of the bottom of a clear jar to make a target.

Observe until they have shown you that they can pour correctly a few times. If one of your pitchers is smaller than the other, they'll need a reminder to watch their container closely to figure out where to stop.

Kids will truly enjoy the practice time with this activity. You can move from dry beans to rice, and then let them try water. It may surprise them the first time because liquid behaves so differently than solids! Expect some spills (that's what the towel is for).

You may need to demonstrate again, to show your child how quickly you need to pour with water so that it doesn't dribble down the pitcher and go everywhere. Allow some guided practice time.

How to Coach to Independence

It won't take long before you're comfortable walking away while your children explore, circling back to make sure they're being safe and remembering their skills.

After your kids get some experience with dry and liquid pouring, give them some challenges.

- Can they pour into a tiny shot glass without spilling?
- Can they pour into a tall wine glass without knocking it over?
- Can they pour exactly to a certain line on a liquid measuring cup? (Make this fun, choosing their age or the number of kids in the family or the "100 Club" on the mL measurements.)
  - Remind your child to "Get Level with Liquids" (from the Foundations 101 lesson on page 39). This one is great number identification practice too!

This station, either dry or liquid (likely not both) can be set up anytime for independent practice. It's so fun, some kids will request it!

If you have Intermediate kids, invite the Beginners to pour syrup on the pancakes – or on your family's next pancakes, waffles, oatmeal, etc. Put some (real) maple syrup in a little creamer pitcher. I recommend suggesting that they make dots of syrup instead of lines, and do take the time to demonstrate. For some reason even the most careful child can end up gushing when they try to switch from dots to lines – there's something "fast" about moving the pitcher around while pouring that is a different skill/age level.

> "If you have Intermediate kids, invite the Beginners to pour syrup on the pancakes – or on your family's next pancakes, waffles, oatmeal, etc."

Practice: Making Gelatin Together

Refer to the recipe in the KCRF recipe book. To find gelatin get access to the KCRF resource page by visiting www.KitchenStewardship.com/kcrfresources

You can make this section as guided or as independent as you're comfortable with. Some of the pouring is with hot liquids (adult job!), but it's just so fun to make what most recognize as the trademarked "Jello" that I couldn't help but include it. Always invite your child to "Get Level with Liquids" and tell you when to stop measuring the juice, and you should be able to guide them while you pour the gelatin into a casserole dish.

> "Once they've practiced their patience waiting for the gelatin to set, I know your kids will love using cookie cutters to make shapes!"

It's also another good opportunity to practice dry measuring skills by using a butter knife to level the tablespoon, and Beginners get their first real practice with whisking, too (Foundations 101 lesson on page 33). *Note: The gelatin will still set with quite a range of gelatin amounts, so your little ones don't have to shoot for perfection while measuring the gelatin.*

Once they've practiced their patience waiting for the gelatin to set, I know your kids will love using cookie cutters to make shapes (if you choose to make the gellies)!

Challenges You Might Encounter

The Overflow. When kids either aren't paying attention, don't care, or don't have the motor control to stop pouring, they'll surely make a spill. That's what the cookie sheet or baking dish is for! Work together to get the dry goods back into their pitcher or sop up major water spills. You won't have to say much for them to put it together that if they are more careful, they will spend more time pouring and less time cleaning up. Let experience speak for itself on this one.

The Fall Over. If kids accidentally rest their pitcher on the edge of what they're pouring into, they might knock the whole thing over. Another really good lesson learned in a safe environment!

The Back and Forth. You may have to remind your children several times to be sure to pour with his or her Crayon Hand and not take the easy route and pour left to right because it's fun. Use an upbeat voice, "Is that your Crayon Hand?" and remind yourself that it's important training in both following directions and doing it right for the long term...even if you have to repeat it 50 million times. If you have to literally get out a crayon and hand it to them, do it. PS – It's actually good for the kids, developmentally, to do things with both hands. So...if they're just practicing and you're cool with it, they can go back and forth. However, I don't really want them pouring milk with their off hand, so I enforce the Crayon Hand rule consistently around here.

The Drinker. Once you switch to water, some kids will want to drink what they pour. If your containers are clean and that's ok with you, they certainly can (as long as they remember to practice too). If you don't want them to drink the water, set that expectation when you begin. You could also have a special juice treat for the *end* of the practice that they know they'll get to drink when they can demonstrate to you that they'll pour without spilling.

The Dumper. Some kids will consistently "dump" their entire pitcher into the other one quickly – which works great until the second container is smaller. Others will spill on purpose because it's fun. We don't want them to practice this way, so you can choose to redirect with your words or simply give them a smaller container purposely to teach by experience. An incentive like "The Drinker" works well too: "I want to let you pour your own milk, and I can only do that when you show me that you know how to do it without spilling."

I Don't Like Using Food as a Tool. If it bothers you to have the children pouring rice or beans, you could also use grainy, pourable sand or beads instead.

Don't forget to create opportunities to practice this skill throughout the week!

You might integrate this one into daily life by inviting the child to pour milk on cereal or porridge, syrup on pancakes, or pour their own juice or water. You'll find many opportunities if you keep your eyes peeled!

Extension Recipes to Apply this Skill:

- Once you start thinking about it, many recipes include some pouring, so be sure to include your Beginner kids in cooking and baking with you and remind them that they can practice their pouring skills.

Recipes in *Recipes for Kids Cook Real Food*:
- Oil and vinegar based salad dressings
- Homemade Mayonnaise

Find these recipes online at *www.kidscookrealfood.com/recipes*:
- Gelatin with citrus juices
- Immune-boosting elderberry syrup gellies

If you don't have the KCRF recipe books visit *www.kidscookrealfood.com/recipes* to get access.

Next Week's Grocery List:

- Lettuce
- A variety of colors:
- Carrots
- Red, yellow or orange peppers
- Green onions
- Purple onions
- Cauliflower
- Tomatoes (to dice or cherry tomatoes)
- Shredded or feta cheese
- Sunflowers seeds
- …plus more to your preference!
- Optional: homemade salad dressings (see KCRF recipe book)

Flipping Pancakes: Intermediate

Don't forget to create opportunities to practice last week's skills:

- Stovetop Safety and Cooking Rice

How We Apply the Skill Today:

- Making our favorite pancake recipe

Skills That Loop into this Lesson:

- Measuring Ingredients (Foundations 101)
- Reading a Recipe (Int. Lesson 1)
- Cracking Eggs (Int. Lesson 3)
- Making a Recipe by Yourself (Int. Lesson 4)
- Stovetop Safety (Int. Lesson 5)

Tools Needed:

- Measuring cups and spoons
- Large bowl
- Whisk or spoon
- Griddle or frying pan
- Spatula
- *Recipes for Kids Cook Real Food*

Time Needed:

- Hands on Time: 30-45 minutes

Food Needed:

- 9 Eggs
- Can of pumpkin or homemade puree (squash or sweet potato is fine too)
- Cinnamon, cloves, ginger, nutmeg
- Salt, baking powder
- Vanilla
- Maple syrup
- Coconut flour (OR almond flour, whole wheat flour, GF flour blend)
- ...OR ingredients to make your own favorite pancake recipe

Adults Should Prepare:

- Select which pancake recipe to make
- Make or thaw homemade puree if necessary

Today's Recipe:

Pumpkin Pancakes

Extensions: how else could this basic skill be used?

- Flipping applies to not only pancakes, but also to meat patties, crepes, grilled cheese, tortillas, and more. Fried eggs are taught in the Advanced Level because they require more finesse and skill.

Allergy Notes and Substitutions:

- Since the goal is flipping, feel free to use any pancake recipe you want. There are plenty without all common allergens.

Daily Nugget:

"Eat Breakfast Every Day"

Our bodies need fuel for our day, and we need to start out
by giving ourselves some energy with a healthy breakfast.
Don't miss it!

Notes:

_____

_____

_____

_____

_____

_____

_____

_____

_____

_____

_____

_____

_____

_____

_____

_____

Lesson Overview: Flipping Pancakes

Pancake flipping is a very helpful, fairly simple skill with a few finer points that will make things run more smoothly. The All-Kid lesson flipping practice is extremely helpful to do first, for the wrist motion and the ability to land the flip in the same place, using the plate as a target.

Making the batter gives your Intermediate kids another chance doing a whole recipe without the adult touching anything!

The pumpkin pancakes we chose are a nice recipe because they're more slow-cooking, so your child won't have to rush so much to get all the pancakes poured before flipping. Of course any recipe will work, but you want to be aware of the slow-ness of this age group at the stove. Definitely turn the heat down so the pancakes cook slower, especially if you have a more traditional flour-based recipe. Some of them cook so fast! We don't want to stress out the young cook.

Catch Phrases to Remember:

Catch phrases help kids to remember the principles and the skills that they are learning. Try to incorporate these phrases into your lesson to help these ideas stick in your kids' minds. Additionally, be sure to cut out or photocopy the flash cards (page 363) and keep them handy throughout the week.

How to Tell When Pancakes are Done:

- Dry around edges
- Edge changing color
- Bubbles popping on top
- Peek underneath: See brown? Is it holding together?
- You might have to pat down to be thinner if they're thick pancakes and browning too fast.

Note: This veggie-based recipe cooks slowly because the majority of the ingredients are very wet: the pureed squash or pumpkin, the eggs. Most pancake recipes will have a few cups of flour and a cup of liquid and an egg, and those will likely cook much faster. Very thin pancakes cook very fast, so shoot for a recipe that yields a thick and hearty batter.

How to Demonstrate

As you cook a batch of pancakes, talk about what you're doing in as many steps as possible:

- What pan and utensils are you going to use? Take a moment to talk about why that utensil fits your pan well (no metal on nonstick or enameled cast iron pans, for example). Be sure to have a place for the utensil to be set down.
- How hot do you set the stove? Remember, it's okay keep the temperature a bit low to give your child more time.
- How long to preheat? We like the "Sizzle Test" – dripping a bit of water onto the hot surface to make sure it's ready.
- How much and what kind of fat will you add? Show how you "drive it" around the pan with the spatula using the Lawnmower stir.
- How do you know how much to pour onto the griddle or fry pan? Bigger pancakes are harder to manage, so start small.
- Where will you pour first? We use a top to bottom, left to right order in our house, and that helps us remember where to start flipping so it can be in the same order as pouring.
- What do you look for to know if the pancakes are ready to flip? For most recipes, this includes dry edges, slight color change around the outside, bubble forming and popping on the top surface, and the ability to get the spatula under the pancake while it holds together instead of flopping apart.
- How do you flip your pancakes? Flip side to side but aim for the same spot you started so all your pancakes don't bump together.
- How do you know when the pancakes are completely done after flipping? Remember, the second side always cooks faster.
- Where will you put them? Have your pancake plate ready!

How To Guide

Definitely stay very close for the first few batches. Help your child feel safe and comfortable at the stove with the heat and the busy-ness of pancakes, and be sure to turn the heat down lower if they need more time to not panic. You can also pour fewer pancakes or even turn the heat completely off to have a breather if your child is stressed out by the pace.

As they work at this skill, some problems may arise. Be there to help troubleshoot:

- If the pancakes are getting too brown on the outside but not cooking in the middle, turn down the heat slightly for the next batch. You can demonstrate how to pat down the pancakes so the middle batter oozes out and gets a chance to cook, and also how to re-flip the pancake to cook the oozy part.
- If the pancakes are falling apart, your child is probably trying to flip them too soon. Demonstrate a little peek to make sure the pancake holds together. (I love our thin metal spatula on cast iron for this – thicker plastic spatulas tend to snowplow the pancake into a bunch, even if it is ready to flip sometimes. Visit the KCRF resources page at *www.KitchenStewardship.com/kcrfresources* for our kitchen tools of choice. There are very thin, flexible plastic spatulas available too if you have nonstick pans.)
- If some of your pancakes are consistently cooking faster than others, make sure the pan hasn't started to scoot off the burner.
- If your pancakes seem to be sticking (despite being thoroughly cooked) you may need to add more butter/fat to the pan.
- For flipping troubleshooting, see "The Perfectionist" below.

> "If the pancakes are getting too brown on the outside but not cooking in the middle, turn down the heat slightly for the next batch."

How to Coach to Independence

You'll likely be able to feel if your child is ready to be more alone on this task. For some kids, their last few batches may be with you across the room; for others, you'll have to continue to guide for weeks or months until you're both confident.

When the pancakes are served, see if your family can guess the spices used in the pancakes to pull the All-Kid Lesson 3 back around!

Challenges You Might Encounter

Range Stranger. If kids haven't seen a *range* of ingredient measurements before, they might be confused (as mine were) by the "1-2 tablespoons" syrup in the pumpkin pancake recipe. My answer was: "Think about whether you want your pancakes a little more sweet or less sweet, and people can always add syrup at the table if you choose less sweet." We did this as well in Lesson 1 with the vinegar in the dressing; it's great to get kids thinking about how they are in control of the recipe and the function of various ingredients.

"This Takes too Long!" I feel the same way about flipping pancakes, don't you?! I'm hoping for you that the novelty of working at the stove keeps the task interesting enough, but you might want to add some music to the activity or give your kids a break every few batches so they make it all the way to the end.

Stovetop Skill Amnesia. It's okay if your child still panics at the stovetop. For some, this may still be an overwhelming new skill. Go back to Lesson 5 on page 191 and review the stovetop basics. Remember, the goal today is to practice flipping. At the very least, have them practice flipping the finished pancakes off the stove and onto a plate.

The Perfectionist. Ah, what to do about imperfect flips? They're going to happen, and kids will react to them in different ways. For those who may tend toward a bit of drama over less-than-perfect results, this is a great opportunity to remind them that even adults don't create perfect circles every time, and that it still tastes good no matter how it looks!

For actual flipping troubleshooting:

- Sometimes the pancakes will "splat" a bit because they're flipped too early and the uncooked batter is too plentiful. Coach your child to wait a bit longer and watch for more dryness on the edges, bubbles popping on top (with traditional flour-based pancakes; if you're using the orange vegetable recipe in *Recipes for Kids Cook Real Food*, you won't really see the bubbles). "Splat" may also mean that the pancakes are a bit thick or the flip a bit boisterous.
- Often, thick pancakes won't get quite done in the middle. Easy to fix – just put them back on the hot surface (in a cooler spot or lower heat) and press down a little to get the uncooked batter as close to the

heat as possible. It might squish out the sides and make a funny shape, but that's ok.

- When a pancake gets folded in half, that's a little harder to fix (but not impossible!). Sometimes it can be unfolded, but that's so tricky (and hot) that it's not even something I'd want young kids to attempt. The adult guide can either step in to help after asking if it's ok with the cook, or just instruct your young cook to flip that pancake an extra time or two and add some time to make sure the now-thicker part gets fully cooked. If your perfectionist is really worked up about the shape, well...don't they know that adults actually LOVE foldy pancakes? You got dibs on that one and no one else better try to take it from you!

Hot Spots. Everyone's cooking surfaces will be different, but if you know yours has "hot spots" that cook pancakes much faster than others, be sure to train your kids to watch for signs of doneness. Even though a cook would usually flip the pancakes in the order they were poured, you may have to go out of order or do some fancy dancing to move pancakes around from the "hot spots" to the "not spots" and make sure everything is done evenly. Make it like a game if you can: "You're going to the on-deck circle!" "Your turn, pancake!" "Time out for you, you're cooking too fast!" "Score for the cook, no burnt pancakes!" My grandmother always says it's okay to talk to your food and appliances as long as they don't talk back.

Don't forget to create opportunities to practice this skill throughout the week!

You might integrate this one into daily life by choosing one day per week that your kids will make breakfast. This will also give you a chance to talk them through things like planning ahead, another important skill!

Extension Recipes to Apply this Skill:

Recipes in *Recipes for Kids Cook Real Food*:
- Whole Wheat Pancakes
- Gluten-free Pancakes
- Grain-free coconut flour blueberry pancakes

Find these recipes online at www.kidscookrealfood.com/recipes:
- Potato-Vegetable Pancakes (Latkes)
- Grain-free Almond Apple Pancakes
- Silly "All-Pancake" Meal Idea
- Sourdough Pancakes
- Salmon Patties

If you don't have the KCRF recipe books visit www.kidscookrealfood.com/recipes to get access.

Next Week's Grocery List:
- White whole wheat flour (not traditional whole wheat)
- Solid fat (palm shortening, lard, butter, coconut oil)
- Whey
- Salt
- If no Advanced kids, plan something to go in homemade tortillas (although they're quite delicious plain). Options include butter/cinnamon/honey, taco night, shredded cheese to make quesadillas, or egg burritos for breakfast.

Cooking Eggs: Advanced

Don't forget to create opportunities to practice last week's skill:

- Cooking Dry Beans

How We Apply the Skill Today:

- Scrambled Eggs, Soft and Hard-fried eggs

Skills That Loop into this Lesson:

- Cracking Eggs (Int. Lesson 3)
- Flipping (All-Kid and Int. Lesson 6)
- Whisking and more (Foundations 101, Stirring Specialties)
- Stovetop Safety (Int. Lesson 5)

Time Needed:

- Hands on Time: 20 minutes

Food Needed:

- Eggs!
- Sour cream, cottage cheese, or milk
- Salt and pepper
- Optional: Shredded cheese
- Optional: add-ins

Tools Needed:

- Frying pan or griddle
- Appropriate spatula for pan
- Whisk
- Medium bowl
- Small bowl
- *Recipes for Kids Cook Real Food* (and/or flash cards from page 363)

Today's Recipe:
Scrambled Eggs & Soft and Hard-Fried Eggs

Adults Should Prepare:

- Decide if you will be using any add-ins (like onions, peppers, salsa) and have them ready to go. The goal for today is to focus on making eggs, though you can always practice Lesson 2 skills by cutting onions and peppers.

Extensions: how else could this basic skill be used?

- Your kids can keep being creative with omelets, egg scrambles filled with goodies, egg sandwiches, and more. Next they can learn poached eggs or other ways of frying eggs.

Allergy Notes and Substitutions:

- If your family can't have eggs, then this whole lesson won't really apply. Choose anything else at the stove that would make sense – stir frying meats, making a soup, or a favorite family sauce recipe would work. Boiling potatoes is another possibility that is taught in the Intermediate Bonus Lesson on page 307.

Daily Nugget:

"Runny Yolks Run Thick with Nutrition"

Cooking eggs can denature some of their health benefits – so runny egg yolks or slow-cooked scrambled eggs retain more nutrition.

Notes:

_____

_____

_____

_____

_____

_____

_____

_____

_____

_____

Lesson Overview: Cooking Eggs

Eggs are our family's easiest and most common breakfast. They are as versatile as they are quick, and we dress them up in all sorts of ways...we also often have basic eggs, because creativity might not be awake at 6:30 a.m. some days.

If your Advanced child did fine with the All-Kid flipping practice they are probably ready to go on this. You may choose to give them an opportunity to practice the Lawnmower and Roller Coaster Stirs they'll need for scrambled eggs in a pan off the heat source, especially if they're still a little tentative at the stove.

How to Demonstrate

Use the flash cards to help your children remember the steps. Start by talking about your particular pan and appropriate utensils.

Catch Phrases to Remember:

Catch phrases help kids to remember the principles and the skills that they are learning. Try to incorporate these phrases into your lesson to help these ideas stick in your kids' minds. Additionally, be sure to cut out or photocopy the flash cards (page 363) and keep them handy throughout the week.

Making Scrambled Eggs:
- Pre-heat On Medium
- Add the Fat (+ Meat or Veggies)
- Pour in eggs
- WAIT: Let it Sit First Before Stirring
- "Low and Slow" to Cook
- Push Runny Egg to the Hot Middle
- Lawnmower and Roller Coaster Stir

Making Fried Eggs:
- Sizzle Test!
- Crack Into a Bowl if it Helps
- Grease the Pan
- See White – Lots of It – Before Flipping

I suggest demonstrating hard-fried eggs first because they're easier, but I've also been known to say I'll demonstrate the "soft-fried" or "over easy" style of fried eggs first, because then if I break the yolk on accident, ta da! Now I'm demonstrating hard-fried eggs.

As always when you demonstrate, see how minutely you can break down your actions for your child, even at this Advanced level:

- What sort of spatula will you use, wood, metal, plastic? (What your pan is made out of will determine what tools you can or can't use. Example: Don't use metal on nonstick pans.)
- What angle will you choose for the spatula?
- Do you test to see if the egg is done enough to flip or just go for it?
- What motion is your wrist making?
- Where are you aiming the egg?

- How long will you let it cook on side two?
- When do you salt and pepper the egg, if at all?

We preheat cast iron or stainless steel pans on medium but turn it to medium-low for cooking eggs because they taste better (and retain more nutrition) that way – this pulls in the Daily Nugget. *(Nonstick pans don't really require a preheat.)*

Don't forget to Sizzle Test to make sure the surface is hot enough! Then explain to your child whether your pan needs fat or not and how much to use.

> **"To make fried eggs as easy as possible, consider using a small bowl to crack the egg into and then gently pour onto a hot skillet or griddle."**

To make fried eggs as easy as possible, consider using a small bowl to crack the egg into and then gently pour onto a hot skillet or griddle. This gives your child a chance to pick out any errant shells and also makes it easier to aim well onto the hot surface and not drop from too high and break the yolk.

Watch the egg cook and discuss the changes you see – another chance for a mini science lesson. When the edges are very white and solid, it's probably time to flip.

The trickiest part of soft-fried eggs is, of course, the flip. Do your best to demonstrate a gentle flip. It may be easier to allow extra space for the egg so you can just flop it over onto an adjacent space, rather than having to lift the egg up and aim for the same spot.

The spatula you have makes a massive difference in my experience – I love our thin, sturdy metal spatula for cast iron, and I used to have a very thin plastic one when I used non-stick. I highly recommend having one on hand.

You can test the second side for doneness with a little peek, and as soon as the white part is cooked, remove it to a plate. If you wait too long, the yolk will cook too.

Then demonstrate the hard-fried egg, which is basically the same motions but you'll purposely break the egg yolk.

How Do You Like Your Eggs?

Soft Fried/Over Easy – runny yolks, fully cooked whites; made by flipping over to slightly cook the yolk. "Over Medium" just means the yolk is cooked a bit more but still pretty runny.

Hard Fried – solid yolks, fully cooked whites; usually flipped over to cook both sides.

Sunny Side Up – runny yolks, cooked whites; usually cooked with a lid and no flip, hence the "up" part of the name.

Scrambled – fully mixed yolk and whites, moved around and in pieces.

Egg "Hash" – I use this term to refer to scrambled eggs with a bunch of meat and veggies mixed up in it. Easier to make than an omelet!

Omelet – fully mixed yolk and whites, in a flat pancake style; usually stuffed with meat and/or veggies.

Poached – a whole egg dropped into water and cooked; can have a runny or hard yolk. There are special appliances for poaching eggs, but they're not necessary.

Soft-Boiled – uncracked and boiled in water; yolk slightly soft.

Hard-Boiled – uncracked and boiled in water; longer cook time than soft-boiled so the whole thing is hard.

Baked Eggs – whole eggs cracked into small dishes, then baked in a large pan filled partway with water. Simple and delicious!

How To Guide

Now your child gets a chance to try the whole process for themselves, with you nearby guiding – ideally with words only.

Once you're both satisfied with how it all went, you can move on to scrambled eggs. I suggest cracking eggs into a bowl, whisking them up with a Hula Hoop stir, adding some dairy to make them fluffy (milk, cottage cheese, or sour cream), and cooking in plenty of fat over low heat. "Low and Slow" is the mantra for scrambled eggs.

Note: In our family we're split on the whole "bowl" thing for scrambled eggs. I like to save time and dishes and break the eggs directly into the pan; my husband goes with a bowl and adds milk. Feel free to teach your child the "direct to pan" method if that's your thing, but it is a little less risky to have a bowl to catch stray shell pieces.

To guide, *first* allow the eggs to sit and cook on the bottom for a minute or two (this saves a lot of hassle if you're using a cast iron or ceramic pan). Then you might demonstrate the first Lawnmower stir for your child and talk about what you're doing – scraping the entire bottom of the pan with quite a bit of pressure (unless you have a non-stick pan), using a pattern like going around the hands of a clock to make sure the surface is scraped thoroughly.

"Low and Slow is the mantra for scrambled eggs."

You can let them take over after that, but stay close to discuss how the eggs are cooking, what part needs stirring, and whether you'll add shredded cheese.

How to Coach to Independence

I truly hope that your kids can get excited about mastering this skill – even if they've cooked eggs before, they can improve their fried egg perfection for runny yolks, add a veggie sauté before pouring the eggs in, or work to cook multiple pieces at once, like sausage patties alongside or making a smoothie.

Challenges You Might Encounter

Broken Yolks. Even accomplished home chefs who are adults sometimes have trouble flipping a fried egg while keeping the yolk intact. There is another way to get nearly the same result if you have a lid for your pan: add a tiny bit of water around the eggs and put the lid on for a minute. Pac Man the Lid to peek and see if the white part on top of the egg looks cooked. Once it is, you can remove the egg with a nice, soft-fried yolk.

Bored Kids. So you've done this before…okay. We can work with that. Breathe some life into the lesson by making a challenge (even if it's just you vs. one child). Have a competition to see who can make the best "over-easy" yolk or hit "over-medium" just perfectly (after you Google what it's supposed to look like). Who can make the most delicious egg scramble – or cook eggs with the least sticking to the bottom as possible? Maybe it's time to try poaching eggs. The challenges are endless!

Don't forget to create opportunities to practice this skill throughout the week!

You might integrate this one into daily life by choosing one day per week that your kids will make breakfast. This will also give you a chance to talk them through things like planning ahead, another important skill!

Extension Recipes to Apply this Skill:

- Think of all the foods you can sauté (Lesson 3 skill) and put a nice soft-fried egg on top of.
- Fried egg sandwiches on toast (put mustard and lettuce on them - trust me!)

Find these recipes online at *www.kidscookrealfood.com/recipes*:

- Tastes Like Pizza Breakfast Hash
- Homemade Sausage

If you don't have the KCRF recipe books visit www.kidscookrealfood.com/recipes to get access.

Next Week's Grocery List:

- Onions
- Garlic
- Cumin
- Carrots
- Dry or canned chickpeas (garbanzo beans)
- Tahini or peanut butter (optional)
- Parsley, dried or fresh
- Any kind of flour
- Baking soda, salt
- Fat for frying
- Optional: cheese, zucchini
- Toppings: homemade ranch, lettuce, cheese, red onion, cucumbers
- If you don't have intermediate kids: Tortillas

Class 7

Kids Cook Real Food
Class 7: Adult Information

The classes today will help you, the adult guides, teach children in your life basic cooking skills. Remember that great teaching and learning includes demonstrating, guiding, and finally coaching to independence. You are a vital part of that process!

You should demonstrate each step of today's skills for your child learner(s). Nothing can replace the guidance you will provide as your child first attempts today's new skills. Be sure to help them on each step - and then step back.

As the child begins to be comfortable with the skills, use your voice to redirect them or refocus them if necessary, but the ultimate goal is for you to fade into the background. Let's dive into today's skill so you feel prepared to work with the children.

What Adult Guides Need to Know

We're stepping up our game today and making another entire dinner – salad (Beginner), a bean-based main course (Advanced) with homemade tortillas (Intermediate), and if you're really motivated, you could have your Intermediate or Advanced kids use their rice cooking skills to make the side dish.

These recipes are a little more challenging than we've had, especially for the Advanced level.

Remember that on the first go round, you're always working *together*. Don't expect the kids to do it all today, and try to make sure they don't expect it either. Next time, they might be able to take over more (if they're strong enough to lift the full pan of veggies).

If you only have one or two levels, remember to focus on the skill being taught and don't worry about the greater meal (unless you want to just cover for the other levels and work together on dinner anyway).

- **Beginner only?** Plan any sort of dinner with a salad.
- **Intermediate only?** Their tortillas could be part of a cold wrap, taco night, or even as dessert with butter, cinnamon and honey. Or skip the tortillas and make homemade crackers for a snack or one of the other extension recipes with dough rolling.
- **Advanced only?** At this stage of the game, the Advanced kids could possibly handle doing all the parts – just not all at once. You might have them make tortillas one day, the salad well before the dinner hour, and then the main course right on time.

Challenges You Might Encounter

If you've never made anything like the chickpea wraps yourself, you may want to try the recipe before doing it with kids (unless you have one of those lovely flexible personalities that I…don't have). It is delicious, but a bit complex.

Tortillas, on the other hand, while a bit time-consuming, are just fun. You can't mess them up – who doesn't love a square tortilla with a hole in it? Even if they're new to you, jump in and enjoy it, m'kay?

No matter what, give yourself and the children LOTS of extra time before dinner hits – double the time you expect to need to prepare the meal. Definitely do *not* do this lesson on a rushed evening when you have to go somewhere after dinner.

Developmental Readiness
and Kid-friendly Reminders

Beginner: This lesson is one of my favorites for the academic connections. You'll cover colors, numbers, and a bit of science, so take that as far (or not) as you wish. Developmentally, young children are still in an "ego" phase where they are seeking their own self-interests most of the time. Making a salad that they might not even eat is pulling them out of their own self-centered world to serve others.

Note: Never assume that kids won't like, eat, or want to try something. Present it as an option, and you can encourage them to try the salad (but don't make a big deal of it). It should be their choice to try some, all or none of it today.

Intermediate: Their muscles are finally strong enough to do a good job of rolling, and they have the stove skills and flipping skills to complete the project. It's almost a form of exercise once you get going!

Advanced: Although pushing buttons on an appliance can be done by a 2-year-old, the Advanced group is likely tall enough and strong enough to actually manage the "rest" of the machine. Use your judgment on that of course. We're putting together a lot of skills in today's lesson, and although kids are not very good at multi-tasking, it's nice to get them practicing, to think critically about things like, "How can I be most efficient?" and, "What do I need to be doing next?" without pausing between each action.

All-Kid Lesson

This topic of washing produce fits best with the Beginner group today, since they're the ones using lots of colorful fresh vegetables. Your Intermediate and Advanced kids should already know how to wash produce since they've been working with it all along, but it's always a good reminder (and if you've been helping/prepping for your Intermediate and Advanced kids, time to let them test their wings).

As the Adult Guide, you should simply remind kids why washing produce is important (fruits and veggies grow in the ground, get dirty, bugs walk on them, and sometimes there are chemicals sprayed that we don't want to eat...). Then show them how YOU wash vegetables – which may be very different from how I do it, and that's ok.

Tips for Teaching Multiple Age Groups

If you're juggling all three modules, I highly recommend having the Intermediate group make their tortillas far in advance of the meal, even as early as mid-morning. Both Intermediate and Advanced will need to start their recipes the day before, so plan for that.

The Beginner level is a quick one for the adult participation, so you can really juggle them with the Intermediates well. Make the dough with your Intermediates and start them on kneading their dough, then get the Beginners to join you at the table and start their lesson with the counting and colors.

Once they get going making their salad, you can go back to the Intermediate group and demonstrate the rolling process. Then hand the beginners a ball of dough once they finish their salad, and they'll be occupied for hours.

The Advanced group's recipe is pretty involved, so try to set aside time to work with them alone as dinner approaches. If your Intermediate kids did really well with the rice cooking lesson and you did the extension of Mexican rice already, they might be able to handle making chicken rice-a-roni while all the chickpea wrap busy-ness is going on (or start the rice before you get the food processor going).

I can't wait to hear about how this kid-made dinner goes!

Salad Masters: Beginner

Don't forget to create opportunities to practice last week's skill:

- Pouring

How We Apply the Skill Today:
- Making a colorful salad

Skills That Loop into this Lesson:
- Peeling (Beg. Class 1)
- Slicing (Beg. Class 2 and 3)
- Pouring (Beg. Class 6)

Time Needed:
- Hands on Time: 10 minutes

Food Needed:
- Head or two of lettuce, unwashed
- Various salad ingredients (see "Adults Should Prepare")
- Salad dressing (optional, some recipes in the KCRF recipe book)

Tools Needed:
- Salad spinner (if you have one; clean towel if you don't)
  - Salad bowl
  - Tongs (optional)

Today's Recipe:
Dinner Salad

Adults Should Prepare:
- Cut many colors of veggies to incorporate into the salad. Ideas include purple onion, white cauliflower, red, orange, and yellow peppers, cherry tomatoes or diced tomatoes, green onion, cheese, or really anything you like on your salad. See the Simple Salad Ideas chart in the KCRF recipe book for a comprehensive list of ideas.

Extensions: how else could this basic skill be used?
- Children could help choose different colors of produce while shopping and they could wash and tear any leafy greens (for example, de-rib kale or Swiss chard for cooking).

Allergy Notes and Substitutions:
- Any allergies can be worked around – if you don't eat greens at all for whatever reason, perhaps the child can make a trail mix or a salad made of diced veggies and a sauce (they'd get to practice their good stirring skills from the Foundations 101 lessons).

Daily Nugget:

"Different Colors Have Different Superpowers"

Food with different colors helps keep different parts of your body healthy – so try to eat lots of different colors at every meal!

Notes:

_____

_____

_____

_____

_____

_____

_____

_____

_____

_____

_____

_____

Class 7: Beginner

Lesson Overview:
Washing and Tearing Lettuce & Making a Salad

This lesson is really all about eating healthy food and giving these young children something that they can do completely independently and feel super proud about. The discussion about colors, counting, and "making it pretty" is as important as what they're doing with the food (if not more so).

The kids love spinning the spinner and are the perfect target market for tearing tasks. Release your quest for perfect-looking food. :) This skill is awesome because the kids can't really mess anything up.

Catch Phrases to Remember:

Catch phrases help kids to remember the principles and the skills that they are learning. Try to incorporate these phrases into your lesson to help these ideas stick in your kids' minds. Additionally, be sure to cut out or photocopy the flash cards (page 363) and keep them handy throughout the week.

- Tear Bite Sized Pieces
- Choose a Rainbow of Color

How to Demonstrate

You should start at the sink with a head of lettuce. Show the children how you prefer to wash lettuce. In our family, we wash the whole head, then tear it up into bite-sized pieces, then wash it again in our salad spinner.

You might point out a piece that is too big (make a joke about how you wouldn't be able to fit it in your mouth and demonstrate being silly trying to eat a whole leaf of lettuce). Otherwise tearing lettuce is easy-peasy.

If you don't have a salad spinner, no big deal. You can show the kids how to rinse the lettuce leaves individually (in a colander is helpful), shake the water off, then roll the whole bunch up in a clean dish towel. The lettuce can actually be stored that way in the fridge, but for eating now the kids can tear it up – after first rolling and unrolling the lettuce gently to get excess liquid off.

"You may not think you'd need to demonstrate how to make a salad, but it's actually a good idea to show the kids a bit about quantity, for example."

You may not think you'd need to demonstrate how to make a salad, but it's actually a good idea to show the kids a bit about quantity, for example. Grab 1-2 of each item and add it to the salad bowl and talk about how we mix up all the colors but not too many of each one. You can decide if the child makes an individual salad or a large serving bowl.

The first time I did this lesson with my kids, I didn't show the them anything about cilantro, and I ended up with huge stalks of cilantro thrown into the salad. *Oh. Right. I do actually have to demonstrate everything...* Ask for what you want or you might be surprised!

How To Guide

Other than catching any egregious misses of dirt globs on particularly dirty lettuce, this is the rare skill that really needs little guidance (unless your salad spinner is difficult to get going).

How to Coach to Independence

The great thing about making a salad is that the skill can just build and build. If you've done all the lessons up until now, check out how many prior skills you *could* choose to integrate into salad prep:

- Peeling vegetables (Beg. Class 1)
- Cutting with a dull knife (mushrooms, cucumbers, cheese cubes) (Beg. Class 2 and 3)
- Measuring spices to create a salad dressing recipe (Beg. Class 4)
- Pouring dressings (Beg. Class 6)

You can see how easy it can be to practice prior skills while working on a new one.

For early writers, you can encourage them to connect their cooking to the classroom by writing down their own "recipe" for a salad or drawing pictures of what they created.

Challenges You Might Encounter

The Salad Hater. Some little ones may be so "anti-salad" that they don't even want to make it for someone else. You'll have to know your child on this one, but I'd encourage the philanthropy issue. See if you can get your child to feel good about *serving* someone else and promise them they won't be required to try it if that's a stumbling block to even participating.

The Sensory Hater. If your child struggles with sensory stimulation, some may find the texture of lettuce repulsive. That's okay! Your kids might refuse to touch lettuce but maybe they'll love baked kale chips – because they are crunchy. If the flimsy/slimy nature of lettuce is throwing your child for a loop, consider having them munch on the crunchier part of a romaine stalk. Or have them create a lettuce-less salad. Remember, the goal is exposure to vegetables and to give them independence to make their own salad.

Don't forget to create opportunities to practice this skill throughout the week!

You might integrate this one into daily life by providing salad ingredients for dinner meals and inviting the children to help create a rainbow of color.

Extension Recipes to Apply this Skill:

Recipes in *Recipes for Kids Cook Real Food*:
- Use any dressing from the recipe book to dress up the salads

Find these recipes online at
www.kidscookrealfood.com/recipes:
- Kale Chips
- Wash and prepare greens to have in scrambled eggs
- Sausage Bean and Greens Soup
- Prepare garden produce for dehydrating
- Sautéed Greens with Garlic

If you don't have the KCRF recipe books visit
www.kidscookrealfood.com/recipes to get access.

Next Week's Grocery List:
- Whole wheat flour
- Honey
- Egg
- Olive oil
- Salt
- Yeast
- *GF substitutes and ideas for folks without a bread machine include: cornbread, cut biscuits, soda bread, or any favorite dough recipe.*

Rolling Dough: Intermediate

Don't forget to create opportunities to practice last week's skill:

- Flipping pancakes

How We Apply the Skill Today:

- Making homemade tortillas

Skills That Loop into this Lesson:

- Following a recipe (Int. Class 1 and 4)
- Measuring and stirring (Foundations 101)
- Stovetop safety (Int. Class 5)
- Flipping (All-Kid and Int. Class 6)

Tools Needed:

- Mixing bowl with lid or plate to cover
- Pastry blender or two knives
- Measuring cups and spoons
- Large cutting board or other clean surface to roll dough
- Rolling pin(s)
- Griddle or fry pan
- Spatula
- *Recipes for Kids Cook Real Food*

Time Needed:

- Hands on Time: 15-30 minutes on day one; 30-45 minutes on day two

Food Needed:

- White whole wheat flour (not traditional whole wheat)
- Solid fat (palm shortening, lard, butter, coconut oil)
- Whey
- Salt

Today's Recipe: Homemade Whole Wheat Tortillas

Adults Should Prepare:

- Strain yogurt to get whey if desired. More details at *www.kidscookrealfood.com/recipes*
- Plan a 2-day lesson – making the dough one day and rolling and cooking the next (or skip the soak).
- If no Advanced kids, think of something to go in the tortillas (although they're quite delicious plain).

Extensions: how else could this basic skill be used?

- Pizza dough, Stromboli, making homemade bread dough into sandwich pouches, homemade crackers, biscuits, pie crust

Allergy Notes and Substitutions:

- Find a recipe for grain-free tortillas at *www.kidscookrealfood.com/recipes*
- Note that grain-free tortillas roll MUCH differently than wheat tortillas. Use waxed paper or parchment paper and lots of patience. We've also enjoyed grain-free crackers (recipe also at the above link), which are easier to roll than tortillas.
- For dairy-free, omit the whey from the recipe above and add 2 tsp. apple cider vinegar to the water instead.
- For gluten-free tortillas, try a masa mix (found in many grocery stores) to make corn tortillas. An even better gluten-free option is to make gluten-free crackers (in the book: *More Recipes for Kids Cook Real Food*).

Daily Nugget:

"Soaking Whole Grains Helps Your Tummy"

Sometimes whole grains are hard on people's tummies. We can make our dough or batter the day before with a little whey or vinegar and let it sit on the counter overnight. That "soaking" can help the whole grains be easier to digest.

Notes:

_____

_____

_____

_____

_____

_____

_____

Lesson Overview: Rolling Dough

Playdough finally has a purpose!

I remember when we were in our first year of the transition from standard American food to a real food diet. I'd get to the end of taco night and, exhausted, marvel at how many steps there were to what used to be a simple meal!

1. Make taco seasoning.
2. Soak, roll and fry tortillas. (With freshly ground wheat, one more step!)
3. Cut veggies for fresh salsa (in the summer).
4. Brown beef and make taco meat.
5. Soak and cook dry beans for refried beans.
6. Make the refried beans.
7. Make Mexican rice.
8. Cut veggies and salad.
9. Make guacamole.
10. Stand back and marvel at the mess in the kitchen, hoping someone else would clean it up.

I've gotten better at batching things so it takes less time because we love taco night (and sometimes we fall back on tortilla chips instead of homemade tortillas, truth be told). Now that my kids can make tortillas on their own, I think they'll be back in our rotation – in quadruple batches so we can freeze them for easy meals another day.

Catch Phrases to Remember:

Catch phrases help kids to remember the principles and the skills that they are learning. Try to incorporate these phrases into your lesson to help these ideas stick in your kids' minds. Additionally, be sure to cut out or photocopy the flash cards (page 363) and keep them handy throughout the week.

- Soak Grains at Room Temperature (on the counter) Overnight
- Kneading Dough: Fold and Press
- Roll Dough From the CENTER Out, Like a Compass: N, S, E, W

How to Demonstrate

Here is a chance to remind your children of good recipe-following procedure: read the whole recipe together, collect the ingredients to the left of your bowl, and work through each step together.

The tortilla recipe will require a bit of parent participation because for most kids at this level, cutting in the fat is a new skill. It's not hard, you're just looking for a powdery consistency with the clumps of fat being about the size of a pea.

If you don't have a pastry blender, no big deal – you can use two knives and criss-cross them back and forth against each other, through the fat and flour. It's more time consuming but not terrible. A food processor does the job quickly, too.

"Tortillas are a great starter recipe for cutting the fat."

With many pastries, like pie crusts and biscuits, the key to flaky success is NOT handling the dough very much. Thankfully, that's not a concern with tortillas. Since they are going to be kneaded, there's no worry about over-handling the dough or making it tough and chewy. That makes tortillas a great starter recipe for cutting the fat.

In this recipe, we soak the dough overnight at room temperature to make it more easily digestible. That just means to leave the dough out, not to make a pool of water to float the dough in! *(Full adult explanation of soaking grains at* www.kidscookrealfood.com/recipes) Cover the bowl to keep dirt and bugs out. You can leave yogurt or whey at room temp overnight without risk.

If you don't want to soak the dough, that won't affect the end product. Simply mix the salt and flour at once, then cut in the fat, then fork in the plain water -- no whey needed.

I recommend making the dough together the first time with the goal of moving toward independence for the child on the second or third attempt.

Demonstrate the kneading process:

1. Press (smash) with the heel of your hand.
2. Fold the dough over with your fingertips.
3. Press again.
4. Rotate and flip dough occasionally.
5. If you soaked the dough and added the salt last, you'll need to make sure that it all gets fully incorporated.

Note: Working at the table is often a great height for petite kids. They don't have to worry about being on a chair when they're moving their upper body so much.

Also demonstrate the rolling pin procedure with one ball:

1. Flour your surface well.
2. Start in the CENTER and Roll Out, Like A Compass -- North, South, East, West.
3. Go back to the center and repeat.
4. Either turn the rolling pin for the "East/West" motion or turn the circle of dough 90 degrees.
5. When the tortilla circle is as thin as you can get it, put it off to the side and roll another ball.

How To Guide

Give each child their own dough ball to knead and let them have at it. You'll likely not need to guide via touch unless they have trouble getting the right angle for pressure. This is a nicely low-risk technique. Simply remind them to keep the dough moving so they are always folding and pressing different parts of the dough ball.

Fun note: If you have beginner kids, share a dough ball with them. They'll love playing with it and will wait with bated breath for their turn to explore the rolling pin!

When it comes time to use the rolling pin, children may need your hands on theirs to help them get the rhythm and then simple reminders about starting each roll in the CENTER and Rolling Out, Like A Compass – N, S, E, W.

> "When it comes time to use the rolling pin, children may need your hands on theirs to help them get the rhythm."

When all the dough is rolled out, turn the griddle or fry pan to medium high (400F on an electric griddle).

Give a little reminder of stove safety habits and show the children how to safely place one tortilla circle on the hot surface. Time the cooking for about one minute and check for brown specks on the bottom of the tortilla. Demonstrate a careful flip, and after about 30 seconds more, the tortillas are done and can be moved to a plate (I like to use the same plate that covered my dough overnight). *Sometimes it doesn't take that long; really as soon as you see a bit of brown, they are ready. Overcooked tortillas are still tasty but will become crispy.*

How to Coach to Independence

With the flipping skills they already have, kids should be able to fry the tortillas without much help already. Tortillas are actually easier to flip than pancakes, so you should be able to do other kitchen work (but hang close with stovetop safety reminders, of course).

Remember to get the child up high enough to see what they're doing and reach safely, especially if you're using a griddle that goes over two burners and ends up far from the child. Also set up the plate and a place to put the spatula down so there's no wondering what to do when hot things are happening.

> "Remember to get the child up high enough to see what they're doing and reach safely..."

Enjoy watching bubbles form in the tortillas – see who can get the biggest one, and then pop it – or eat it!

Eventually, many people can get into a rhythm with tortillas where they can roll some dough while others are cooking. For children, it's good to start with one step at a time so they're not trying to rush the rolling or the stove work. They can stand and watch a tortilla cook with much more patience than I can!

Challenges You Might Encounter

Roly Poly Troubles. It can be challenging to get the dough both thin enough and even enough, so that there aren't thick patches that make cooking difficult. It's ok for an adult to do "finishing touches" and even things out, and it's also not a huge problem to cook uneven tortillas. Since there aren't perishable ingredients like eggs, if a section is a tiny bit doughy or another section a bit crispy, it won't hurt.

Sticky dough can be tricky too, but just adding flour like with any bread dough will fix that up quickly.

High Speed Chase. Keeping up with tortillas is much like pancakes, although if you roll out all the dough in advance, it's less hectic. If kids are having trouble managing multiple tortillas, just do one at a time. As they get more accomplished, you might be able to get the rhythm of roll one, place on griddle, roll another, flip first tortilla, put second on griddle, roll number 3, remove number 1, flip number 2, ETC. That's a lofty goal for a child to reach though!

Don't forget to create opportunities to practice this skill throughout the week!

You might integrate this one into daily life by planning a tortilla meal this week and also making homemade crackers for a snack.

Extension Recipes to Apply this Skill:
Find these recipes online at
www.kidscookrealfood.com/recipes:
- Homemade Crackers
- Homemade Pizza Dough
- Homemade Biscuits
- Beef and Cabbage Sandwich Pouches
- Homemade Healthier Toaster Tarts
- Homemade Pie Crust
- Kifli Cookies

If you don't have the KCRF recipe books visit *www.kidscookrealfood.com/recipes* to get access.

Next Week's Grocery List:
- Ground meat
- Plus whatever you might want to make with the ground meat; choose a recipe in advance (if you have Advanced kids, we'll make something together).

Using a Small Appliance: Advanced

Don't forget to create opportunities to practice last week's skill(s):

- Making eggs

How We Apply the Skill Today:

- Shredding cheese, slicing zucchini, making meatless chickpea wraps

Skills That Loop into this Lesson:

- Knife skills (Adv. Class 1, 2 and 3)
- Stovetop safety (Int. Class 5)
- Sautéing (Adv. Class 3)
- Cooking dry beans (Adv. Class 5)
- Flipping (All-Kid Class 6)
- Making rice (optional; Int. Class 5)
- Measuring skills (Foundations 101)
- Following a recipe (Int. Class 1)

Tools Needed:

- Food processor
- Frying pan or skillet
- Knife and cutting board

Adults Should Prepare:

- If making the chickpea wraps, you'll need the KCRF recipe book.
- Plan a 2-day lesson with soaking beans the night before.
- If you want the kids to focus on one skill only, you can make a rice side dish and tortillas yourself – or let them do each recipe one at a time.

Time Needed:

- Hands on Time: 45-90 minutes (plus soaking and cooking beans)

Food Needed:

- Onions
- Garlic
- Cumin
- Carrots
- Dry or canned chickpeas (garbanzo beans)
- Tahini or peanut butter (optional)
- Parsley, dried or fresh
- Any kind of flour
- Baking soda, salt
- Fat for frying
- Optional: cheese, zucchini
- Toppings: homemade ranch, lettuce, cheese, red onion, cucumbers
- If you don't have intermediate kids: Tortillas

Today's Recipe:
Chickpea Wraps & Homemade Chicken Rice-a-Roni

Extensions: how else could this basic skill be used?

- Kids will be ready for more complicated recipes after this, anything that uses a food processor, plus working toward planning and balancing a whole meal. Extend your kids to other small appliances in your household, too, like blenders, grain mills, dehydrators, stick blenders, stand mixers and more.

Allergy Notes and Substitutions:

- For Paleo eaters, try making homemade almond butter or coconut milk.
- No nuts? Omit the tahini or nut butter without need for any substitutions.
- If you don't have tortillas, these are fine over rice, on a salad, or just plain with a nice dip.

Daily Nugget:

"The Value of Shredding It"

Did you know "stuff" is added to store shredded cheese? If you want to be in charge of the ingredients and get the best taste, shred your own.

Notes:

_____

_____

_____

_____

_____

_____

_____

_____

Lesson Overview: Using a Small Appliance

This lesson is a bit different than most because it has to be so adaptable – if you don't have a food processor, you may have to completely switch up the content and recipe, but that's really okay.

Alternatives to use the chickpea wrap recipe if you don't have a food processor:

Catch Phrases to Remember:

Catch phrases help kids to remember the principles and the skills that they are learning. Try to incorporate these phrases into your lesson to help these ideas stick in your kids' minds. Additionally, be sure to cut out or photocopy the flash cards (page 363) and keep them handy throughout the week.

- Pulse for Onions
- Wash once, Use Lots

1. An immersion blender (a.k.a. stick blender) would do the job in a nice big bowl. You'd want to crush the garlic separately and just add all the ingredients at once, so that the moisture from the sautéed veggies can help the blender get through the chickpeas at the same time. Then just stir in the flour/salt/baking soda by hand.
2. A high-powered blender like a Vitamix or Blendtec could knock out this recipe no problem. Use the tamper on the Vitamix and the jar with the scrapers on a Blendtec.
3. If you'd like to try using a regular blender, I'd recommend splitting the recipe up into 2-3 portions so that the blender can process it sufficiently. Just add some chickpeas and sautéed veggies, blend, and remove to a large bowl. Repeat. Then stir in the additional ingredients by hand.

I wanted to include something like this because I thought about the time adults spend using their helpful kitchen machines, and I felt it was important to ensure that our kids get a chance to learn how to use those machines too, whatever they are.

So consider what small appliance you use most often in your house, choose a favorite recipe, and teach your child using that framework. If you want to make this chickpea wrap recipe for dinner, it's a great challenge and a yummy result!

I like to use a small appliance for multiple tasks if I'm going to have to do dishes, so we shred cheese, slice zucchini for another recipe the next day, and then make the chickpea wraps. We use the food processor to dice the onion, mince the garlic, shred the carrots, mince the parsley and puree the chickpea paste! Efficiency is a great conversation to have...and if the child doesn't understand, just have him/her do dishes. :)

How to Demonstrate & How to Guide

Using a small appliance – and this complicated recipe – are both examples of co-working skills. You and the child(ren) should work together, and after a practice or two, the child might be able to work independently.

You can structure what you choose to do – will you shred and slice first, or just jump into the recipe? Will you teach another small appliance entirely?

"Using a small appliance – and this complicated recipe – are both examples of co-working skills."

I'm not going to walk you through each step of the process, because the recipe should do that sufficiently. Just know that your child may not be strong enough to lift a frying pan full of onions and carrots and scrape it into the food processor, so that's a good "helping" job for the adult to take care of.

This recipe provides more sautéing, stovetop, and flipping practice as well, along with the important skill of managing many items at once. The cooking may be done on a griddle or in a skillet.

How to Coach to Independence

I encourage you to expand into other small appliances in your kitchen – we only have one more class of the official *Kids Cook Real Food*, so it's time to start thinking about "what happens next." Talk to your child about other recipes and tools s/he might want to learn when cooking school is over.

"...we only have one more class of the official *Kids Cook Real Food*, so it's time to start thinking about 'what happens next.'"

We sat down and made a list of family recipes the kids wanted to learn to make, and it was so nice to have it all written down so that we could pull from it for each weekly "kids' cooking night."

To pull the class three lesson on spices back in, you might ask if people can identify the flavors in this dish (cumin) or what other sauces you might put on top that would coordinate well with the seasoning.

Challenges You Might Encounter

Patty Problems. How big do you make the patties of chickpea mush? How do you know when they're done?

Shoot for about 1/2-inch thick patties, 3 inches or so across. The "mush" is very sticky so that can be tricky. I personally prefer to use my hands (well floured!) to form the patties, but some kids have trouble with that and prefer to use a spoon. You can always add a tiny bit of water, either to the mush or to your hands, to make it easier to manage with less stickiness. We like to make them on the smaller side so that there's more of the crispy outside and less of the mushy inside.

There's no egg or raw meat in the patties, so "done" is basically when they're browned on both sides. They will still be very soft in the middle lest they become too dried out, so don't expect the final texture to be like a hamburger patty.

Too Much Going On. Are you concerned your child will forget to put the lid on the blender? Burn something on the stove while they're wrestling with a small appliance? Remember the co-working strategy here, and never feel like you have to let a child go on their own with more than you think they can handle. Stoves can always be turned off while something else is happening. If you're concerned about kids not using a small appliance correctly, you might make an index card of step-by-step rules for its use.

Don't forget to create opportunities to practice this skill throughout the week!

You might integrate this one into daily life by planning meals that use the small appliance you taught.

Extension Recipes to Apply this Skill:

Recipes in *More Recipes for Kids Cook Real Food*:
- Almond Apple Pancakes
- Potato Vegetable Pancakes (Latkes)
- Black Bean Brownies
- Blended Soup
- Sausage Zucchini Bake

Find these recipes online at www.kidscookrealfood.com/recipes:
- Homemade Dried Fruit & Nut Bars
- Hummus

If you don't have the KCRF recipe books visit www.kidscookrealfood.com/recipes to get access.

Next Week's Grocery List:
- Broccoli or green beans (something to steam, can be frozen)
- Milk
- Cheddar cheese
- Arrowroot starch or flour
- Cooked rice
- Spices
- *If you don't have intermediate kids: ground meat*

Class 8

Kids Cook Real Food
Class 8: Adult Information

The classes today will help you, the adult guides, teach children in your life basic cooking skills. Remember that great teaching and learning includes demonstrating, guiding, and finally coaching to independence. You are a vital part of that process!

You should demonstrate each step of today's skills for your child learner(s). Nothing can replace the guidance you will provide as your child first attempts today's new skills. Be sure to help them on each step - and then step back.

As the child begins to be comfortable with the skills, use your voice to redirect them or refocus them if necessary, but the ultimate goal is for you to fade into the background. Let's dive into today's skill so you feel prepared to work with the children.

What Adult Guides Need to Know

It's your last class! (Sniff, sniff)

Today I love that I get to challenge children to be kitchen artists and let their wings spread a little. We'll make a "leftover bowl" using bits and pieces from each group's lesson – it turned out to be a super kid-friendly way to serve vegetables, a nice discovery!

You have a few decisions to make before you get started:

Beginner

You can use a bread maker, a stand mixer, or knead by hand to make today's rolls. The roll recipe in the accompanying KCRF recipe book uses a bread maker, but you can adapt it to kneading by hand (instructions in Beginner lesson), use the Stir-and-Pour recipe in the recipe book, or switch to biscuits or cornbread (GF versions included). The goal is to give the Beginners something they can do that is both tactile and able to be completed outside the normal dinner-hour rush.

Intermediate

We're browning ground meat today, so you'll need to decide what kind of meat to use, what recipe you'll make with the finished product, and most importantly, the one you won't think of until it's upon you because it's well short of glamorous: how the grease will be drained (ideas in the lesson section).

Advanced

The oldest group is steaming vegetables today, and the "finishing" of that process is similar to the grease-draining above. There's some dangerous heat going on, so you need a plan for how your young ones will remove the boiling water or steamed veggies from the pot, taking their height, strength and experience into account.

Challenges You Might Encounter

Fear of the Stove? Just wait. Don't push. The kids have to be ready and feel comfortable before they can master the stove!

Fear of Creativity. Not all kids will feel comfortable with trying seasonings on their own. If you've got a "salt and pepper" sort of child who doesn't want to commit to trying anything new, help them to bridge what they know with where they can go. Encourage (or require) them to choose *one thing* to add to your leftover bowl. Have them smell spices with you often as you're cooking (revisit the All-Kid Lesson from Class 3 anytime), and allow them perhaps to choose a new recipe that has a seasoning in it that you've never tried before. Being cautious is normal – nobody likes to put work into something and then not enjoy it, and remember that kids literally have more taste buds than adults, so their sensory sensitivity is much higher than yours. Look for ways to stretch their horizons outside a recipe whenever you can (more ideas below).

Developmental Readiness and Kid-friendly Reminders

Today instead of talking about what your children are learning IN the course, I want to leave YOU with some challenges as the adult guide, to keep everyone moving in the right direction in the kitchen: growing, learning new things, helping out the family.

Beginner

Let's make a goal for our little ones to have a few totally independent tasks that they can do to help the family. For us, it's definitely peeling and cutting cucumbers, making guacamole (nearly independent), and rolling the rolls from today's lesson.

In other words, our Beginners know a lot of *pieces* of kitchen work. With a little prep from an adult, they can use spreading skills, for example, to prepare their own snacks or breakfast.

Intermediate

This level has so many skills that make good things to eat: dressings, muffins, pancakes, tortillas. They can do some things from start to finish independently and can be given more responsibility.

In other words, our Intermediate kids know how to make *snacks* completely on their own and could be asked to head up one snack or breakfast each week (or perhaps teamwork with an Advanced sibling on a whole meal).

Advanced

Choose a meal and delegate! I recommend choosing a meal that doesn't have any time crunches, which may mean a weekend breakfast or dinner. Schedule it in the calendar and do your best to keep it consistent from week to week so the kids always know when "their meal" is coming. Include them in the menu planning, especially figuring out how long before dinner they'll need to get in the kitchen and get started.

In other words, our Advanced group knows how to make an entire *meal* using the skills they've learned.

For all three age levels:

I highly encourage you to make some lists with your kids:

- Snacks they know how to make
- Snacks they want to learn to make
- Meals they know how to make (or parts)
- Meals they'd like to learn

And if you'd like an activity to do with your kids, work together to create a "favorites" cookbook or stack of recipe cards with their most-loved recipes so that they have something special to pull out each time they get to work in the kitchen.

All-Kid Lesson

In the All-Kid lesson today, I challenge every level to find a way to try something new with the skills they have, to use new seasonings or new vegetables and create something wonderful to eat.

We enjoy the "leftover bowl" that we created in the Advanced Level lesson. No matter the age of your kids, it's awesome to have ideas like this in your mind. We took cooked rice, homemade cheese sauce, herbs that the boys chose, steamed broccoli, and cooked ground beef and simply mixed it all up into a one-bowl meal (with the Beginners' rolls served on the side).

You can apply this formula to any leftovers you have:

- *Choose a base:* Cooked rice, quinoa, beans, pasta, or veggies.
- *Add a protein:* Ground meat, shredded chicken, leftover taco meat or slow cooked roast, beans, or eggs.
- *Add some veggies:* What do you have around? If you always have a few pieces of steamed vegetables left after a dinner and they end up tossed because you're not sure what to do with them, save them in the freezer for this!
- *Make a sauce:* Cheesy sauce like we used, spaghetti sauce, cream of chicken/mushroom/etc. soup, shredded cheese on its own, any dressing (they're not just for salads!).
- *Choose seasonings:* See Class 3 All-Kid lesson for more ideas.

- *Add something fresh:* Professional cooks know to add a hint of "something fresh" to awaken the flavors of leftovers. Try frozen peas, raw veggies (like onion, green onion, radishes, diced tomatoes), fresh herbs, a squeeze of citrus juice or zest, or something fun like feta or Parmesan cheese. You can *really* think outside the box and add fruits, too!
- Stir and serve!
- Write down what you try so you can remember it if you find a huge winner.

When we made ours, each child got to season his own bowl, and it was funny to watch one boy being almost overly adventurous (I had to tell him 3 seasonings, maximum) and one playing it safe (salt, pepper, garlic powder). And they were both yummy!

For your kids who feel like they couldn't cook without a recipe, explain to your child that recipes are just building blocks, and we can take different parts we know to build new creations...like Legos. That may connect the dots for some of your kids too!

Another Make-it-Your-Own Idea

If you have a food processor, you can invite kids to choose ingredients for "snack balls" including dried fruits, nuts or seeds, coconut, cocoa powder, spices, and anything you can think of. As long as you get enough sticky stuff (dried fruit or a bit of honey) they'll stick together.

Use the ratio from my *Healthy Snacks to Go* eBook of 1/2 cup dried fruit and 1/4 cup dry mix-ins (nuts, etc.). You might need more dried fruit if yours isn't very moist, or add a teaspoon of water to help it stick together. Dates are a good base, but raisins will do if you don't stock dates!

If you need more recipe ideas to start with you can go to www.KidsCookRealFood.com/recipes and grab Healthy Snacks to Go for 40% off with the coupon KCRFHSTG40

Tips for Teaching Multiple Age Groups

Although all the parts come together into a meal so nicely, the time aspect of balancing multiple levels isn't great on this class because you have two groups working on the stovetop.

If you're juggling all three, I'd recommend something like this:

- The Beginner group has to start early because of the time bread dough takes to rise. I might even start them in the morning so that their tasks are completely done by dinnertime. If it's better to work all together, plan the bread dough to be ready to roll into rolls about an hour and a half before dinner. That means you and the little ones are mixing up the dough 2 1/2 hours before that OR the day before to soak.
- You can start cooking class by training Beginners to make the rolls and then let them work semi-independently (you're checking on them a lot) at the table while you get the Intermediate crew started at the stove.
- If your Advanced kids need to do any cutting for their veggies, they can do that while you're working with the Beginners. It should be an independent job by now.
- If you have to cook rice, start it now on a back burner or in a rice cooker.
- Because the meat can wait around without losing quality, start the Intermediate group next. Once you're comfortable that the meat will be taken care of and the child will be safe, move on to the Advanced cheesy sauce, and finally, the steamed vegetables.
- Your Advanced kids can get an opportunity to practice their oven skills by putting the rolls into the oven at the right time, as well as taking them out and doing the "tap test" to see if they're done.
- While the older groups are seasoning and mixing the leftover bowl meal, the Beginner kids can be spreading butter on their rolls.
- And everyone can serve dinner with massive satisfaction on their faces – including you!

What's Next?

A Bonus Class of Sorts

I don't want to leave you with all these skills and nowhere to go, so there's one extra set of lesson plans to help you teach another official lesson. Hopefully you are comfortable with the 3-step teaching process and can break down skills into kid-friendly segments. You can teach the kids anything they want to know about what you do in the kitchen!

Keep Going in the Kids Cook Real Food Classes!

Beginner and Intermediate kids are certainly invited to continue with the next level of the *Kids Cook Real Food Course* as soon as you think they're ready. If you don't already have it you can grab the recipe book, *More Recipes for Kids Cook Real Food*. It has lots of recipes to keep going with, written in the KCRF kid-friendly style to save you time.

> Kids Cook Real Food was originally created as an online video eCourse. If you'd like access to the videos that compliment the lessons in this book, visit *www.kidscookrealfood.com/printbook*

Get Great eBooks

KitchenStewardship.com is my online home and has plenty of great recipes – but the best, most-tested and comprehensively written ones are in my eBooks. I'm happy to give you a 35% off coupon for any book or already-discounted package – check them out by going to *www.KitchenStewardship.com/ebooks* and use the coupon KCRFPRINTDISCOUNT

You might start with *Healthy Snacks to Go* for Beginners and Intermediates, and try *Better Than a Box* for Advanced kids and adults. More info on each book is on the last page of this book.

Thank you so much for joining us in this course! My kids and I had a wonderful time preparing all the material for you, and we're thrilled to hear about kids cooking with us all over the world!

Working with Dough: Beginner

Don't forget to create opportunities to practice last week's skill:
- Making a colorful salad

How We Apply the Skill Today:
- Making homemade rolls

Skills That Loop into this Lesson:
- Spreading (Beg. Lesson 1)
- Measuring (Beg. Lesson 4)
- Stirring (Foundations 101)
- Measuring Liquids (Beg. Lesson 6, Foundations 101)
- Pouring (Beg. Lesson 6)

Time Needed:
- Hands on Time: 20+5+45 minutes (over two days)

Food Needed:
- Whole wheat flour
- Honey
- Egg
- Olive oil
- Salt
- Yeast
- Butter

Today's Recipe:
Easy Whole Wheat Happy Rolls

Tools Needed:
- Measuring cups and spoons
- Liquid measuring cup
- Stirring spoon
- Bread maker (if you have one)
- Cookie sheets or stoneware trays
- Tea towel (or similar to cover rolls while rising)
- *Recipes for Kids Cook Real Food*

Adults Should Prepare:
- Plan out your timing, since bread dough needs to be visited a few times over hours (or 2 days)

Extensions: how else could this basic skill be used?
- Working with dough can extend into cutting biscuits, helping roll tortillas, crackers, or pie dough, and eventually kneading one's own bread dough.

Allergy Notes and Substitutions:

- **Gluten-free adaptation:** The point of this lesson is to make a recipe together and enjoy it, plus find a little piece that the youngest children can do on their own if possible. I know gluten can be a touchy subject and that not everyone has a bread machine.

  Cornbread, cut biscuits, soda bread, any favorite dough recipe or even quick bread or a savory dinner muffin are all great alternatives (see extension recipe list at the end of this lesson). Independent possibilities for those activities include cutting the biscuits with a small glass and moving to a tray, lining muffin tins with paper liners (and spooning batter into cups if your child is on the older end of the age range and careful about it), or adding mix-ins like raisins or nuts to a quick bread recipe.

- **Paleo adaptation:** Your favorite coconut flour or almond flour recipe is certainly a great idea, or move to the extension lesson plan and teach peeling hard-boiled eggs, a skill that is totally possible for little tots and super helpful for a Paleo household.

- **Egg-free adaptation:** The egg in the dough recipe serves as a dough conditioner, but it's not vital to the rolls. Leave out the egg and add a bit of water to compensate if the dough seems dry, or use a "flax-egg" of 1 Tbs. ground flax + 3 Tbs. water.

Daily Nugget:

"One Bread at a Time"

We don't want to fill up on breads all the time, so just one on the plate at a time. Starches (as explained in Lesson 1) are quick energy. We want foods that will give us our "super power" energy for a long time so we eat the meat (protein) and fats first.

Notes:

_____

_____

Lesson Overview: Making Dough

This project is a bit of the classic "bake together" scenario, but with one special part that littles can do independently, which has definitely been our theme in this course. The most time-consuming part of making homemade rolls for me (because I rely on my bread maker for the kneading part) is actually forming the rolls – and that's the part that kids can totally do on their own.

And better yet, because of the time it takes for bread to rise and bake, this task is almost always done *before* the dinner rush (plus rolls can be reheated), so it's nice to incorporate our youngest kids when we're not stressing about time.

Catch Phrases to Remember:

Catch phrases help kids to remember the principles and the skills that they are learning. Try to incorporate these phrases into your lesson to help these ideas stick in your kids' minds. Additionally, be sure to cut out or photocopy the flash cards (page 363) and keep them handy throughout the week.

- Sticky? Take a Dip!
- Rolls the Same Size

How to Demonstrate

Assembling the ingredients for the recipe is a chance for kids to practice their measuring skills and uniform mixing, to observe you moving ingredients from left to right as you use them (Intermediate, Lesson 1), and it's something to enjoy doing together.

Be sure to take the opportunity to ask kids to put measuring cups in order, identify the ones you need, practice "Get Level with Liquids" and their good pouring skills and use "Let it Fall Like Snow" to measure the flour.

Note: We "soak" whole grains in our house, which means we'll mix up most of the dough a day prior to when we want to bake the rolls. The flour and wet ingredients rest at room temperature for 12-24 hours to make the rolls more digestible. If you don't want to do this step, it won't change the outcome of your rolls. Just mix all the ingredients together at once and proceed with the recipe without soaking.

A few recipe notes:

- If you have it, use some whey for soaking or a few tablespoons of yogurt.
- Measure the oil first, then honey, so it slides right out.
- Flour is a great chance to practice Snow Plowing It Flat.
- If you're hoping to substitute different flours: White and red (traditional) whole wheat both work great (or a combo), but whole wheat pastry flour just isn't the right choice for rolls. Spelt will likely do okay but I have not tested it (charts online recommend reducing the water to 1 1/4 cup). I have not tried a gluten-free flour blend.
- Because we were soaking, we measured the salt and yeast into a small bowl to save for the next day since the measuring spoons were out. It was just a time-saving technique.
- When adding the egg, allow the child to put their hand over (or under) your own to practice feeling how hard you crack it. Invite them to put their thumbs on your thumbs to break the shell open over a bowl – this is all preparation for Intermediate Lesson 3!

I use a bread machine simply because I appreciate how easy it is, but kneading dough is a great skill too! Of course you can teach your child "real" bread making without a bread maker too.

When it's time to form the rolls, you'll want to demonstrate the size and process as an adult first before your kids dig their hands into the sticky dough.

If you're using the recipe from the KCRF recipe booklet, we shoot for about 24 rolls, each the size of a Clementine orange. If you have a Clementine or appropriate-sized ball, putting it on the table for comparison is really helpful for little eyes and brains!

"We can see when the dough is too sticky, because it gets legs!"

Put some extra flour in a bowl for kids to dip their fingers into, and show them how you can sprinkle flour on top of the dough as well, so your hands don't stick to everything. We dip our fingers and the dough into the flour and talk about how we can see when the dough is too sticky, because it gets legs!

How To Guide

You may find that some kids aren't ready to judge the size of the dough, or that their hands are simply too small to break off a piece from the large hunk of dough. That's okay! It's still good practice (and a great tactile experience) for little ones to roll the balls after an adult hands them the right amount.

Particularly for very young children, portioning the dough for them will allow them to practice one skill at a time - first rolling the dough, then judging size later.

Try some hand-on-hand technique to help kids make the circular motion needed to get the dough into a ball. "Bi-lateral" work (where the two hands are going in opposite directions) is not easy but is a very important skill to develop at this young age. Be sure to discuss where the rolls should go and how far apart they need to be. We find that 3 in a row is just perfect.

As an adult doing this recipe for the first time, you should know that they will take 45 minutes to rise and 15-20 minutes to bake. That helps you plan when to start. (Kids will take at least 30 minutes to make the rolls. Trust me.) If you don't have time to waste, turn the oven on to preheat 30 minutes after setting the rolls to rise, and it will be ready the second your 45-minute rise timer goes off.

"As an adult doing this recipe for the first time, you should know that they will take 45 minutes to rise and 15-20 minutes to bake."

The rolls are done when they're golden brown on the outside and sound hollow when you tap them. (If you have Advanced kids, this is a great opportunity for them to practice oven skills and the technique of testing when bread is done.)

How to Coach to Independence

After a few times practicing, kids should be able to roll the balls all on their own and really help mom out, and mixing up the dough will be an optional "togetherness" activity.

Each time you make rolls, check the first few rolls for size and shape, give some pointers, and remind the children how far to space them apart on the tray. We learned the hard way that all that info doesn't necessarily get retained (i.e. I set my kids to work in a rush and ended up with dozens of tiny piles of dough on a tray, ahem...).

Challenges You Might Encounter

Way Too Sticky! If your dough is simply too moist, add a half cup flour and knead it in, then try making the dough balls again.

Bread Dough #Fail. If you're a novice bread baker yourself, don't be concerned about perfection. Bread baking is a process, and you're just at the beginning. Embrace the opportunity to demonstrate graceful failure and laugh at yourself in front of your kids, and determine to try again another time. Bread dough can be at once easier and more difficult than you expect, but don't let it intimidate you. You can do this!

Small Hands. I already mentioned this above, but some kids just won't be able to grab the right sized handful of dough, either because their hands are too small or they don't have the judgment to eye it up yet. Just make "plops" of dough for them and let them manipulate those into the best "ball" they can. Focus on how much they're learning by exploring with the dough and having a positive feeling about working in the kitchen!

Can't Ball It Up. The rolling motion to make an actual ball can be tricky for little ones, much like moving their feet in opposite directions to pedal a bicycle or tricycle. Encourage them to keep trying, allow them to use a hand-on-hand technique with you to practice, and show them other methods to make nice ball shapes by patting the dough with cupped hands.

Don't forget to create opportunities to practice this skill throughout the week!

You might integrate this one into daily life by continuing to include your young children in making dinner and making sure they have some independent activities they love to do.

Extension Recipes to Apply this Skill:

Recipes in *Recipes for Kids Cook Real Food*:
- Stir-and-Pour Rolls
- Homemade Tortillas

Recipes in *More Recipes for Kids Cook Real Food*:
- Homemade Crackers
- Gluten-free Cornbread

Find these recipes online at www.kidscookrealfood.com/recipes:
- Homemade Biscuits
- Gluten-free Bacon and Green Onion Dinner Muffins
- Whole Wheat Cornbread
- Pie Crust Dough

    If you don't have the KCRF recipe books visit *www.kidscookrealfood.com/recipes* to get access.

Next Week's Grocery List:
- Eggs
- Potatoes
- Pickles
- Olive oil
- Mustard

Browning Ground Meat: Intermediate

Don't forget to create opportunities to practice last week's skill:
- Rolling dough

How We Apply the Skill Today:
- Browning ground meat

Skills That Loop into this Lesson:
- Stovetop Safety (Int. Lesson 5)
- Stirring (Foundations 101)

Time Needed:
- Hands on Time: 15 minutes

Tools Needed:
- Skillet or Dutch Oven
- Tool for breaking up meat: wooden spoon, spatula, potato masher, other tool of choice

Food Needed:
- Ground meat

Today's Recipe: Taco Meat or Other Options with Ground Meat

Adults Should Prepare:
- Choose a recipe for the meat
- Thaw meat if necessary

Extensions: how else could this basic skill be used?
- The basics of being at the stovetop are becoming more common for this age level, and kids should be able to move into sautéing vegetables (Advanced, Lesson 3) with confidence.

Allergy Notes and Substitutions:
- Vegetarians and those who don't eat meat might choose to teach how to use a meat substitute like TVP or tofu or a simple stovetop skill like sautéing onions (we do teach how to sauté vegetables in the Advanced Level, but that includes all veggies – onions are pretty easy and just take a lot of stirring).

"Happy Cows Make Healthy Meat"

Cows who get to be outside and eat grass have healthier tummies and their meat has more goodness for our bodies, too. (Same goes for chickens who get to be outside and eat grass and even bugs, just like they were designed to – their eggs have more nutrition than other eggs, whether they're brown, green, white or even blue!)

Notes:

_____

_____

_____

_____

_____

_____

_____

_____

_____

_____

_____

_____

Lesson Overview: Browning Ground Meat

This skill cannot be underestimated as far as how helpful it is to have a child who knows how to do it. Myriads of family-friendly recipes are now unlocked for this child to help or take the lead on!

Start as always with some stove safety reminders. *(Need a refresher? Check out Intermediate Lesson 5.)* While you're on the safety subject, explain about raw meat/juices and how important it is to use sanitary habits when working with meat. *When should you wash your hands? What would you like children to do if some raw meat gets on a counter?* Adult guides should definitely think this through and discuss with their children.

Catch Phrases to Remember:

Catch phrases help kids to remember the principles and the skills that they are learning. Try to incorporate these phrases into your lesson to help these ideas stick in your kids' minds. Additionally, be sure to cut out or photocopy the flash cards (page 363) and keep them handy throughout the week.

- From Pink to Brown
- Break it Up
- Scoop, Lift, Flip – to the Center

How to Demonstrate

To get started, once you've determined where the cooking utensil should go and everything is ready, ask your child to turn on the stove to medium heat.

Adults will need to decide how the raw meat gets out of the packaging and into the pot. Personally, I wanted to retain control of that process with my 7-year-old, so I did it for her. Older children could certainly be trusted, with proper training, to care for raw meat waste and utensils.

> "Adults will need to decide how the raw meat gets out of the packaging and into the pot."

I demonstrate by turning the heat down a little bit, both because cooking grass-fed ground beef at a lower temp and slower rate tends to yield tastier results and so that nothing is moving too quickly during the learning process. I also emphasize safety by holding the handle appropriately before I even get started.

Show a little bit about breaking up the meat, and demonstrate how the meat turns brown on the bottom and what to do with that. The goal of browning beef is to get all the pink/red parts brown as evenly as possible. To do so, we push the pink parts into the center of the pot, and move the brown parts to the outsides and top. We use a Roller Coaster stir and gently flip over each bit that we can scoop underneath.

I joke that when we learn to break up the meat we have to remember that we don't want to make little hamburgers here, we want ground beef.

How To Guide

You could certainly use two pounds of ground meat and demonstrate with the first and allow practice with the second. Cooked ground meat is very handy to have in the freezer! For kids who feel confident jumping in, it's certainly okay to share one pound: you demonstrate for a minute, and then let them take over.

A bit of hand-on-hand practice is good for kids, because it can be surprising to learn exactly how much force one needs to exert upward in order to flip cooking meat over – but not flip it out of the pan. There's a balance there! A deeper pot like a Dutch oven may be a nice security blanket so your kids don't have to worry as much about the flipping-out part.

How to Coach to Independence

Particularly if you've already observed your child being successful with pancakes and tortillas at the stove, you should feel comfortable turning over the reins even during this first pound of meat. Stay close and give tips about how much to break up the meat, getting the pink parts toward the center, and figuring out how to get the pink parts to the bottom and the brown to the top.

An excellent way to use this pound of practice is to go on to make taco meat – not only is it a generally a well-loved meal in the kid arena, but you might have Taco Seasoning from the Beginner lesson (or find the recipe in *Recipes for Kids Cook Real Food*). Our closing dinner that all the kids cooked for their parents was a Mexican meal, and it was so nice to have our girls with "browning meat" skills taking care of that step for everyone.

Draining the Grease

When there is enough grease to get rid of, we teamwork this part in our family. It just seems too tricky for a child to do on their own due to the need to tip a heavy pot or pan on an angle.

Sometimes I'll just do this part, and other times I tip the pot and invite the child to dip out grease into an old jar with a small metal ladle. We do it all with the heat off, of course.

Note: if you are using lean ground beef, ground turkey, or even ground beef from pastured cows, there may not be any/enough grease to drain. It's perfectly okay to leave a little grease in for extra flavor. Also many families save the grease and use it for cooking later on.

Challenges You Might Encounter

"Little Hamburgers." Whether it's inattention or lack of strength to push down and break up the meat, some kids run the risk of frying up little burgers. Just help them to understand the importance of pressing their utensil all the way to the surface of the pan and wiggling or twisting it to get through the meat completely.

Whoops! Sometimes meat will go flying. In fact, it's almost inevitable the first few times if you're using a skillet. Demonstrate how to clean up a grease smear on your surface (or floor) and whether you want the meat to go back in the pan or in the trash. Guide their hand on a Roller Coaster stir, scooping under the meat, gently lifting, and rolling it over to flip it, rather than trying to lift and flip all at once, which is usually the cause of flying meat.

Don't forget to create opportunities to practice this skill throughout the week!

You might integrate this one into daily life by inviting your child to help brown some beef or sausage for a few meals and even help you plan some favorites.

Extension Recipes to Apply this Skill:

- Your favorite chili recipe

Recipes in *More Recipes for Kids Cook Real Food*:
- Cheeseburger Soup

Find these recipes online at
www.kidscookrealfood.com/recipes:
- Homemade Sausage
- Beef and Potato Casserole
- Dad's Cheeseburger Helper
- Lasagna or Spaghetti Squash Lasagna
- Shepherd's Pie
- Mexican Stuffed Peppers

If you don't have the KCRF recipe books visit *www.kidscookrealfood.com/recipes* to get access.

Next Week's Grocery List:

- Eggs
- Potatoes
- Pickles
- Olive oil
- Mustard

Making a White Sauce and Steaming Vegetables: Advanced

Don't forget to create opportunities to practice last week's skill:
- Using a small appliance

How We Apply the Skill Today:
- Homemade cheese sauce with a roux/béchamel and steamed broccoli

Skills That Loop into this Lesson:
- Measuring (Foundations 101)
- Following a Recipe (Int. Lesson 1)
- Stovetop Safety (Int. Lesson 5)
- Cooking Rice (Int. Lesson 5)
- Cutting Vegetables (Adv. Lessons 1-4)
- Using a Small Appliance (to shred cheese) (Adv. Lesson 7)

Time Needed:
- Hands on Time: 30 minutes

Food Needed:
- Broccoli or green beans (something to steam, can be frozen)
- Milk
- Cheddar cheese
- Arrowroot starch or flour
- Cooked rice
- Spices
- Ground meat

Tools Needed:
- Measuring cups and spoons
- Medium pot
- Steamer basket and appropriate pot
- Whisk
- Liquid measuring cups
- Food processor with shredding attachment or a grater for shredding cheese
- *Recipes for Kids Cook Real Food*

Today's Recipe: Simple Cheese Sauce or Grain-Free Cheese Sauce

Adults Should Prepare:
- Cook rice before hand (or have kids do it)
- If no Intermediate kids, cook ground meat

Extensions: how else could this basic skill be used?

- Steaming veggies is an incredibly helpful skill that applies to all vegetables, and knowing how to make a roux/béchamel and thicken a sauce extends to making "cream of" soups, pasta sauces, gravy, and more. The cheese sauce itself can go over vegetables, become nacho cheese, be served mixed with salsa as an appetizer dip with chips, and the list goes on.

Allergy Notes and Substitutions:

- **Dairy-free:** It's possible to make a dairy-free sauce with chicken broth and starch – this will be a thick sauce like gravy, but it won't be as creamy. Use half coconut milk or almond milk if desired. You might add nutritional yeast for cheese flavor!

- **Grain and Gluten-free:** The second recipe using arrowroot starch is both grain-free and gluten-free. Another gluten-free option is to use buckwheat flour in place of the whole wheat flour in a roux/béchamel.

Daily Nugget:

"Cooking Kills Some Vitamins"

Some of the healthy vitamins in vegetables and fruits are damaged by heat - so lightly steaming is better than boiling to retain more nutrients. Boiling makes some of the good stuff go into the water (soups are easier to digest). The tomato is an exception – lycopene, a healthy nutrient, is actually released by cooking.

Notes:

_____

_____

_____

_____

Lesson Overview: Making a White Sauce and Steaming Veggies

We'll be juggling two pots at once today for our Advanced kids, which is some good practice for cooking a whole meal by themselves!

I like to teach my kids that they need to think through the whole meal to figure out what to start on first. In this case, one of the two dishes can "hold" on warm without changing much, whereas steamed vegetables will either get cold or overcook if they have to wait around for a sauce to finish, so the choice is clear. You'll start the cheese sauce first, then the veggies.

If using fresh veggies instead of frozen, your kids get a chance to practice their sharp knife skills once again. Emphasize the importance of cutting same-size chunks, especially with things like broccoli stems. (*Note: Frozen veggies cook faster than the timing chart. All timing begins when water is boiling already.*)

Catch Phrases to Remember:

Catch phrases help kids to remember the principles and the skills that they are learning. Try to incorporate these phrases into your lesson to help these ideas stick in your kids' minds. Additionally, be sure to cut out or photocopy the flash cards (page 363) and keep them handy throughout the week.

How to Make a Roux:
- 1 Tbs. fat
- 1 Tbs. flour (or starch, but less)
- 1 cup milk

Steaming Vegetable Timing Chart:
- Broccoli 5-6 min
- Carrots 4-5 min
- Green Beans 5-8 min
- Peas 4-5 min
- Potatoes 10-12 min
- Spinach 2-6 min
- Zucchini 4-6 min
- *(frozen veggies cook faster)*

How to Demonstrate

Unless you want a LOT of cheese sauce and steamed vegetables around, you can probably trust your kids at this point to listen and follow directions without you making the whole thing first. You might demonstrate a good sharp whisking motion, or just tell them about some culinary terms (that you also may have just learned, and that's okay!):

Roux – a 1:1 mixture of fat and flour, usually intended to thicken a sauce or soup.

Béchamel – a white sauce or cream sauce. To make one, add a liquid (milk, water, stock) to a roux and bring to a boil, which will then thicken up without getting lumpy.

To make a roux, melt 1 Tbs. fat in a pot, then stir in 1 Tbs. flour. Cook for a minute or so to get out the flour taste. Your could invite the kids to taste flour on their fingertips to understand why you don't want "flour taste" in your sauce!

Pour in a cup of milk or cream to make a béchamel (a white sauce). Bring to a gentle boil while stirring and that's what will thicken up the sauce.

> "To make a roux, melt 1 Tbs. fat in a pot, then stir in 1 Tbs. flour. Cook for a minute or so to get out the flour taste."

If you decide you want to make a thicker sauce, double up on the flour/ starch and the fat, but do not double the liquid.

The second recipe in *Recipes for Kids Cook Real Food* will lead your Advanced kids through the process of making a **slurry,** a mixture of liquid and starch/flour. You can use arrowroot for that to remain completely grain-free.

How To Guide

Let's see how well our oldest kids can follow a recipe.

Help them get out all the ingredients, shredding cheese if necessary. Talk through any tough parts of it with them and make sure they understand the framework: fat, thickener (flour or starch), milk.

Then fall back a little bit and observe, only stepping in if a mistake is about to be made.

Once the sauce is made, show your kids your steamer basket (there are lots of different variations). After they understand the process of steaming veggies, talk to them about how the veggies cook, that the lid needs to be on, and how long they'll steam the vegetable they chose (check the timing chart in the flash cards, remembering that frozen veggies cook more quickly).

The most important piece Adult Guides won't want to miss is to make an end-game plan: *How will your child get the cooked vegetables or the boiling water out of the pot?* (You can't just turn off the heat if the water is still in the pot or the veggies will over-cook.)

With our steamer basket, we're able to lift the basket out with a spoon handle, set it on the chopping block, pour the water in the sink and put the steamer basket back in the pot to stay warm. You might want your kids to remove all the vegetables to a serving bowl with a slotted spoon, pour the entire contents of the pot into a colander to drain the water, or something completely different. Discuss, plan ahead.

> "The most important piece Adult Guides won't want to miss is to make an end-game plan: *How will your child get the cooked vegetables or the boiling water out of the pot?*"

How to Coach to Independence

While the timer is ticking, tell your kids that no matter what the timer says about the food being done, it's best to just test the vegetables to see what you like. Encourage kids to pull out a small piece before they're "supposed" to be done, cool and taste, and to do it again when the timer goes off. If they're not in love, set a timer for 2 more minutes and taste again.

Your child should take note of what the color of their "perfectly cooked" vegetable is and how their fork pierces it (how soft it is), because experienced cooks usually can tell their steamed veggies are done not by the clock, but by the color.

Challenges You Might Encounter

I don't have a steamer basket. You can use a cheater steamer – just a tiny bit of water on the bottom of a smaller pot, so most of the food doesn't touch the water because it's all stacked on each other. (But a steamer really is a wonderful basic kitchen gadget. I recommend some on our resource page which you can find at www.KitchenStewardship.com/kcrfresources

Sauce doesn't thicken. Add more starch/flour, but WAIT! Don't just sprinkle it in (that's what makes lumpy gravy). Mix a bit more cold milk with your starch *or* flour thoroughly, like shaking it in a jar, and pour into the boiling, thin solution. As the milk in the pot comes up to temperature it will thicken. Keep in mind that this cheese sauce thickens a LOT as it cools.

Don't forget to create opportunities to practice this skill throughout the week!

You might integrate this one into daily life by assigning "side vegetable" to your Advanced graduate for the next week.

Extension Recipes to Apply this Skill:
Find these recipes online at
www.kidscookrealfood.com/recipes:
- Cream of Potato Soup
- Creamy Stuffing Chicken Casserole
- Pasta with White Bean Sauce
- Spicy Cheese Chicken Dip

If you don't have the KCRF recipe books visit www.kidscookrealfood.com/recipes to get access.

Next Week's Grocery List:
- Eggs
- Potatoes
- Pickles
- Olive oil
- Mustard

Bonus Class

Kids Cook Real Food
Bonus Class: Adult Information

Congratulations on moving your child(ren) through 8 weeks of incredible cooking lessons!

You must feel very accomplished...perhaps a little tired...and perhaps wondering what comes next. I thought I'd give you one more set of lesson plans to help bridge you to "going it on your own" – a bit of me practicing what I preach by providing a "guide" lesson for you as the teacher in your kitchen.

This is the "Guide" step for me as a teacher and you as a student. You are ready to take on any new skill that you want to teach your kids – you know how to break it down into tiny steps, make it fun for them, and how to demonstrate first and then guide and coach to independence.

I'm really excited to hear about your successes cooking real food with your whole family!

What Adult Guides Need to Know

For years my kids and I have brought homemade potato salad to family gatherings, parties and potlucks. My trick for getting my kids to eat well at parties is always to bring something we love to eat to make sure they have at least one big serving of wholesome food – and this is the thing!

I also love that my kids can each have a genuinely helpful job to do in the process, so not only is our whole kitchen busy as we prepare, but I can also build them up when we're out by sharing how they all pitched in. They beam!

If you choose to teach this lesson, here's what your young chefs will be practicing and learning:

Beginner:

- **Practice:** cross-hatch pattern on cooked eggs (and possibly potatoes)
- **New skill:** peeling hard-boiled eggs

Intermediate:

- **Practice:** sharp knife skills on pickles
- **New skill**: hard boiling eggs and boiling potatoes (tandem skill)

Advanced:

- **Practice:** sharp knife skills on raw potatoes, new-ish skill of peeling (raw) potatoes
- **New skill:** making homemade mayo

Tips for Teaching Multiple Age Groups

If you have all 3 levels, I'd recommend this order of operations:

1. Intermediate kids: Start with hard boiling eggs and scrubbing potatoes (you might even hard boil the eggs the day before if you are at home).
2. Advanced kids: peel and cut potatoes (if using raw cubes) OR scrub and bake potatoes (if you want your Beginner kids to cut cooked potatoes)
3. Intermediate: cut pickles and get potatoes boiling (if using raw)
4. Beginner: peel eggs (if done the day before, this can happen at any time)
5. Advanced: make mayo
6. Beginner or Intermediate: cut eggs into dices
7. Everyone: stir it all together and season – then taste test!

Developmental Readiness and Kid-friendly Reminders

I wanted to use this section today in my last chance with you to offer some ideas for other skills that each age level should be capable of tackling.

Beginner:
- Unload dishwasher
- Sort clean utensils into the drawer
- Wipe the floor for spills
- Put muffin liners in tins
- Help scan and bag groceries in the checkout line
- Learn to scrape the sides of the bowl/food processor cleanly
- Separate pumpkin or squash seeds from the "guts"
- Making simple trail mixes
- Refill bulk beans, grains and spices (if you can handle some spills)
- Sweep the floor with a small broom/dustpan
- Scrape leftovers on plates into trash
- Put away groceries
- Your kids may be ready to tackle the Intermediate Level of the course!

Intermediate:
- Drying dishes
- Serving own breakfast
- Cooking pasta
- Making toast
- Creating own new recipes with basic granola bars, pancakes, muffins, dried fruit/nut balls, etc.
- Figuring out change at the Farmer's Market and learning to choose good looking produce
- …but mostly, these kids are likely ready to tackle the Advanced Level of the course and all that it entails!

Advanced:
- Washing dishes
- Creating new recipes for salads, simple main courses
- Making many soup and casserole recipes start to finish
- Separating eggs
- Whipping egg whites or cream
- Working with raw meat

- Grilling skills
- Cooking fish
- Searching for new recipes online (supervised as necessary)
- Planning meals
- Helping with grocery shopping, list-making
- Understanding shopping on a budget

Don't forget to check out the book
More Recipes for Kids Cook Real Food
for more kid-friendly, kid-worded recipes.

Go to *www.KidsCookRealFood.com/recipes*
for a link to order the book, and for more ideas for
your kids to cook using the skills they have learned.

Peeling Hard-Boiled Eggs: Beginner

Don't forget to create opportunities to practice last week's skill:
- Working with dough

How We Apply the Skill Today:
- Making potato salad

Skills That Loop into this Lesson:
- Cross-hatch pattern cutting (Beg. Class 3)
- Stirring (Foundations 101)

Time Needed:
- Hands on Time: 20 minutes

Food Needed:
- Eggs
- (+ other potato salad ingredients if you don't have kids at other levels; see KCRF recipe book)

Tools Needed:
- Bowl of water
- Bowl for shells
- Mega large bowl for potato salad
- Knife, cutting board
- *Recipes for Kids Cook Real Food*

Today's Recipe:

Homemade Potato Salad

Adults Should Prepare:
- If you have Intermediate or Advanced kids, nothing. Otherwise you'll need to boil some eggs and cook the potatoes.

Allergy Notes and Substitutions:
- If you have egg allergies obviously you won't want to teach this skill, but you could perhaps teach how to peel a Clementine orange or how to mix up a pasta salad (or some other family favorite party recipe that your littles will recognize and enjoy).

Lesson Overview: Peeling Hard-Boiled Eggs

This lesson is a great teamwork activity if you have kids at all levels (see Adult Guide section for more info). If you just have Beginners, it's still awesome to teach how to peel hard-boiled eggs since it really is something they can do independently.

Make it easier on them by cooking eggs that are easy to peel. Here are 4 ways that work:

1. **The Secret Crack.** Tap the narrow end of each egg gently, just enough to hear a "crack" sound but not a *break*. Cover with cold water, bring to a boil, turn off the heat and set a timer for 12 minutes. Cool in ice water and peel as soon as they are cooled.
2. **Steam the Eggs.** Using a steamer basket, steam whole eggs for 12-15 minutes (in a single layer). Cool in cold or ice water.
3. **Use a Pressure Cooker.** If you have an Instant Pot or other pressure cooker, you may already have discovered the joy of peeling eggs.
4. **Bake the Eggs.** Place eggs in mini muffin tins and bake at 325F for 30 minutes. Cool in ice water.
5. Peeling hard-boiled eggs is also much easier with the addition of water to the process – that's why we'll have a little bowl of water on the table for your kids to dip the eggs into. (Adults might simply peel under running water at the sink, but I feel like little ones take so long that it's just too much water!)

How to Demonstrate

Show your Beginner kids the set up, left to right:

Phase One:

- Cooked and cooled hard-boiled eggs
- A bowl of tap water (if you cool your eggs in water, you can likely use the same bowl of water here)
- A "garbage bowl" or "GB" for the shells
- A clean bowl for the peeled eggs

Phase Two:

- A cutting board and dull knife
- A large bowl for the potato salad (this is where the diced eggs will go)

To demonstrate peeling the eggs, take one egg. Crack it allllll over on all sides (this can be made quite fun for the kids!).

Dip and roll it in the cool water, pressing gently on all sides to allow the water to get in between the shell and the egg membrane. (*Note: if you have steamed eggs, they might be so easy to peel that you can skip this step.*)

Show the children how to find a piece of eggshell that is ready to come off and how you can pick it off and put it in the GB (garbage bowl). Often you are able to grab large sections of shell all at once – some kids will enjoy challenging themselves to get huge pieces and delight in themselves when they accomplish it. Make it a game!

"Be sure to emphasize that all shells go into the GB, then once the egg is peeled, dip it in the clear water again to get any tiny shell fragments off."

Be sure to emphasize that all shells go into the GB, then once the egg is peeled, dip it in the clear water again to get any tiny shell fragments off. Inspect the egg for shells (again, this can be made to be fun, like a silly detective with a fake magnifying glass, for example). Place the peeled egg into the holding bowl.

I recommend having your child peel all the eggs first, then move on to cutting. If you haven't done the cross-hatch pattern since Class 3, you should definitely demonstrate that again as well, but it's wise to wait until all the eggs are peeled so your little cook can focus on one multi-step skill at a time.

Cutting eggs:

1. Use Up and Over Soldier to make two cuts if possible, or just in half if making 3 pieces is too difficult for younger kids.
2. Lay each piece flat.
3. On each flat section, make 2 cuts in one direction, then turn like a clock and make 2-3 cuts the other way (Top Chop can be handy).

Note: If you'd like your Beginner kids to have even more to do, you can bake whole potatoes for potato salad or boil them whole, and Beginners can be in charge of the cross-hatch pattern once they're cooled.

How To Guide

I definitely recommend the adult to stay close for the first egg, to make sure all the steps are being followed and be there to help if the egg is difficult to peel. (Although hopefully if you use one of the methods above, you won't have any problems!)

Remind your child to take their time and do a thorough job, something they can be proud of.

Once they have peeled all the eggs, move on to the cutting board job, which is review.

> "Remind your child to take their time and do a thorough job, something they can be proud of."

How to Coach to Independence

As your child works, pass by the table to check on progress, giving little reminders from time to time. Other than troubleshooting the occasional "throwing away too much egg white" and rejecting diced eggs that are too large, you shouldn't have to micromanage this process too very much.

If anyone in your family likes to eat hard-boiled eggs for breakfast or lunch – especially your Beginner kids – plan to have them 1-2 times a week for a while until the child feels totally proficient at peeling them. Hopefully, they'll enjoy it and want to help.

Challenges You Might Encounter

The Overpeeler. Overzealous kids may get more than their fair share as they peel, removing many bits of egg white in the process. This can be especially a problem if the eggs are difficult to peel, because the whites will come with the shell accidentally. Emphasize the importance of taking one's time and how we don't want to throw away good food (and perhaps choose a different method to cook the eggs next time). Hopefully most kids will have the patience to peel at least one or two eggs properly, but some simply won't be ready yet.

The Underpeeler. Leaving a few chunks of shell on the egg isn't all that nice for your eaters. Have a "quality control" check where the adult looks for shells, and really make it a "blue ribbon" event when you find perfectly peeled eggs. Positive appreciation will go further than negative comments. If you do find shells on the peeled eggs, try to keep it fun and upbeat, and just hand the egg back for a re-do.

The Tough Egg to ~~Crack~~ Peel. If your eggs are really tough to peel, the water is the key. Soak well cracked eggs in water and perhaps allow your child to work under running water. In the future, use a different method to cook the eggs OR be sure to peel them as soon after cooking as possible. That can really help facilitate an easier peel. Farm fresh eggs are also problematic – set aside a dozen eggs in the fridge for 2-3 weeks and then hard boil them and they'll peel easier as well.

The Pokes. Eggshells can be sharp. If your child complains about getting poked, show them how to crack the egg more thoroughly all the way around, squeeze a little to loosen, use water, and use the flat edge of your thumb to try to get larger pieces.

The Slippery Egg. When cutting eggs, they *are* challenging because they're so roly-poly round and slippery. Remind the children of the "Up and Over Soldier" hold and encourage them to cut the egg in half the long way first, then lay both halves flat to eliminate rolling.

The Big Chunker. Don't want 2-inch pieces of egg in your potato salad? Remember the power of demonstration – teach your kids how many slices to make, counting if you have to.

The Micro Chopper. With an activity as involved as peeling and chopping, your little chefs may hit attention fatigue – which could result in either silliness or hyperactivity. If you find that they are chopping the eggs to bits, feel free to pull the plug on the situation and explain the importance of treating our food with respect. It's perfectly okay to split up the peeling and the dicing into two work sections. Just make sure you keep your cooked eggs in the fridge, no matter where they are in the process. The alternative? Make mashed egg salad.

We hope to see our Beginner kids in the Intermediate Level someday! Happy Cooking!

Boiling Eggs and Potatoes: Intermediate

Don't forget to create opportunities to practice last week's skill:

- Browning ground meat

How We Apply the Skill Today:

- Making potato salad

Skills That Loop into this Lesson:

- Sharp Knife Skills (Int. Class 2)
- Stovetop Safety (Int. Class 5)
- Washing Produce (All-Kid Class 7)
- Stirring (Foundations 101)

Tools Needed:

- 2 pots with lids
- Slotted spoon
- Large bowls
- Sharp knife
- Cutting board
- *Recipes for Kids Cook Real Food*

Time Needed:

- Hands on Time: 1-2 hours

Food Needed:

- Potatoes
- Eggs
- Pickles (spears or whole)
- Mayo (if no Advanced kids)
- Mustard

Today's Recipe:

Homemade Potato Salad

Adults Should Prepare:

- If you have Advanced kids, nothing. If not, you might have to make homemade mayo or provide a purchased version.

Allergy Notes and Substitutions:

- If your family cannot use eggs, please focus on the skill of boiling potatoes. You can still make a good cold potato salad, classic German potato salad, or perhaps teach mashed potatoes. Making a pasta or cold grain salad or other family-favorite potluck dish is a great thing to teach your Intermediate kids.

Lesson Overview: Boiling Eggs and Potatoes

This lesson is a great teamwork activity if you have kids at all levels (see Adult Guide section on page 298 for more info). If you just have Intermediate kids, there are plenty of dishes you can make with boiled potatoes and hard-boiled eggs, if you don't choose to make the entire potato salad. Although – if you like potato salad, your Intermediate kids can nearly complete the entire process

How to Demonstrate

Although we hope your Intermediate kids are confident at the stove now, boiling a big pot of water still has its challenges – we don't expect this age group to be able to actually *drain* anything safely; it's just too heavy.

Boiling Potatoes

Having a child who can boil potatoes independently all the way to the draining point is awesome, whether for a side dish like boiled red potatoes, mashed taters, Shepherd's Pie topping, or this potato salad.

Here's how you can demonstrate or do a tandem job with the kids (some parts of the skill are better suited for Advanced kids, like cutting raw potatoes):

1. Scrub potatoes well
2. Peel or don't peel – your choice
3. Dice small (parent may have to do this if no Advanced kids) OR you can boil in big chunks or even whole if they're small "new" or red potatoes
4. Cover with cold water
5. Add generous dash of salt (1/4 - 1/2 teaspoon if you need to measure)
6. Turn the burner on high, put the lid on, and watch for foam and bubbles
7. When the pot reaches a boil, turn the burner to low with lid on.

"Although we hope your Intermediate kids are confident at the stove now, boiling a big pot of water still has its challenges..."

8. Ten minutes is usually enough if you have small dices for potato salad. Add 5 more minutes for mashed potatoes, and it will take longer for bigger chunks.

9. Teach the kids how to poke the potatoes with a fork to test for doneness. They should feel completely soft all the way to the center.

10. When finished, turn off the heat. Kids can remove potatoes to another bowl with a slotted spoon OR the adult can drain into the sink. Be sure to demonstrate this process so the kids understand how to safely scoop one item at a time without dropping anything into boiling water. Ouch!

11. If you boiled large chunks or whole potatoes and you need to cool them off to dice, fill the bowl with cold water and ice and it won't take long at all. Don't leave the potatoes in the water any longer than necessary – they'll get sticky/slimy.

Health note about boiling vegetables – some of the vitamins go into the water, which can be great for making soup and stocks, but not always great for veggies. Potatoes are no big deal, but we don't usually boil carrots, broccoli, or other non-starchy vegetables. Steaming, as taught in the Advanced Level, Class 8, or sautéing, Advanced Class 3, are the preferred methods for cooking vegetables.

Hard Boiling Eggs

There are a couple neat ways to make "hard-boiled eggs," including steaming, baking, and traditional boiling. If you like traditional boiling, here's the process you can use to teach this first time:

1. Crack the raw eggs slightly on the narrow end (It sounds like this: "clunk, clunk, cshhhh") – stop at the first non-clunk! It's that sound of, "Ooops, the egg cracked!" but not nearly as much as when you make a bullseye.
    - This strategy allows just a little bit of water to get between the shell and the membrane while the eggs cook, making them much easier to peel. Just emphasize that you are NOT trying to actually break the egg open. Nothing should come out.
    - If you are not using farm fresh eggs, this strategy may not be necessary.
2. Put the eggs in a single layer in a pot.
3. Cover with cold water.

4. Add a generous dash of salt (1/4-1/2 teaspoon).
   - This brings the temperature of the water up to a boil faster and prevents egg from coming out of the cracks in the shells.
5. A parent might need to help carry the pot to the stove.
6. Turn the burner on high and put the lid on the pot.
7. When it comes to a rolling boil, turn the burner off. Leave the lid on the pot.
8. Set a timer for 12 minutes (12 = a dozen eggs, easy to remember).
9. Prepare a big bowl with ice water.
10. When the timer beeps, remove eggs one at a time with a slotted spoon to the ice water bowl.
11. Peeling the eggs as soon as they are cool helps make that process easier as well. (*More peeling tips in the Beginner Lesson plans.*)

Sometimes traditionally cooked hard-boiled eggs aren't the easiest to peel, even with my secret "sorta crack" trick – especially if you use farm fresh eggs. Here are 3 alternative ways to cook eggs that can be much less difficult to peel:

- **Steam the Eggs.** Using a steamer basket, steam whole eggs for 12-15 minutes (in a single layer). Cool in cold or ice water.
- **Use a Pressure Cooker.** If you have an Instant Pot or other pressure cooker, you may already have discovered the joy of peeling eggs.
- **Bake the Eggs.** Place eggs in mini muffin tins and bake at 325F for 30 minutes. Cool in ice water.

More instructions for all those methods can be found at www.KidsCookRealFood.com/recipes

How To Guide

"This entire lesson is a co-working process."

This entire lesson is a co-working process. I'd expect the adult and child to be working together completely the first go round, and then on subsequent opportunities to practice, you can talk over the technique verbally beforehand, then stay to watch/guide the child through the steps as they gain independence in boiling.

How to Coach to Independence

Depending on what other ages you have in your home, your Intermediate kids might get to do other jobs on the potato salad.

Pickles need to be diced, which is a perfect job for Intermediate level sharp knife skills. I recommend demonstrating one – how you would make 2-4 long strips, then turn those strips to cut into dices.

If you don't have Beginner or Advanced kids, other jobs include:

- Peeling eggs
- Dicing eggs and cooked potatoes (or the adult can dice raw potatoes before boiling)
- Eyeing up the ingredients
- Stirring it all together

Be sure to follow the potato salad recipe in the KCRF recipe book to put it all together – there are lots of little pieces for kids to help with! And then the best part...tasting. Mmmmmm!

Challenges You Might Encounter

Hot Water Issues. Dealing with boiling water is a little scary. Make sure your kids are set up in a safe place, with the pot and their receiving bowl close together and no risk of them wanting to lean over the pot to get anything else. Remind kids that a potato or egg falling back into the water and splashing would really hurt them, so they must be careful as the remove each item. Demonstrate a steady hand! Don't forget you can review stovetop safety in Intermediate Class 5.

When is it Done? If kids are having trouble determining when the potatoes are fully cooked just by poking with a fork, don't hesitate to let them pull one out, rinse it in cold water to make it palatable, and taste it. Focus on the very center. It's pretty clear when the center is not soft enough; it's just not a very pleasant experience!

The Tough Egg to ~~Crack~~ Peel. If your eggs are really tough to peel, you may be able to save the day by adding water to the mix. After cracking a hard-boiled egg all the way around, place it in a bowl of cool water.

Gently squeeze it to allow water to get between the shell and the inside of the egg. You could also allow your child to work under running water (although I feel like that uses too much water personally). In the future, use a different method to cook the eggs OR be sure to peel them as soon after cooking as possible. That can really help facilitate an easier peel. If your eggs are very fresh, setting a dozen aside for 2-3 weeks and then boiling them will make a positive impact on peeling as well.

We hope to see our Intermediate kids in the Advanced Level someday! Happy Cooking!

Making Homemade Mayo: Advanced

Don't forget to create opportunities to practice last week's skills:
- Steaming veggies and making a white sauce

How We Apply the Skill Today:
- Making potato salad

Skills That Loop into this Lesson:
- Cracking Eggs (Int. Class 3)
- Using a Small Appliance (Adv. Class 7)
- Washing Produce (All-Kid Class 7)
- Sharp Knife Skills (Adv. Classes 1-4)

Tools Needed:
- Immersion blender or food processor
- Wide-mouth pint jar
- Liquid measuring cup
- *Recipes for Kids Cook Real Food*

Time Needed:
- Hands on Time: 10 minutes for mayo, 1-2 hours for potato salad

Food Needed:
- Egg
- Olive oil (or similar)
- Apple cider vinegar or lemon juice
- Parmesan cheese
- Dry mustard, garlic powder, paprika,

Today's Recipe: Homemade Mayo and Potato Salad

Adults Should Prepare:
- Hopefully nothing! Mayo works best when the eggs are at room temp, so think ahead an hour before you want to start with your kids.

Allergy Notes and Substitutions:
- There are ways to make egg-less mayo, and I once made a cashew/coconut milk vegan mayo. See www.KidsCookRealFood.com/recipes
- You could certainly teach how to boil potatoes via the Intermediate lesson, as well as peeling potatoes (a very different skill from the straight peeling we taught in the Beginner class) and dicing them. Mashed potatoes are often a favorite kid-friendly side, and as long as your family can eat them, that's a great skill for your Advanced kids to learn.
- An egg-less sub for the whole potato salad recipe might be a basic German potato salad.

Lesson Overview: Making Mayo

If you've never made mayo before yourself, this will be a fun experience for you and your kiddo!

However – a note:

I'd rather you buy mayo to make this potato salad and spend time with your kids rather than get hung up on the task of mixing up your own mayo and not trying the recipe at all. Making mayo is a surprisingly easy activity -- but it can seem daunting at first. Above all, the goal is to have your kids broaden their experiences in the kitchen. So don't be afraid to experiment or try!

How to Demonstrate

Read through the recipe from *Recipes for Kids Cook Real Food* together carefully, making sure you both understand each step.

Test your immersion blender in the jar to make sure it fits.

Then simply follow the instructions exactly and troubleshoot along with your child if necessary.

Note: If you don't have an immersion blender, you can also make mayo in a food processor by running it constantly and very very slowly drizzling the oil in the top while it's running – but it's much messier to clean up and moving the mayo from the food processor into a jar is another step.

> "Read through the recipe from *Recipes for Kids Cook Real Food* together carefully, making sure you both understand each step."

314

How To Guide

If you'd like to make potato salad with the mayo, especially if you have a Beginner but no Intermediate, you can ask your Advanced cook to do the jobs of boiling potatoes and boiling eggs.

How to boil potatoes:

1. Scrub potatoes well.
2. Peel or don't peel – your choice.
3. Dice small.
4. Cover with cold water and add salt.
5. Turn the burner on high, put the lid on, and watch for foam and bubbles.
6. When you reach a boil, turn to low with the lid on.
7. Set a timer for 10 minutes.
8. Demonstrate how to check with a fork for doneness.
9. Remove to another bowl with slotted spoon OR the adult can drain.

Alternatively, you could show how to make baked potatoes – and then Beginners can dice the cooked potatoes for potato salad.

Hard Boiling Eggs

There are a couple neat ways to make "hard-boiled eggs," including steaming, baking, and traditional boiling. You can find more info and instructions for each method at *www.KidsCookRealFood.com/recipes*. If you like traditional boiling, here's the process you can use to teach this first time:

1. Crack the raw eggs slightly on the narrow end (It sounds like this: "clunk, clunk, cshhhh") – stop at the first non-clunk! It's that sound of, "Ooops, the egg cracked!" but not nearly as much as when you make a bullseye.
    - *This strategy allows just a little bit of water to get between the shell and the membrane while the eggs cook, making them much easier to peel. Just emphasize that you are NOT trying to actually break the egg open. Nothing should come out.*
    - *If you are not using farm fresh eggs, this strategy may not be necessary.*
2. Put the eggs in a single layer in a pot.

3. Cover with cold water.
4. Add a generous dash of salt (1/4-1/2 teaspoon).
   - *This brings the temperature of the water up to a boil faster and prevents egg from coming out of the cracks in the shells.*
5. A parent might need to help carry the pot to the stove.
6. Turn the burner on high and put the lid on the pot.
7. When it comes to a rolling boil, turn the burner off. Leave the lid on the pot.
8. Set a timer for 12 minutes (12 = a dozen eggs, easy to remember).
9. Prepare a big bowl with ice water.
10. When the timer beeps, remove eggs one at a time with a slotted spoon to the ice water bowl.
11. Peeling the eggs as soon as they are cool helps make that process easier as well. (*More peeling tips in the Beginner Lesson plans.*)

> "There are a couple neat ways to make "hard-boiled eggs," including steaming, baking, and traditional boiling."

How to Coach to Independence

Advanced kids have all the skills to make a homemade potato salad all by themselves. See the recipe in the KCRF recipe book for all the steps. If this is something you could bring to a party or potluck like our family likes to do, see if you can assign the task to your big kids – and watch them shine!

Challenges You Might Encounter

Broken Emulsification. Emulsifying is the process of a liquid oil blending with an egg yolk (or in this case, a whole egg) to make a semi-solid. It's pretty cool – until it doesn't work. Troubleshooting fixes are in the recipe book. Just remember that it's always fixable – don't despair!

Raw Egg Heebie Jeebies. If you've never eaten raw egg before, let's talk about that. First of all, have you had a bite of cookie dough? We say, "Oh, you're not supposed to do it," but most of us do anyway. If so, you've had raw egg.

Here's the risk with eating raw eggs: It's not really that the egg itself is raw, but that IF there were any contaminants like Salmonella on the *outside* of the eggshell, they would likely cross-contaminate into the cracked egg, and if not cooked, they would still be there when consumed. If you'd like an extra layer of protection, simply wash the outside of your eggs well with hot soapy water to remove any potential contaminants. *Disclaimer: I cannot be held responsible for any illnesses contracted from eating raw eggs – or anything else! – recommended in the course. You know I have to say that…but I wouldn't tell you to make homemade mayo if I didn't think it was safe.*

**Thank you for joining us in the
Kids Cook Real Food Course! Happy Cooking!**

Resources

Guidebook to Cooking Dry Beans

(for Advanced Level and Adult Guides working with Beginners)

There are many ways to soak beans (believe it or not!) and also ways to cook without soaking. The method detailed below results in, some say, the most digestible beans, and there are other options provided afterward.

Step 1: Measure and Rinse Dry Legumes

I highly recommend cooking beans in bulk, one to two pounds at a time. Simply use what you need for a recipe and freeze the remainder.

Sort through the dry beans for any stones or other debris. I've actually found a pebble and clumps of dirt before, so don't skip this step any more than you would eat lettuce from your garden without washing it. I also toss out any strange-looking or overly wrinkly beans. I don't trust them.

Rinse the dry beans in a colander thoroughly under cool water.

If you're using lentils, mung beans, or split peas, it's possible to skip the soaking and cook them dry. However, if you want to really maximize your nutrition, include the next step anyway: *soaking*.

Step 2: Soak and Rinse Dry Legumes

All dry beans and legumes, even those mentioned above that *can* be cooked without a soak, *should* be soaked before cooking. Soaking may shorten the cooking time and is supposed to make the beans more digestible.

Choose a large pot. Dry beans expand quite a bit when soaked, which is why you need to really drown them in water. Never fill your pot more than 1/3 of the way with dry beans.

To soak, cover the rinsed beans with water to double the depth. The optimal soaking temperature is 140° F (60° C), but room temp is just fine, especially when working with kids. Let's not complicate it.

Soak overnight or for 12-24 hours, covered to keep things from falling in. The long soak is what makes the beans more digestible. Note: You do not need any salt, vinegar, or lactic acid medium added to the soaking water. In fact, those may hinder the bean's ability to soften. Recommendations vary on this though – some say to add a teaspoon of salt while cooking to help keep the beans intact. Nothing needed to soak though.

I always soak right in the pot I'll use to cook the beans, which is often the pot I'll use for the final bean recipe. Why wash more dishes than necessary?

An option to reduce flatulence: It is said that if you pour off the water mid-soak and replace with fresh water, you can cut down on the flatulence that is sometimes blamed on beans and legumes.

Step 3: Cook and Rinse Dry Legumes

- Drain, rinse, and return the beans to the pot.
- Add water to cover beans twice as deep.
- Bring to a gentle boil and use a large spoon to skim off any foam that appears, pouring it into the sink. (Foam is supposedly impurities and junk; again, some sources say skimming isn't necessary so don't feel badly if you forget. It makes me feel good to get rid of that stuff though!)
- Keep heating over high until you see a rolling boil.
- Reduce heat and simmer, covered, for 4-8 hours until soft. (It is said that simmering for the first hour or so *uncovered* may reduce "wind.")

It is very important to note that a simmer for dry beans is a different beast than the "low heat" you want for something like rice. It's more of a "high simmer," which on my gas stove is about a 2 or 4 out of 9 (5 is dead center "medium"). You don't need to see a rolling boil the whole time, but if steam is rising, that's a good sign that the water is hot enough. I put the lid on after the first hour or so, which allows me to keep the temp at just above the lowest setting.

Bottom line: Keep the beans at a higher heat than "warm" but lower than a true boil.

I always plan to start cooking the beans in the morning after breakfast, because it's okay if they're finished a little early. They'll wait for dinnertime just fine with the heat off, drained or undrained. If I don't have time in the morning or forget, I always figure the last possible chance to get them started (with this cooking strategy) is by the end of lunch or about 1:00. That way I know they'll be ready by dinner prep time.

Troubleshooting Crunchy Beans:

Unbelievably, some beans can cook for 8 hours and *still* be crunchy, which is very frustrating. Hitting a good rolling boil at the start is one step to avoid this.

If your beans *are* crunchy after 4-6 hours, add a *pinch of baking soda* to the water and crank the heat up a bit. The one comfort in this process is that you can't burn them or irreparably mess them up! (Note: Beans that struggle to cook may split and look less than desirable for cold bean salads, but you can always use them in soups.)

Additional Notes:

- 1 cup dry beans yields 2-2 ½ cups cooked.
- 1 can of store-bought beans is roughly 1 ¾ cups cooked beans. Typically, you can just measure 2 cups for a recipe that calls for a can.
- Kidney beans (red or white) require a 10-minute vigorous boil because they contain a certain toxin that must be neutralized. (No kidneys in a slow cooker.)
- Both salt and acids (vinegar, lemon juice, tomatoes) can disrupt the cooking and result in crunchy beans, so do not add either one while soaking or during the first hour of cooking.
- Measure out extra cooked beans for frozen storage. Store in 2 or 4-cup portions to be ready for any recipe.
- Find more on how to cook dry beans, including comparing to cans, price checking, and the awful (funny) story of the first time I ever worked with dry beans at *www.KidsCookRealFood.com/recipes*

This information on cooking beans is an edited excerpt from one of my eBooks: The Everything Beans Book. If you enjoy using dry beans, this cookbook has great family-friendly recipes for every course of the meal, even dessert! Visit www.KidsCookRealFood.com/recipes to get a special discount!

The Why on Soaking

If you're new to whole foods or traditional cooking, here's a quick background peek at why one might bother to soak beans (which also applies to nuts, whole grains, and seeds).

As a seed, a legume (dry bean) is the plant's chance to reproduce. Therefore, it's not in the plant's best interest for the seed to both be eaten and digested. If the plant got to choose, the seed would simply be replanted – or eaten by an animal, not chewed well or digested, and "deposited" elsewhere to germinate and grow.

Kind of disgusting, right? My third graders used to love this lesson!

The seed is thus designed for the benefit of the plant – to be quite indigestible. It's our job as human eaters to break through the seed's defenses in order to commandeer for our own benefit the nutrients the seed holds within.

Soaking begins the process of germination by which the seed grows a tiny plant. Once that process begins, the seed's defenses are down because it's getting ready to release the sprout – and thus the nutrients too. The long, slow cook for legumes also helps to break down other "anti-nutrients" that make the seed all the more indigestible.

Visit *www.KidsCookRealFood.com/recipes* and scroll down to the beans section for more than you'll ever want to know!

Other Ways to Soak and Cook Dry Beans

Note: If you're cool with just cooking beans the way I do it, and you don't like having more options than necessary or are prone to overwhelm, stop reading now. If you like many options and want to know some shorter cook times, press onward.

Quick-Soak
(Less healthy, but works in a pinch if you forget to soak)

1. Bring (unsoaked) beans to a boil for one minute, cover, turn off heat, and let sit for one hour.
2. After an hour, boil furiously, uncovered, for ten minutes.
3. Cover, lower heat, and simmer for 1-2 hours, until tender.

Slow Cooker Soak Method

1. Rinse and pick the beans.
2. Cover with water to double the volume of beans and soak for 6 hours or overnight.
3. After soaking, drain water and add fresh water to twice the height of the beans.
4. Cook soaked beans in a slow cooker on low for 8 hours or high for 4 hours.
5. Important note: Do not use the slow cooker for kidney or cannellini beans, as they have a toxin that needs a hearty boil to neutralize.

Slow Cooker No-Soak Method

1. Rinse and pick the beans.
2. Place beans in crockpot, filling no more than 1/4 full of beans.
3. Add water to three times the height of the beans (since they aren't soaked and will absorb much more water).
4. Cook unsoaked beans on low for 12 hours or high for 6 hours.
5. Important note: Do not use the slow cooker for kidney or cannellini beans, as they have a toxin that needs a hearty boil to neutralize.

Pressure Cooker Method

If you have a pressure cooker, it likely came with instructions for cooking dry beans. It's very quick, typically only 8-25 minutes after pressure is attained (less than hour total for even the longest cooking bean, chickpeas).

Be sure to follow the instructions and specific steps for your pressure cooker and be aware that the timing is quite different for different kinds of beans.

Refer to my blog post on the topic at:
www.KitchenStewardship.com/pressurecookbeans

How to Make Perfect White Rice*

1. Measure Rice

2. Pour into the Pot

3. Measure Water (usually twice as much as rice)

4. Pour into the Pot

5. Gentle Stir

6. Put the Lid On

*For brown rice, the process is much the same, but cook 45 minutes instead.

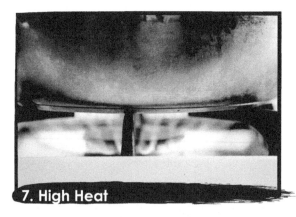

7. High Heat

8. Bring to a Rolling Boil

9. This is Hot...but Not Close Enough

10. Turn Heat to Low, Lid On

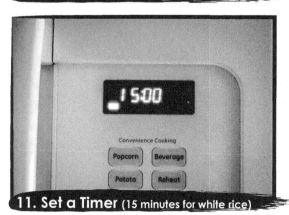

11. Set a Timer (15 minutes for white rice)

12. No Peeking!

Craters everywhere!

13. Craters on Top Show that the Rice is Done

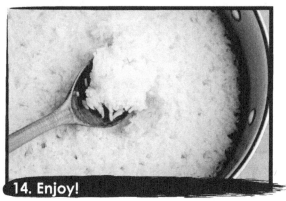

14. Enjoy!

Resources: Perfect White Rice

Tools Needed Checklist

This checklist is designed to give you a rough idea of what tools will be used in the Kids Cook Real Food Course and how often you may use them. You may use these tools more frequently than what is listed below; the list merely shows when a tool will be a special focus. Be sure to check the Tools Needed list at the beginning of every lesson for specific items you will need.

Naturally, the goal of this course is to help YOU teach YOUR kids how to cook in YOUR kitchen. You may have your own favorite specialty tools that you use for certain jobs, like a special liquid measuring cup or a Pampered Chef Mix 'N' Chop for the stove. Those will be great to use!

However, if you're looking for specific recommendations on ingredients and supplies – like a kid-friendly chef knife, my favorite measuring spoons, or great quality cutting boards – head over to *www.KitchenStewardship.com/kcrfresources* to my resource page with a list of links to tried-and-true items.

Key
B = Beginner
I = Intermediate
A = Advanced
(Number corresponds to class lesson.)

- Butter Knife (B1, B2, B3, B4)
- Chef's Knife (A1, A2, A3, A4, A5, A7)
- Colander (B5, I2, B5, A5)
- Cookie Sheet with Sides (B6, B8, A4)
- Cooking Spoon (I8)
- Creamer Pitcher (B6)
- Cutting Board (B1, B2, B3, I2, I7, A1, A2, A3, A4, A5, A7)
- Flat Spatula (I6, I7, A6)
- Food Processor (A7)

- Garlic Press (A3)
- Glass Casserole Dish (B6)
- Glass jar or Salad Dressing Container (I1)
- Hand Towel (B6)
- Immersion Blender or Potato Masher (A5)
- Jars with Lids (B4)
- Large Bowl (B2, B3, B7, I3, I4, I7, A1, A2, A4, A6)
- Large Pitcher (B6)
- Large Pot (B5, I5, I6, A3, A5)
- Large Spoon (I1, I4, I5, I6, A4)
- Liquid Measuring Cup (B6, I1, A5)
- Little Bowl (B4, A6)
- Measuring Cups (B4, B5, B6, I4, I6, I7, A5)
- Measuring Spoons (B4, B6, I1, I4, I6, I7, A3, A5)
- Medium Pot with Lid (A8)
- Muffin Liner (I4)
- Muffin Tin (I4)
- Oven Mitts (A4)
- Paring Knife (I2)
- Pastry Blender/Cutter (I7)
- Rolling Pin (I7)
- Shot Glass, Coffee Mug, Wine Glass (B6)
- Skillet or Frying Pan (I6, I7, I8, A3, A6, A7)
- Small Plate (B1)
- Small Pot (B6)
- Spreader (B1)
- Steamer Basket (A8)
- Swim Goggles (A2)
- Tongs (B7, A3)
- Vegetable Brush (A1)
- Vegetable Peeler (B1)
- Whisk (B6, I1, I3, I4, I6, A6, A8)

Optional
- Bread Machine (B8)
- Cheese Grater (A5)
- Crinkle Cutter (B2, B3)
- Plastic Freezer Bags (A2)
- Salad Spinner (B7)
- Scoops (B4)
- Small Tongs (B2)
- Toothpicks (B2)

Beginner: Food Shopping List

Class 1
- Celery
- Peanut butter
- Raisins
- Butter, softened at room temp (or alternative to spread: cream cheese or hummus and crackers or cucumbers, jam on toast, guacamole)
- Bread (or toast)

Class 2
- Bananas (at least one per child plus one to demonstrate)
- Melon (cantaloupe or honeydew)
- 8 oz. block of soft cheese (like mozzarella, not aged sharp cheddar)

Class 3
- Whole mushrooms
- Cucumbers
- Zucchini (Remember to have at least one extra of each for the demonstration step.)

Class 4
- Paprika
- Cumin
- Onion powder
- Garlic powder
- Cayenne pepper
- Arrowroot starch or corn starch
- Dried dill

Class 4, *continued*
- Dried parsley
- Dried chives
- Black pepper
- Salt
- Bulk salt, sugar, cornmeal, or something granulated for measuring spoon practice
- Dry flour
- Oats or rice (for measuring cup practice)

Class 5
- Dry black or pinto beans (or any dry beans)

Class 6
- Gelatin
- 100% juice (grape is great)

Class 7
- Head or two of lettuce, unwashed
- Various salad ingredients (see "Adults Should Prepare" on page 245)
- Salad dressing (optional)

Class 8
- Whole wheat flour
- Honey
- Egg
- Olive oil
- Salt
- Yeast
- Butter

Intermediate: Food Shopping List

Class 1
- Extra virgin olive oil
- Red or white wine vinegar
- Dijon mustard
- Garlic powder
- Italian seasoning
- Salt and pepper
- Sour cream (or alternatives)
- Ranch mix (from Beg. Lesson 4) OR herbs to make it (see recipe book)
- Something to taste the ranch dip with *(cut carrots are great)*

Class 2
- Strawberries
- Mushrooms
- Pineapple
- (or other soft fruits or veggies)

Class 3
- Eggs (lots)

Class 4
- Whole wheat flour or GF flour blend
- Pumpkin or pureed squash
- Cinnamon
- Nutmeg
- Cloves
- Baking powder
- Baking soda
- Salt
- Sucanat (or cane sugar)
- 2 eggs
- Butter or coconut oil

Class 5
- Rice (white or brown)
- Tomato sauce (if making Mexican Rice)
- Taco seasoning (see recipe book, if making Mexican Rice)

Class 6
- 9 Eggs
- Can of pumpkin or homemade puree (squash or sweet potato is fine too)
- Cinnamon
- Cloves
- Ginger
- Nutmeg
- Salt
- Baking powder
- Vanilla
- Maple syrup
- Coconut flour (OR almond flour, whole wheat flour, GF flour blend OR Ingredients to make your favorite pancake recipe)

Class 7
- White whole wheat flour (not traditional whole wheat)
- Solid fat (palm shortening, lard, butter, coconut oil)
- Whey
- Salt

Class 8
- Ground Meat (ex: beef, turkey)

Advanced: Food Shopping List

Class 1
- Carrots
- Cucumbers
- Celery

Class 2
- Onions (sweet are best)
- Bell peppers

Class 3
- Cooked rice
- Eggs
- Garlic
- Onions and peppers (from freezer)
  (OR 1/2 c. pepper, 1/2 c. onion)
- Zucchini
- Stir fry vegetables
- Olive or sesame oil
- Rice vinegar
- Soy sauce (optional)
- Stir fry spices (curry, ginger, etc.)

Class 4
- Cantaloupe or honeydew
- Watermelon
- Apples

Class 5
- Dry pinto or black beans
- Olive oil, lard, or coconut oil
- Onions
- Ground cumin
- Garlic
- Mexican or regular oregano
- Salt
- Cheddar or jalapeño jack cheese block (optional)

Class 6
- Eggs (lots)
- Sour cream, cottage cheese, or milk
- Salt and pepper
- Shredded cheese (optional)
- Add-ins for eggs (optional)

Class 7
- Onions
- Garlic
- Cumin
- Carrots
- Dry or canned chickpeas
- Tahini or peanut butter (optional)
- Parsley, dried or fresh
- Any kind of flour
- Baking soda
- Salt
- Fat for frying
- Cheese (optional)
- Zucchini (optional)
- Toppings (homemade ranch, lettuce, cheese, red onion, cucumbers)
- Tortillas

Class 8
- Broccoli or green beans (veggies to steam, can be frozen)
- Milk
- Cheddar cheese
- Arrowroot starch or flour
- Cooked rice
- Spices
- Ground meat

Measuring for Pre-Readers

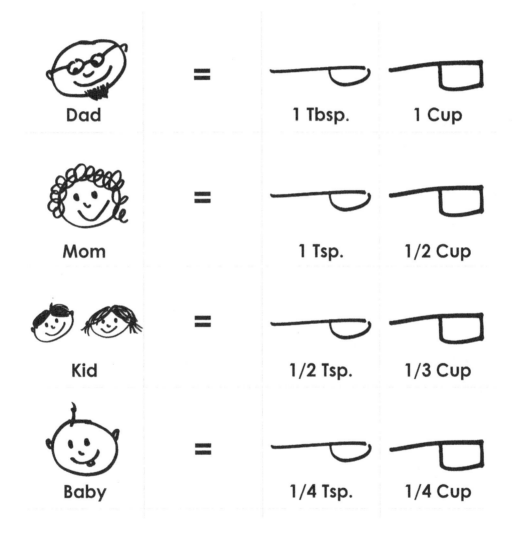

Dad	=	1 Tbsp.	1 Cup
Mom	=	1 Tsp.	1/2 Cup
Kid	=	1/2 Tsp.	1/3 Cup
Baby	=	1/4 Tsp.	1/4 Cup

Ranch Dressing Mix

Dill	Parsley	Chives
2 Dad (Tbsp.)	2 Dad (Tbsp.)	2 Dad (Tbsp.)

Onion Powder	Black Pepper	Salt
4 Dad (Tbsp.)	2 Mom (Tsp.)	2 Mom (Tsp.)

Cayenne Pepper		
1 Baby (1/4 Tsp.)		

Taco Seasoning

Chili Powder

2   Dad (Tbsp.)

Paprika

1   Dad (Tbsp.)

Arrowroot or Corn Starch

3   Dad (Tbsp.)

Onion Powder

2   Mom (Tsp.)

1   Kid (1/2 Tsp.)

OR

Onion Powder

2   Mom (Tsp.)

1   Kid (1/2 Tsp.)

Garlic Powder

2   Mom (Tsp.)

1   Kid (1/2 Tsp.)

OR

Garlic Powder

2   Mom (Tsp.)

1   Kid (1/2 Tsp.)

Cumin

1   Dad (Tbsp.)

1   Mom (Tsp.)

1   Kid (1/2 Tsp.)

OR

Cumin

1   Dad (Tbsp.)

1   Mom (Tsp.)

1   Kid (1/2 Tsp.)

Optional: One baby cayenne pepper (grab the card from Ranch Dressing Mix) if you like your taco seasoning spicy.

St. Peter's Spicy Fish Seasoning

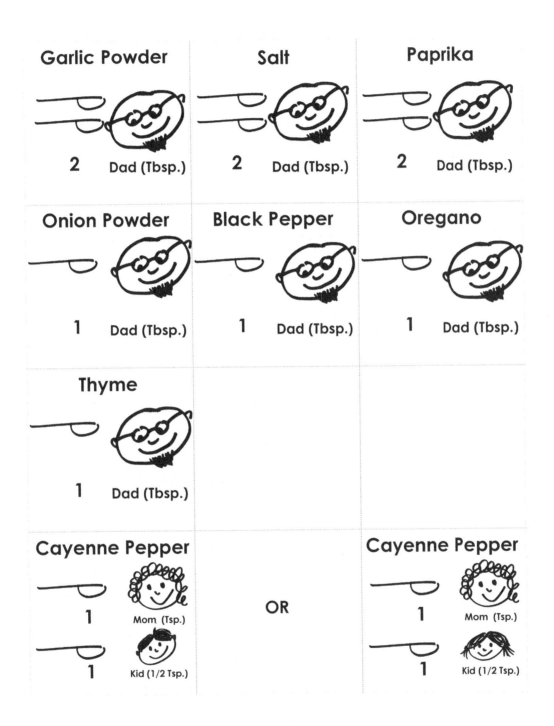

Garlic Powder

2   Dad (Tbsp.)

Salt

2   Dad (Tbsp.)

Paprika

2   Dad (Tbsp.)

Onion Powder

1   Dad (Tbsp.)

Black Pepper

1   Dad (Tbsp.)

Oregano

1   Dad (Tbsp.)

Thyme

1   Dad (Tbsp.)

Cayenne Pepper

1   Mom (Tsp.)

1   Kid (1/2 Tsp.)

OR

Cayenne Pepper

1   Mom (Tsp.)

1   Kid (1/2 Tsp.)

Adobo Seasoning

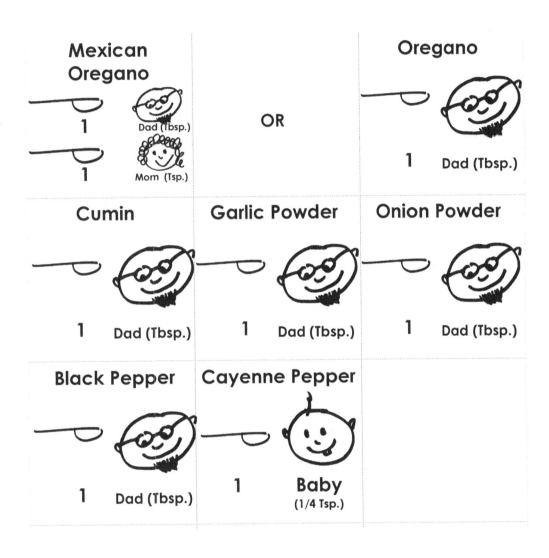

Mexican Oregano

1   Dad (Tbsp.)

1   Mom (Tsp.)

OR

Oregano

1   Dad (Tbsp.)

Cumin

1   Dad (Tbsp.)

Garlic Powder

1   Dad (Tbsp.)

Onion Powder

1   Dad (Tbsp.)

Black Pepper

1   Dad (Tbsp.)

Cayenne Pepper

1   **Baby** (1/4 Tsp.)

Guacamole

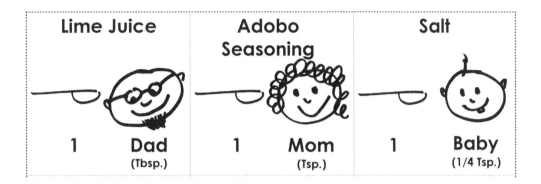

Lime Juice	Adobo Seasoning	Salt
1 Dad (Tbsp.)	1 Mom (Tsp.)	1 Baby (1/4 Tsp.)

Make Your Own Spice Cards:

Use the blank cards below to make your own spice cards for your pre-readers to use while they learn to cook. Simply print them out, and write the spice and the amount next to the measurement. Laminate them to reuse them over and over again!

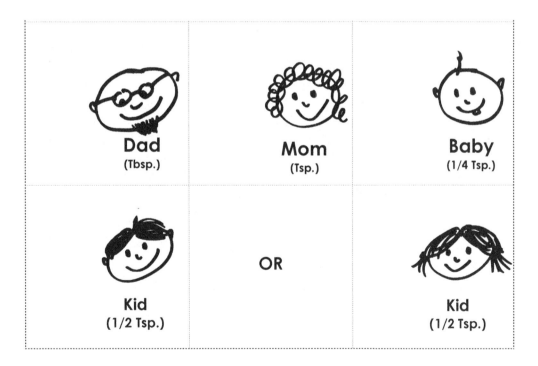

Dad (Tbsp.)	Mom (Tsp.)	Baby (1/4 Tsp.)
Kid (1/2 Tsp.)	OR	Kid (1/2 Tsp.)

Daily Nugget Cards

Cut Your Own Cheese

If your cheese comes all wrapped up in slices that someone else cut, it's probably fake cheese with weird ingredients. Cut your own so you know it's real cheese.

KCRF: Daily Nugget
Beginner: Class 2- Slicing with a Dull Knife, Level 1

Swim the Salty Oceans

Too many spice blends have lots of white salt in them. REAL salt in nature has lots of colors, and white salt needs to be processed. The natural is healthier with more minerals, so we use that.

KCRF: Daily Nugget
Beginner: Class 4- Measuring Ingredients

Bread with Butter is Better

Different foods help your body be healthy in different ways. We should eat things from more than one food group together – butter with your bread, veggies and nuts, fruits and cheese or yogurt. Balance!

Parents may want to understand: Fat slows down the digestion of starch and helps the body use vitamins in vegetables better.

KCRF: Daily Nugget
Beginner: Class 1- Dull Knife Skills: Spreading and Peeling

Don't Slip on the Skins

There are lots of nutrients in and near the edible skins of many fruits and veggies – so if you don't have to peel something, don't do it!

KCRF: Daily Nugget
Beginner: Class 3- Slicing with a Dull Knife, Level 2

Start Your Day with a Glass of Water

Every body needs water, so get a glass in as soon as you wake up – pour it yourself!

One Bread at a Time

We don't want to fill up on breads all the time, so just one on the plate at a time.

Parents may want to understand: Starches (as explained in Lesson 1) are quick energy. We want foods that will give us our "super power" energy for a long time so we eat the meat (protein) and fats first.

Balance Beam Beans

Beans keep us balanced because they have protein and carbs.

Different Colors have Different Superpowers

Food with different colors helps keep different parts of your body healthy – so try to eat lots of different colors at every meal!

Raw Foods Have Workers Inside

Raw food has enzymes, things that DO actions in our bodies – important jobs like digestion. You don't have to eat everything raw, but it's a good idea to eat something raw at every meal, like the fruit we're cutting today, raw veggies, or salad.

Sugar is a "Sometimes" Food

Recipes that have as much sugar as flour are always desserts – we try to cut down the sweetener whenever we can and only it eat "sometimes" – if at all.

Natural sweeteners like honey, maple syrup, and sucanat are better, but still should be eaten in moderation.

Olive Oil is so Cool

Olive oil has the most nutrients when cold. It doesn't stand up to heat really well, so it's best to use it cold – like salad dressings! Also don't store it near heat or in the light (clear containers aren't great).

Eggs have God's Packaging

A lot of food is packaged by humans – sometimes with lots of ingredients and weird stuff that's icky for your body. The way the egg comes – one ingredient, two parts, lots of nutrition – is just perfect.

Eat Breakfast Every Day

Our bodies need fuel for our day, and we need to start out by giving ourselves some energy with a healthy breakfast. Don't miss it!

KCRF: Daily Nugget
Intermediate: Class 6- Flipping Pancakes

Happy Cows Make Healthy Meat

Cows who get to be outside and eat grass have healthier tummies and their meat has more goodness for our bodies, too.

(Same goes for chickens who get to be outside and eat grass and even bugs, just like they were designed to – their eggs have more nutrition than other eggs, whether they're brown, green, white, or even blue!)

KCRF: Daily Nugget
Intermediate: Class 8- Browning Ground Meat

Rice is Nice

Rice is an unprocessed food, whole grain or white. Brown and white are just different. Brown has a longer cook time and all the parts of the seed, but white is still ok – both have their strengths.

KCRF: Daily Nugget
Intermediate: Class 5- Cooking Rice/ Stovetop Safety

Soaking Whole Grains Helps Your Tummy

Sometimes whole grains are hard on people's tummies. We can make our dough or batter the day before with a little whey or vinegar and let it sit on the counter overnight. That "soaking" can help the whole grains be easier to digest.

KCRF: Daily Nugget
Intermediate: Class 7- Rolling Dough

Onions are Powerhouses

Onions are good for your heart, for your immunity, for preventing cancer, are anti-inflammatory, AND the good parts don't go away when cooked or boiled -- they go into the water!

KCRF: Daily Nugget
Advanced: Class 2- Sharp Knife Skills, Level 2

Eat the Whole Fruit, Skip the Juice

God made a whole package in each fruit with a balance of nutrients. Juice doesn't have the fiber to balance out the sugars. Did you know that fresh fruit even gives your body water for your daily needs?

KCRF: Daily Nugget
Advanced: Class 4- Oven Safety and Cutting Whole Fruits

Fermented Foods Feed our Guts

With your sharp knife skills, you could make lacto-fermented veggies, like real pickles, Dilly Beans, Kimchi, etc.

Eating fermented foods adds probiotics to your meals and feeds the ONE TRILLION bacteria in our gut! Wow! You can also eat a yogurt dip with your raw veggies to get healthy probiotics.

KCRF: Daily Nugget
Advanced: Class 1- Sharp Knife Skills, Level 1

Free Nutrition Inside Garlic

Did you know that garlic gets healthier 7 minutes after it's crushed -- and then better yet in another 7 minutes? When you first start cooking, crush your garlic and let it sit and wait.

Garlic can fight sick bugs and infections, is good for your heart, helps prevent cancer, is anti-inflammatory, and is good for digestion, blood pressure, and blood sugar.

KCRF: Daily Nugget
Advanced: Class 3- Sharp Knife Skills, Level 3

Runny Yolks Run Thick with Nutrition

Cooking eggs can denature some of their health benefits – so runny egg yolks or slow-cooked scrambled eggs retain more nutrition.

Cooking Kills Some Vitamins

Some of the healthy vitamins in vegetables and fruits are damaged by heat - so lightly steaming is better than boiling to retain more nutrients. Boiling makes some of the good stuff go into the water (soups are easier to digest).

The tomato is an exception – lycopene, a healthy nutrient, is actually released by cooking.

Beans are Musical for a Reason

Beans can help pull bad stuff out of your body, but they can be hard to digest. That's why we long-soak and long-cook them.

The Value of Shredding It

Did you know "stuff" is added to store shredded cheese? If you want to be in charge of the ingredients and get the best taste, shred your own.

Flash Cards

Peeling

○ Don't Cross the Wall!
○ Turn Your Veggies
○ Clear Your Peels

Dull Knife Skills, Level 2

○ Tip of the Knife is Down (when cutting)
○ Cross Hatch =
   1. Lay Flat.
   2. Cut into Sticks like String Cheese.
   3. Turn Like a Clock.
   4. Cut into Cubes.
○ Make Room for the Knife – Choo, Choo!
   Like a Train Going Through a Tunnel!

Spreading

○ Hand Over Teeth
○ Tip of the Knife in the Spread
○ Corner to Corner, Edge to Edge

Dull Knife Skills, Level 1

○ Always Carry Knives Point Down.
○ Be the Boss of the Knife!
○ Choke Up. (No Finger!)
○ Knife Moves, Eyes Down
○ Food Moves, Knife Down

Measuring

o Flat: No Holes, No Hills
o Flour Falls Like Snow (No Sandcastles!)
o Snowplow it Flat
o Get Level With Liquids

No Rocks in the Beans

Measuring

Dad = 1 Tbsp. | 1 Cup

Mom = 1 Tsp. | 1/2 Cup

Kid = 1/2 Tsp. | 1/3 Cup

Baby = 1/4 Tsp. | 1/4 Cup

Five Ways to Stir

o Merry-Go-Round
o Pogo Stick
o Roller Coaster (toward the center)
o Lawnmower
o Hula Hoop (whisk)

o Mix it Well!
  o Hold the Bowl
  o Uniform Mixture

Making a Salad

o Tear Bite Sized Pieces
o Choose a Rainbow of Color

KCRF CLASS 07(B)

3 Steps for Training Kids in the Kitchen

1. Demonstrate
2. Guide
3. Coach to Independence

Don't forget to Encourage and Practice, Practice, Practice!!

KCRF

Pouring

o Pour with your Crayon Hand
o Up High, in the Center
o Pour with the Spout
o Vocabulary:
   o spout
   o pour
   o center
   o pitcher
   o liquid measuring cup

KCRF CLASS 06(B)

Working with Dough

o Sticky? Take a Dip!
o Rolls the Same Size

KCRF CLASS 08(B)

Measuring

Dad = 1 Tbsp. / 1 Cup

Mom = 1 Tsp. / 1/2 Cup

Kid = 1/2 Tsp. / 1/3 Cup

Baby = 1/4 Tsp. / 1/4 Cup

Five Ways to Stir

- Merry-Go-Round
- Pogo Stick
- Roller Coaster (toward the center)
- Lawnmower
- Hula Hoop (whisk)

- Mix it Well!
  - Hold the Bowl
  - Uniform Mixture

Reading a Recipe

- Read the Whole Recipe First
- Move Ingredients From Left to Right
- Stir a Uniform Mixture Every Time

Measuring

- Flat: No Holes, No Hills
- Flour Falls Like Snow (No Sandcastles!)
- Snowplow it Flat
- Get Level With Liquids

Safe Ways to Hold Food

- Top Chop
- Up and Over Soldier
- Hey Hey, Outta the Way!
- (Never "Pick Me! Pick Me!")

KCRF CLASS 02(I)

Cracking Eggs

- Crack on a Flat Surface
- Bullseye!
- Can't Unbreak an Egg
- Thumbs In, Then Out

KCRF CLASS 03(I)

Intro to Sharp Knife Skills

- Always Carry Knives Point Down
- Be the Boss of the Knife!
- Choke Up (No Finger!)
- Knife Moves, Eyes Down
- Food Moves, Knife Down

KCRF CLASS 02(I)

Ways to Cut

- Rock-a-Bye Knife (knife tip touches the board)
- Drive it Like a Vacuum (knife stays on the board)
- Saw Blade (soft foods and big items)
- Tug-o-War Pull (slicing)

KCRF CLASS 02(I)

Stovetop Safety and Cooking Rice

o Stay Away from the Heat
o Pot Center, Handle Side – Hold it!
o Cooking Rice? NO PEEKING!
o Pac Man the Lid

KCRF CLASS 05(I)

Instructions for Cooking Rice (cont'd.)

6. Keep the lid on the pot.
7. Set the timer (see chart for the kind of rice)
8. NO PEEKING!
9. The rice is done when you see little craters show up on the top surface.
10. Let it sit 5 minutes with the lid on, heat off, for best fluff.

KCRF CLASS 05(I)

Making an Entire Recipe By Yourself

o Read the recipe all the way through first. Ask questions about anything you don't understand.
o Get out all the ingredients.
o Organize them on the left.
o Level measuring! (Use a little bowl for spices and/or eggs to help your confidence.)
o Hold the bowl to stir.
o Proper stirring.
o Move ingredients to the right after you use them.
o Look for a uniform mixture.

KCRF CLASS 04(I)

Instructions for Cooking Rice

1. Measure rice and water into pot. (usually 1 cup rice, 2 cups water)
2. May add salt or oil at this point.
3. Gentle stir.
4. Bring to a boil over high heat, lid on.
5. Turn the heat to very low.

KCRF CLASS 05(I)

Rolling Dough

○ Soak Grains at Room Temperature (on the counter) Overnight
○ Kneading: Fold and Press
○ Roll Dough From the CENTER Out, Like a Compass – N, S, E, W.

3 Steps for Training Kids in the Kitchen

1. Demonstrate
2. Guide
3. Coach to Independence

Don't forget to Encourage and Practice, Practice, Practice!!

How to Tell When Pancakes are Done

○ Dry around edges
○ Edge changing color
○ Bubbles popping on top
○ Peek underneath: See brown? Is it holding together?
○ You might have to pat down to be thinner if they're thick pancakes and browning too fast.

Browning Meat

○ From Pink to Brown
○ Break it Up
○ Scoop, Lift, Flip – to the Center

Safe Ways to Hold Food

- Top Chop
- Up and Over Soldier
- Hey Hey, Outta the Way!
- (Never Pick Me! Pick Me!)

Sharp Knife Skills 2: Onion & Pepper

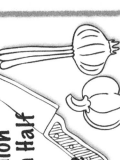

- Cut the Ends Off the Onion
- Flat Side Down, Cut it in Half
- Tear Off the Peels
- Slice Rainbows and Dice Around the Rainbow

Intro to Sharp Knife Skills

- Always Carry Knives Point Down
- Be the Boss of the Knife!
- Choke Up (No finger!)
- Knife Moves, Eyes Down
- Food Moves, Knife Down

Ways to Cut

- Rock-a-Bye Knife (knife tip touches the board)
- Drive it Like a Vacuum (knife stays on the board)
- Saw Blade (soft foods and big items)
- Tug-o-War Pull (slicing)

Flash Cards: Advanced

Oven Safety

KCRF CLASS 04(A)

- Quick but Slow
- Like a Hotel Key in a Slot
- 100% OUT then UP

Five Ways to Stir (review)

KCRF CLASS 04(A)

- Merry-Go-Round
- Pogo Stick
- Roller Coaster (toward the center)
- Lawnmower
- Hula Hoop (whisk)

- Mix it Well!
  - Hold the Bowl
  - Uniform Mixture

Sharp Knife Skills 3: Garlic & Sautéing Veggies

KCRF CLASS 03(A)

- Crush Garlic First: Add Garlic Last
- Pac Man the Lid
- Sauté Long Cooking Veggies First

Measuring (review)

KCRF CLASS 04(A)

- Flat: No Holes, No Hills
- Flour Falls Like Snow (No Sandcastles!)
- Snowplow it Flat
- Get Level With Liquids

Making Scrambled Eggs

- Pre-heat on Medium.
- Add the Fat (+Meat or Veggies)
- Pour in Eggs
- WAIT: Let it Sit First Before Stirring
- "Low and Slow" to Cook
- Push Runny Egg to the Hot Middle
- Lawnmower and Roller Coaster Stir

KCRF CLASS 06(A)

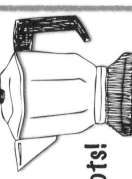

Using Small Appliances

- Pulse for Onions
- Wash Once, Use Lots!

KCRF CLASS 07(A)

Steps to Cooking Dry Beans

1. Pick over for rocks or dirt.
2. Rinse the beans.
3. Cover the beans with LOTS of water to soak overnight.
4. Drain the soak water off the beans.
5. Fill the pot with new water – LOTS of it again.
6. Boil and reduce heat to medium low – Loonnnng cook all day – 4-8 hours.
7. Make sure they're done. (special baking soda trick)

KCRF CLASS 05(A)

Making Fried Eggs

- Sizzle Test!
- Crack Into a Bowl if it Helps
- Grease the Pan
- See White – Lots Of It – Before Flipping

KCRF CLASS 06(A)

Veggie Steaming Cheat Sheet

Vegetable	Steaming Time
Broccoli	5-6 min
Carrot	4-5 min
Green Beans	5-8 min
Peas	4-5 min
Potatoes	10-12 min
Spinach	5-6 min
Zucchini	4-6 min

KCRF CLASS 08(A)

Making a White Sauce

o How to Make a Roux
  o 1 Tbs. fat
  o 1 Tbs. flour (or starch, but less)
  o 1 cup milk

FLOUR

KCRF CLASS 08(A)

3 Steps for Training Kids in the Kitchen

1. Demonstrate
2. Guide
3. Coach to Independence

Don't forget to Encourage and Practice, Practice, Practice!!

KCRF

Be sure to check out the complete collection of recipe eBooks from Katie Kimball! Go to *KitchenStewardship.com/ebooks* for access.

Healthy Snacks to Go
Over 45 recipes to get you on your way with real food, real fast
Fast food doesn't mean processed food. The 2nd edition includes more recipes, more bonuses and covers nearly every food allergy out there – all without a pre-packaged food. Finally, a book filled with truly healthy snacks!

Better Than a Box
How to Transform Your Processed Foods Recipes into Whole Foods Favorites
20 recipe reverse engineering demonstrations, 35 remake resources and 25 ready-to-cook recipes make cooking family-favorite recipes using whole foods a whole lot easier. Get rid of the processed foods and make dinner better than a box!

The Healthy Breakfast Book
Cereal-free Secrets to Starting the Day with Real Food
With over 50 family-friendly recipes, key tips for planning ahead, hosting a brunch and the one food to have on hand to kickstart your family's "5-a-day" fruits and veggies at breakfast, this book will be your guide to healthier mornings.

The Healthy Lunch Box
Sandwich-free Secrets to Packing a Real Food Lunch
45 recipes, 100+ resources and loaded with strategies to streamline your packing process, stock your pantry with emergency backups for your backups, and send healthy, delicious food in the lunch box, no matter how old your eater is – and there's not a sandwich in sight.

The Family Camping Handbook
Real Food in the Big Woods
You don't have to compromise with pre-packaged meals and processed foods just because you're cooking over a campfire. 36 recipes and a Paleo/Primal/Grain-free adaptation guide are at your disposal to make your next frugal vacation a success.

The Everything Beans Book
30 Frugal, Nutrient-Packed Recipes for Every Eater
From nutrition and storage to preparation and kid (and adult) friendly recipes, this book is the A to Z of beans. Beat the rising cost of food prices with thoroughly tested recipes that cover every meal, including dessert!

Smart Sweets
30 Desserts to Indulge your Sweet Tooth
Can dessert really have less sugar, soaked or sprouted whole grains, probiotics, or even vegetables and still taste good? Absolutely! Whip up a batch of healthified cookies, bars, brownies, cakes, pies and more, and win over even the sweetest tooth!

Made in the USA
Las Vegas, NV
26 February 2023

68170719R00214